DINING AT SPEED

DINING AT SPEED

A celebration of 125 years of railway catering

Chris de Winter Hebron

·RAILWAY HERITAGE·
from
The NOSTALGIA Collection

First published in 2004

British Library Cataloguing in Publication Data

A catalogue record for this book is available from the British Library.

ISBN 1 85794 211 6

Silver Link Publishing Ltd
The Trundle
Ringstead Road
Great Addington
Kettering
Northants NN14 4BW

Tel/Fax: 01536 330588
email: sales@nostalgiacollection.com
Website: www.nostalgiacollection.com

Printed and bound in Great Britain

ACKNOWLEDGEMENTS

A book of this kind is a joint effort: it could not have been written without assistance and courteous permission of many people. First, I must acknowledge my debt to the authors of the many sources consulted: they will be found credited in detail in the Notes at the end of the book. I would also like to formally acknowledge the courtesy of those who gave permission for the reproduction of illustrations or extracts, in particular, in the UK, the National Museum of Science and Industry, London's Transport Museum, Cambridge University Press, David & Charles, HarperCollins, Ian Allan Publishing, John Murray, David Jenkinson of Pendragon Partnership, the successors to the Transport Publishing Company, Glossop, and Peter Trewin of BRB (Residuary). In Canada and the USA I would like to acknowledge the courtesy of the California State Railroad Museum, Canadian Pacific Railroad Archives, CSX Transportation, the Minnesota Historical Society, Joseph Shine of Four Ways West Publications of California, and the University of Nebraska Press for permission to reprint the quotations from *History of the Atchison, Topeka and Santa Fé Railway* by Keith L. Bryant Jr (Copyright © 1974 by Keith L. Bryant, Jr.) acknowledged in the Notes

As always, some authors and pictures have proved difficult to trace. Every effort has been made to secure permissions, and give credits, for all material cited or reproduced that is still in copyright, but apologies are offered in advance for any mistakes or omissions, which should be communicated to the author via the publishers.

At the more personal level, I would like to thank Professor Colin Divall of York University; Ed Bartholomew and Richard Taylor of the National Railway Museum, York; Hamp Smith of the Minnesota Historical Society; Brian Radford; Michael Charman and his colleague Chris Turner; Geoff and Sue Woodward of Harpenden Railway Museum; Robin Jones of *Heritage Railway*; David Small and Lydia Contreras of Rail Gourmet; and three particularly generous US contacts – E. S. ('Tod') Hanger of C&O, Bob Johnston of *Trains* magazine, and Marc Frattasio of the NHRR Historical Association. Additional thanks are also due to Les and Margaret Bretherick of Bridport, Dorset, for making available their archive copy of the long-out-of-print 1930s part-work *Railway Wonders of the World*, and to Derek Hill of Salford University, who painstakingly reviewed the draft text chapter by chapter.

I would also like to thank all those currently working in the railway catering industry who helped me: in particular Steve Jones of Anglia Railways, Rob Mulder of Eurostar, David Crome of First Great Western, John Dykes of GNER, Duncan Fraser of Midland Mainline, and Lucy Evans, formerly of Virgin Trains.

And last – but most certainly not least! – I would like to thank my wife Doreen, who has not only put up with me spending many hours over a hot computer screen, but whose expertise in management formulated a range of theoretical approaches to help uncover why things developed as they did.

CONTENTS

FOREWORD
by Colin Divall
Institute of Railway Studies and Transport History, York

If travel were just about moving from A to B and dining merely involved eating, the history of catering on the train would doubtless have followed a far simpler – and more easily researched – path than it did. Taken individually, each of these most basic of human functions has long been tied up with a host of values and expectations reaching far beyond the mere satisfaction of utilitarian need, and reflecting the social and cultural mores of the times. Put the two together and the combination was – and is – stimulating and fascinating, both immediately, at the moment of consumption, and later, from the retrospective point of view of the historian.

The provision of food and drink to passengers on a moving train was a difficult enough feat technically and organisationally in the 19th century, and it remains a not inconsiderable one today, particularly when the underlying economics are inevitably so central to the operation. But the even greater challenge has always been to spot ways in which changing attitudes to eating and drinking can be exploited for the delight and pleasure of passengers and, potentially at any rate, to the financial advantage of the railway. It is surely no coincidence that on-board catering first developed extensively in those two countries, the United States of America and Britain, where in their differing ways the combination of private ownership and government regulation resulted in inter-company competition more in terms of service than fares – the story of train catering requires far more of the historian than merely a knowledge of menus, vehicles, staffing rosters and working diagrams, essential though these were to the successful delivery of the dining experience to the passenger.

The idea and reality of dining at speed epitomises, then, one of the enduring and central paradoxes of the railway: that it was, and is, at the same time one of the most highly industrialised modes of transport, yet also capable of re-enchanting, if only for fleeting moments, the standardised world that made railway travel readily available to large numbers of people. In making this insight central to his study, Chris de Winter Hebron guides us with skill and passion in equal measure through the long menu of possibilities, alternatives, dead-ends and achievements characterising the history of on-board catering. This is a feast of a book: enjoy it.

INTRODUCTION

There is a gap in the literature about on-train dining: both the two main British books, Geoffrey Kitchenside's *The Restaurant Car*[1] and Neil Wooler's *Dinner in the Diner*[2], treat the history of railway dining as something that 'just happened'. But the true story is longer, more complex, and much more exciting than that. It includes an American testifying to Congress before there even *were* any railways in America[3]; Brunel dreaming of taking coffee at 45 miles per hour[4]; the Editor of *Punch* running a spoof news item on the Eastern Counties Railway[5,6]; Charles Darwin missing connections at Birmingham[7]; a Scottish-descended Cockney using the electric telegraph to corner the fast-food railroad provision for the Wild West[8,9]; and the young George Mortimer Pullman persuading the Chicago & Alton to let him have some old railroad cars to play with[10].

It turns on friendships – between Pullman and James Allport[11,12], between Nigel Gresley and Sir Ralph Wedgwood[13,14] – and on enmities such as that between Pullman and Nagelmackers, the founder of Wagons-Lits[15]. It takes in changes in eating habits and notions of comfort, inter-company competition, the rise of consumerism, depressions, world wars, class and democracy, nationalisation, privatisation – and even TQM. And it's as full of mysteries as a detective story – for example, if Allport of the Midland introduced Pullman to Britain, why was the first Pullman dining car service operated by the Great Northern?

But for me, it's also the history of a magical lived experience. I was born in 1933: my first Hornby train set included a crude model of *Silver Link*. One of my earliest boyhood memories is of travelling to Lowestoft to see my grandparents in one of Gresley's 'tourist stock' coaches. Then, post-war, we started to go on holiday to Devon. Devon itself was magical: but that first journey from London to Ilfracombe was appalling. It was August 1945: no restaurant cars had yet been restored. My mother had made honey sandwiches before we left, but we were crammed five-a-side in Third Class with the seat arms up, so getting them out was a problem, let alone eating them. My father had brought ginger beer, but had forgotten the bottle-opener. The journey was over

six hours long, boiling hot. The bread went stale, the butter went rancid, and the honey ran stickily everywhere.

In 1946 we managed to get on to the 'Atlantic Coast Express'. The 'ACE' did have some new corridor stock, and some restaurant cars had also been restored, but rationing was still in force and the fare they could offer was extremely limited. Then, in 1947, my father got wind of a new train – a Pullman called the 'Devon Belle'. Things were never to be the same again.

This time there was no queuing: the Pullman supplement included reserved seats. Followed by a porter with our cases on a hand-barrow, we made our way along the massive line of umber, gold and cream coaches, the impression of length heightened by the first car being the Observation Car; starkly modern, its severe rear slope was unlike anything I'd seen outside science-fiction, and the almost blank wall of the bar, following all that glass, seemed to make it longer still. (Later I learned it wasn't a new car at all – the canny Pullman Corporation had refitted two of its old cars, with seating designed to feel slightly uncomfortable after about 20 minutes, to prevent people hogging the rear view for too long at a stretch.[16]) In our carriage, the dream continued. The seats were palatial – you sank into them, so that if I leaned back my feet hardly touched the floor. There were armrests, too – and the multiplicity of little coat-racks! The napery and silverware!! The table lamps!!! And this was *Third* Class?

We pulled away on the stroke of noon and the liveried attendants began to prepare the service of lunch. As we passed through Surbiton the train, by my reckoning, reached 80mph, and I told my parents so.

'You can always tell when they reach 80 on these trains anyway,' my father replied, 'because that's when they serve the soup.' And sure enough, at that moment the soup arrived. He was right, too: the riding quality of the heavy Pullman stock was superior even to the newest coaches on the 'ACE'. I don't remember that particular lunch menu, but I later learned that to avoid rationing restrictions Pullman during 1947 had tried out the use of ready-

This 1947 SR poster by Savignac advertising the 'Devon Belle' emphasises notions of luxury, speed and modernity. *Courtesy National Railway Museum/Science and Society*

made frozen foods (Lyons' 'Frood') on the 'Devon Belle'. This was one such menu – for the Press Run of 19 June 1947[17], but typical of the period:

Tomato Cream Soup
Chicken Chasseur
Parisienne Potatoes, New Peas and Carrots
Orange Mousse with Rainbow Ice and Devon Strawberries
Coffee

After the meal and coffee, I went back down the train to that fascinating Observation Car. The deliberately uncomfortable seats seemed modernistically bare compared with the plushness of the rest of the train, but enthralled with the speeding rear view (and the sheer volume of *locomotives* one could see) I sat forward on my seat all the way to Exeter.

For me, this was a defining experience – a fantasy of comfort, privilege and luxury that could be lived out by almost anybody at no great cost. I had been overcome by the *idea* of elegant travel, of 'dining at speed'. I knew that often railway travel was crowded, slow, and uncomfortable – but I'd seen what it *could* be like, and I'd been sold on the idea. Ideas of this sort are remarkably strong once they catch hold. This idea has stayed with me all my adult life, and has profoundly affected my attitudes towards travel by train. Having once been infected by it, I have all sorts of rose-tinted memories of other dining journeys.

On the up 'Thames-Clyde Express' in the 1950s, on a September afternoon, sitting bathed in the afternoon sun, eating toasted tea-cakes and drinking pot upon pot of tea…

Another tea-time train, travelling with my new wife on the 'Queen of Scots Pullman' en route to Edinburgh in a 'honeymoon coupé', one of those little private compartments at the end of the coach, isolated by its own side corridor, that were a feature of the old-fashioned Pullman design…

The excitement, during the late 1960s, of trying to make sure my train between Newcastle and London would be one of BR's 'steak-and-kidney pie trains', among the best-kept secrets of 1960s BR catering. With its succulent steak covered by a melting, crisp pie-crust, it was one particular chef's personal creation, and he guarded both it and its recipe closely. Those in the know literally smelled it out, by the rich aromas of the sherry-laced gravy…

Travelling to Lausanne on Train 225, formerly the 'working' 'Simplon-Orient' express, admiring northern France on a summer evening over a Navarin D'Agneau and a half-bottle of Bergerac. (The dining car by then was of the new design with half the seats in rows, airline fashion, instead of round central tables, but the food quality was still better than anything one could expect on most British trains!)

Continental travel's much longer distances, of course, render the provision of dining services very complex. This means that intending 'diners at speed' need to plan their routes and trains with some care – and even then, things can go wrong. My final story, illustrating this, concerns the 'Tauern Express', a train that conveyed coaches from many different destinations – Klagenfurt, Graz, Trieste, Belgrade, even Athens. These all met at the little junction station of Villach, an hour up the line from Klagenfurt, where the restaurant car also came on. That day in 1979 it was a bright, crisp January morning in Klagenfurt: there'd been a fall of snow in the night. I sat in my greatcoat, watched the snowy Alpine scenery, and looked forward to Villach, where we arrived only a few minutes late. But because of blizzards further east, the other sections were later still, and, worse, late *in the wrong order*. (The 'Tauern' splits again further up the line, so at Villach the sections all have to be assembled in just the right order, with the restaurant car added at precisely the right moment.)

What followed resembled some of the more frantic moments from *The Great St Trinian's Train Robbery*. Villach station is a pretty place, with the line out northwards going up a slight gradient among pine tress, overlooking the side of the mountain valley. This morning, however, it was full of bits of train. As each part of the 'Tauern Express' came in, it had first to come up to the arrival platform to set down and pick up passengers, then be moved away again to allow the next bit to do the same. At one point, all the bits had to be shunted off the main line altogether, to allow the 'Austria Express' to come roaring through.

Eventually, though, with a satisfying clang the restaurant car came on. I waited until the train began to pull out of Villach station, then walked forward to it. It was delightfully warm, and the coffee aroma was gorgeous. Only one other person was in it – an old crone, all dressed in black. The attendant approached me. 'Ein kännchen Kaffee extra stark, bitte,' I said. He fetched it, and poured out a cup from the little pot. I savoured the aroma for a moment, then started to drink. There was a grinding jerk, as

the train shuddered to a halt: then another jerk, as we started to move backwards again. We hadn't been on our way at all – we'd simply been clearing the station for the last set of coaches. My hand shook, so did the cup, and most of the delicious black liquid soaked into the tablecloth. The only thing left to do was swear. Casting rapidly round for a language the old lady perhaps wouldn't know, I settled on French. 'Merde!' I cried. 'Tee-hee-hee!' went the old crone, utterly delighted.

This story demonstrates another thing about 'dining at speed' as an idea. Once one has become infected with the idea, the chaos and minor disasters that are bound sometimes to accompany any form of travel become an adventure, or a subject for comedy. It doesn't matter if the train sections are late in the wrong order: at the end of the day, you remain confident that there will be good food, good wine, good coffee, warmth, a comfortable seat, a good view, and attentive service. You have 'bought into' the idea of a special experience, and somehow it feels to you as if the 'buying-in' creates a charmed circle of travel.

The real world doesn't work like that, of course, but that is how it is perceived by the convinced traveller. This perception dominated notions of quality travel for a century or more, steadily becoming available across a larger and larger range of society. It is harder to recapture now on the main-line railways than it used to be – though it is currently reviving among some of the privatised train companies, and its continuing appeal testifies that it still retains its ancient power to enchant. In its heyday it was a fascinating dream, and its spread to ever-widening ranks of society formed no mean part of the democratisation of privilege.

This book is an attempt to tell the story of how and why it happened.

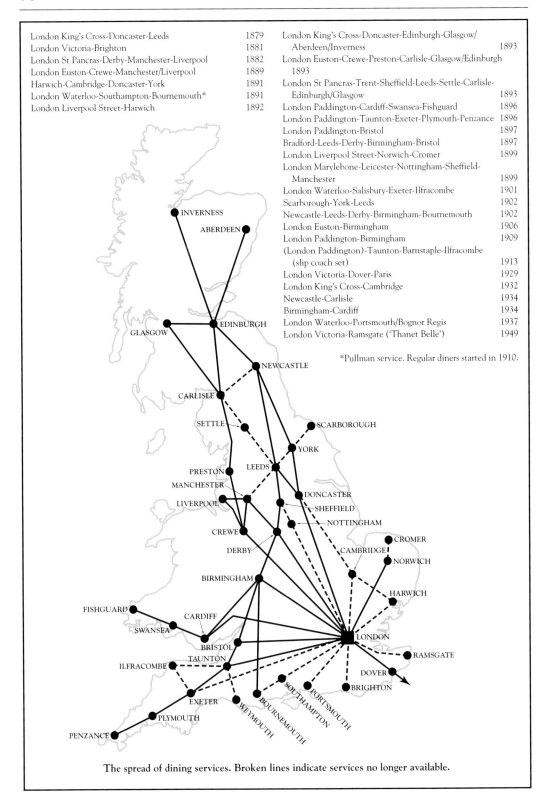

London King's Cross-Doncaster-Leeds	1879
London Victoria-Brighton	1881
London St Pancras-Derby-Manchester-Liverpool	1882
London Euston-Crewe-Manchester/Liverpool	1889
Harwich-Cambridge-Doncaster-York	1891
London Waterloo-Southampton-Bournemouth*	1891
London Liverpool Street-Harwich	1892

London King's Cross-Doncaster-Edinburgh-Glasgow/ Aberdeen/Inverness	1893
London Euston-Crewe-Preston-Carlisle-Glasgow/Edinburgh	1893
London St Pancras-Trent-Sheffield-Leeds-Settle-Carlisle- Edinburgh/Glasgow	1893
London Paddington-Cardiff-Swansea-Fishguard	1896
London Paddington-Taunton-Exeter-Plymouth-Penzance	1896
London Paddington-Bristol	1897
Bradford-Leeds-Derby-Birmingham-Bristol	1897
London Liverpool Street-Norwich-Cromer	1899
London Marylebone-Leicester-Nottingham-Sheffield- Manchester	1899
London Waterloo-Salisbury-Exeter-Ilfracombe	1901
Scarborough-York-Leeds	1902
Newcastle-Leeds-Derby-Birmingham-Bournemouth	1902
London Euston-Birmingham	1906
London Paddington-Birmingham	1909
(London Paddington)-Taunton-Barnstaple-Ilfracombe (slip coach set)	1913
London Victoria-Dover-Paris	1929
London King's Cross-Cambridge	1932
Newcastle-Carlisle	1934
Birmingham-Cardiff	1934
London Waterloo-Portsmouth/Bognor Regis	1937
London Victoria-Ramsgate ('Thanet Belle')	1949

*Pullman service. Regular diners started in 1910.

The spread of dining services. Broken lines indicate services no longer available.

I
'DINING AT SPEED' – THE IDEA AND ITS ORIGINS

The notion of 'dining at speed', however, needs several further characteristics to qualify as an 'idea' in the full historical sense. First, it needs to have *currency*: other people, too, should regard it as a distinct notion. Second, it needs to have *influence*: it should lead to observable developments or to practical applications and effects. We should be able to give an historical account of the idea's origins, developments and applications.

Next, the idea needs to fit into and exhibit connections with the overall intellectual patterns and beliefs of its period. One ought to be able to define the *implications* of the idea in terms of its fit and its connections with those other notions. And one ought to be able to define it also by means of *distinction* from alternative notions in the same area.

And finally, the idea needs to have *explanatory power*. it should enable us to pose and answer questions or problems that simply recounting the sequence of historical events would not enable us to do. It is my belief that the idea of 'dining at speed' possesses all five of these characteristics.

Let's begin with *currency*. Many writers have testified to their perception of a special kind of experience related to dining while travelling. Kitchenside, for example, begins the Introduction to his centennial book thus:

'Eating on a train can be one of life's most enjoyable experiences, with good food well served and a constantly changing panorama as the scenery unfolds before you. Breakfast with dawn breaking over a misty river valley transcends even the finest paintings in the best-known art galleries, while no seascape on canvas could match luncheon on the "Cornish Riviera Express" as it ran beside the beach between Dawlish and Teignmouth, while

dinner on the "Midday Scot" climbing over the Southern Uplands of Scotland in the failing light evoked far greater memories than any sun-sinking-slowly-in-the-west travelogue.'[1]

Wooler opens his own Introduction in similar vein:

'Upon the platform of some great railway junction like York or Carlisle, waiting travellers stand and gaze as a non-stop express sweeps by, the figures within the lighted windows joining some seemingly enchanted feast as their dining car bears them northward into the night. On board, the mystique is equally compelling as, with stewards bustling deftly around, the fortunate passengers tuck into their repast while the restaurant car, crockery enticingly a-jingle, speeds its way past hill and dale.'[2]

And the American historian William A. McKenzie describes the 'dining idea' twice in the same book:

'I claim … that the world is filled with people willing to join me in trumpeting the surpassing enjoyment of western scenery; an amiable steward; friendly, efficient and immaculately clad waiters; and food right out of a dream.
    Little survives of this dream…'[3]

'Where else … can one find that joyous combination of movement toward a goal, food in a pleasing variety, ineffably delightful scenery, service fit for a reigning monarch, and a feeling of intimacy that is totally at odds with time and place?'[4]

Perhaps the most extensive evocation of the 'idea' by a railway historian, however, is that by Charles Fryer, in his Prologue to *British Pullman Trains*[5], in which he describes the experience of First Class Pullman travel on the Metropolitan Railway during the 1930s. It is one of the best descriptions of the power of the idea, in all its connections with privilege and luxury, that I know. I quote a major extract from it below:

'To me it seemed the very acme of luxury travel, utterly beyond my means, only possible to … the top brass of the business world, whom I saw boarding the cars and settling into their armchairs… In the cramped six-a-side accommodation of a Metropolitan compartment coach, I would daydream about what it might be like to belong to the higher echelons…

There they sat, the weary tycoons, each in his *Louis Quinze* chair at his own table, fingering the wine-list. Softly across the carpeted floor the attendant approached them… What would Monsieur like to drink? A gin and tonic, perhaps, after the labours of the day? By the time King's Cross was reached, each having been supplied with his own expensive beverage, their portly frames relaxed as they scanned the *Times* or *Telegraph*. Isolated from the common herd, from the junior clerks and girl typists who thronged the platforms or squeezed into the crowded compartments in front or behind, they could just stare out from plate glass windows like goldfish from bowls and just ignore the lesser bourgeoisie…

From Baker Street onwards there would be no stop for half an hour, and during that time they would most likely nod off. Then … away into the heart of Metroland, halting at Chorley Wood, Chalfont, Amersham, Great Missenden, Wendover, Stoke Mandeville and Aylesbury. At each of these a tycoon or two would ease himself from his seat, retrieve his briefcase and umbrella, have the door opened for him by the attendant, step out on to the platform and walk a few yards to the waiting limousine, thence to be chauffeur-driven to his mock-Tudor mansion among the beechwoods. To be one of *them* now, instead of just a scrubby junior clerk!'[6]

Expressions of the idea by company officials exist also, especially from the Pullman Car Company. From the beginning, Pullman described his cars in terms of luxury, service and privilege: they were 'palace' cars, and his US company was the Pullman Palace Car Co Inc[7]; his first dining car was named the 'Delmonico', after the exclusive New York

restaurant[8]; and he coined an in-house slogan 'Improvement is our Watchword', which anticipates Total Quality Management by more than a century[9]. Pullman inter-war publicity material in Britain regularly carried the slogans 'The Maximum of Luxury at the Minimum of Cost' and 'Pullman and Perfection'[10]. A typical text continues:

'"Pullman" and "Perfection" are synonymous when they refer to Car Building, in which the Pullman Car Company leads the world. In elaborate design, substantial construction, and luxurious finish, Pullman Cars represent the highest standard of excellence. Ingenuity and skill are constantly being applied to the improvement of details with a view to adding to the comfort of travel. Every Car is in charge of an experienced, well-trained Conductor, whose services are always at hand from start to finish of a journey, and invalids and ladies with children can always rely upon ready attention to their comfort and convenience. Cleanliness is also a special feature, coupled with perfect ventilation and good lighting, making travelling a real luxury.'[11]

And in 1962 Sir John Elliot, the Pullman Car Company's last Chairman, was able to remark: '"Pullman" has always meant "super – the best". It is individual, personal – as its American founder, George Pullman, intended it to be.'[12]

Fryer could thus legitimately comment, about the BR 'New Pullman concept' of 1985: 'George Mortimer Pullman gave his name first to a coach, then to a train, and finally to a notion, that of relative comfort in contrast to relative austerity, Sybaris instead of Sparta.'[13]

Examples also exist from sources such as the Midland Railway. Thus in early 1872, James Allport, the General Manager of the Midland, wrote:

'I have felt saddened to see Third Class passengers shunted on to a siding in cold and bitter weather – a train containing amongst others lightly-clad women and children – for the convenience of allowing the more comfortable and warmly-clad passengers (travelling First and Second Class) to pass them. I have even known Third Class trains to be shunted into a siding to allow express goods to pass.'[14]

This remark is particularly interesting because it demonstrates Allport's innovative notion of making comfortable travel available to *all* passengers, not just a privileged few. It dates from shortly before he persuaded the Midland Board to provide Third Class coaches on all trains, which marked the start of the 'comfort revolution' that put Midland travel standards firmly in the front of all UK railways.

By 1906 the Midland is proclaiming itself 'The Best Route for Comfortable Travel and Picturesque Scenery' on its posters, with text stressing a whole raft of comfort-travel facilities, including 'Breakfast, Luncheon, Dining and Sleeping Cars, Corridor Trains and New and Improved Carriages'.[15] To only a very slightly later date, too, belongs the slogan:

> 'The popular British summer resorts ... are conveniently reached by the Midland Railway. To any one of these districts you can make the journey a pleasant part of your holiday if you travel by the Midland.'[16]

Statements of the idea of customer care and comfort travel can also be found in the USA. In the early 1880s Fred Harvey, the catering purveyor for the Atchison, Topeka & Santa Fé, is credited with this response to his staff's treatment of an unruly customer:

> 'Of course he is a crank, but we must please him. It is our business to please cranks, for anyone can please a gentleman.'[17]

And E. Sterling Hanger, in the Foreword to the Chesapeake & Ohio dining car recipes book, comments:

> 'Robert R. Young ... Chairman of the Chesapeake & Ohio ... led C&O to ... [introduce] a magnificent new streamliner to be called the Chessie (named after C&O's famous mascot "Chessie the Kitten") scheduled to operate between Cincinnati and Washington. This wonderful new train would carry such amenities as hostesses, music piped to each individual seat, theatre car, children's playroom, the first domed cars in the east, and myriad additional appointments and services previously unheard of. Naturally, new dining cars were among the train's most touted features...'[18]

Evidence for acceptance of the idea can also be found in the design and furnishing of carriage stock. It is one thing to provide stock that is adequate and

Supposedly based on an actual stowaway kitten found curled up on a sleeping car bunk, the C&O's logo shows a kitten beatifically at rest between the sheets, in a human rather than a feline posture. Note the deliberate associations with luxury and comfort suggested by this drawing. *'Chessie the Kitten' is a proprietary service mark and a copyrighted image of CSX Transportation Inc; image reproduced with permission*

comfortable: it is quite another to require it to be rare and luxurious. Yet that was what several British and US companies actually did. A very good British example is the Great Central Railway's 1896 stock for the London Extension, described by George Dow.[19] 'Those coaches which were to form the main line trains,' he says, 'were bogie corridor vehicles, fitted with ... vestibules and automatic couplers, and electric communication between passengers and attendants.'

The First Class dining cars, which seated just 20 passengers,

> '...were finished in rare woods, upholstered in figured plush and embellished with works of art, the ceilings being decorated in gold and colours. The ends were panelled, moulded and carved to match, and relieved with proof-etchings, the doors ... inlaid with marquetry... The interiors of the Third Class dining cars were finished in light and brown oaks. The ceilings were covered in picked-out and decorated lincrusta. There were seats for 36 passengers, and a lavatory at one end... The kitchen cars ... also embodied two First Class compartments and an attendant's compartment. Cooking was by gas... Compartment interiors were trimmed in morocco, moquette, terra cotta, cashmere, velvet, and green cloth, finished in mahogany and decorated with photographs of places of interest on the Company's system. All the carriages were equipped with portable tables

stacked at the ends of the corridors, and the whole of their floors were covered with cork matting, supplemented by a rug in each First Class compartment.'

Such provision was designed to impress the traveller not only by its opulence, but also with real attention to comfort and travel security. For example, the passenger-attendant communication system (intended to be used to enable buffet snacks to be provided at seat in the carriages) antedates the better-known Southern Railway call system[20] by almost 30 years. Above all, the standard of flooring made the carriages not only sumptuous but warm.

These examples also demonstrate a number of aspects of 'dining at speed' as an idea. The first is that evidence for the idea's *currency* is also often evidence for its *influence*. Thus, the notion of comfort travel leads not only to people expressing themselves in a particular way, but also to specific attitudes to service provision, carriage specifications, or text and designs for posters and brochures. The second aspect is that the evidence for currency is also often evidence of some of the *implications* that the idea gathers to itself as it develops. Thus the examples link the idea of 'dining at speed' with wider notions of comfort and luxury travel, with early moves towards notions of quality management and customer care, and with such ideas as developing general standards of personal comfort, notions of privacy and modesty, the democratisation of what was formerly seen as privilege, and notions of territorial and business competition.

These last notions become particularly important to the development of on-train dining provision, but the link is not a simple one. One of the best explanations of it is given by J. T. Shackleton, in discussing the design and effects of railway posters:

'The images which [a railway] chose to present to the travelling public may not have been a true reflection of its reality; most people, asked to define what a railway means to them, would speak in terms of draughty stations, stale sandwiches and trains which always run late. In poster advertising, we are offered an opportunity to fantasise and escape from all this, into a world of gay holiday travel, luxurious dining cars and hotels, and fast, efficient services. This world immediately excites the imagination; it is, of course, intended to do so and to lure us onto the trains as a result.'[21]

True enough: but there is a further step. Once the railway has proffered this vision to its customers, it has to provide a reasonable approximation to the image of comfort displayed in its advertising if it is not to lose them. The desire to inculcate the idea of comfort travel thus reinforces the production of the carriages and standards of service that in turn reinforce it again. The idea has an aesthetic dimension, which links it to the growth of consumer society, the development of mass capitalism, and the explanatory ideas that that development engenders. A poster like that reproduced here offers what consumer aesthetics describes as a 'promise of use value': this has to be paralleled by the provision of an 'actual use value' if the whole operation is not to recoil on the railway companies' heads.[22]

This Edwardian Midland Railway holiday travel poster invites us to collude with the railway in the idea of railway travel as attainable armchair comfort. The young middle-class couple are shown relaxing in dreamy solitude over a pristine dining table. He is studying the menu, presumably about to recommend a choice to her. Outside the window, a stylised summer view of part of the Settle and Carlisle line floats effortlessly by. The use of warm browns and reds in the original and the easy, comfortable curves of the lettering further enhance the effect. *Former David Brough collection*

The origins of the idea

One commonly occurring mark of an historical idea is that examples of its intellectual existence are likely to precede examples of its application in practice. In 1863, the Philadelphia, Wilmington & Baltimore Railroad used steam baths to keep hot food cooked off the train[23]; the first true dining car in the USA was Pullman's 'Delmonico' of 1868, and the first in the UK was the Great Northern Railway's 'Prince of Wales' of 1879. The earliest references to the *idea* of on-train dining, however, substantially precede all three.

The earliest discussion of providing refreshment on trains even antedates the existence of public railways. In 1819 Benjamin Dearborn, giving evidence to the US Committee on Commerce and Manufactures, suggests that passenger cars of the future railroads be furnished 'with accommodations for passengers to take their meals and their rest during the passage, *as in packets* (my italics); that they be sufficiently high for persons to walk without stooping, and so capacious as to accommodate twenty, thirty or more passengers, with their baggage.'[24] To find aspects of railways being discussed before the advent of public railway systems is not in itself particularly unusual. Like the idea of on-train dining, the idea of public railways was itself abroad for some time before the physical infrastructure came into existence. A British example of such discussion, by Richard Lovell Edgeworth, for instance, dates from as early as 1802.[25]

But if Dearborn is writing before there are any public railroads in the USA, what gave him the idea in the first place? The answer seems to lie in the phrase '*as in packets*'. In Britain the predecessor to the railway was the stagecoach, but in the USA the major predecessor to the railroad was the river steam packet – larger than any equivalent packets in Europe, and, with saloons typically 40 feet long by 11 feet wide, gigantic by the side of British canal narrow-boats.[26] It is this model that Dearborn seems to have in mind, and he carries over into his railroad proposals what he sees as the major characteristics of the riverboat.

After Dearborn, the next early instances of the idea of on-train refreshment and travel comfort move to Britain, where they appear to arise independently, and the story does not return to the USA until around 1853. The early British ideas are a curious group, with far from straightforward connotations – though they do all seem to have one key feature in common.

The earliest British reference to the possibility of refreshment on trains seems to come from Isambard Kingdom Brunel. On 5 December 1831 the young Brunel finds himself in Manchester, visiting his current girlfriend Ellen Hulme. He makes sure to take a ride on the Liverpool & Manchester Railway, and is filled with a mixture of excitement and dissatisfaction. He gets out his diary and, while the train is in motion, begins to draw freehand circles. Against them, he notes: 'I record this specimen of the shaking on the Manchester Railway. The time is not far off when we shall be able to take our coffee and write whilst going noiselessly and smoothly at 45mph. Let me try…'[27]

We can deduce two things from this passage. First, whereas Dearborn offers democratic suggestions for the general improvement of travel for all citizens, Brunel essentially thinks in class terms. By 'we', Brunel means people like himself – members of the rising middle classes, who 'take coffee' and need not only to travel speedily but to be able to work – to 'write' – while on their journeys. The other important point to deduce is his mixture of excitement and dissatisfaction. Brunel is clearly exhilarated by his first train experience, but it is also exasperating – the mode of travel is constricted, uneven, and shaking – and he knows in his heart *it could be so much better*. We shall see that this feeling of 'it could be so much better' is a major wellspring in other minds, too, for generating many of the ideas of comfort travel that make up our story.

Brunel seems to have kept this diary comment in mind, for there are references to him designing in 1838 a 'grand saloon … complete with every convenience and luxury, being most gorgeously fitted up'[28]: details are scanty, but this may possibly be the same as the 'Super 1st Class posting carriage … fitted up in a style not met with in any other railway conveyance in the Kingdom (except the Royal carriages)' described by Vaughan.[29] If he had also acted on the 'taking our coffee' part of the comment, Britain might well have had on-train dining before the USA. But he didn't, for a curious reason.

As the 1830s wore on, the construction of the Great Western Railway ran over budget, and Brunel came under increasing pressure to retrench where possible. In May 1841 he bowed to pressure from his Chairman, and persuaded his contractor, Rigby, to build Swindon Station (which was to include refreshment rooms) and the works village of New Swindon at Rigby's own expense. Rigby's demand in return was the rents from the cottages and the takings from the refreshment rooms for 99 years *with the contractual obligation on the GWR that all passenger trains* (with a very few exceptions) *should stop there for refreshments for at least ten minutes.*[30] Brunel signed, and the GWR built no dining cars until the lease was bought back in the 1890s. And the subsequent refreshment room coffee at Swindon, according to Brunel's own correspondence, was perfectly foul. 'I have long ceased to make complaints at Swindon,' he writes in December 1842. 'I avoid taking anything there when I can help it.'[31]

Our next two British references to the idea of on-train dining suggest in a little more detail how on-train refreshment might be achieved: both come from the mid-1840s. The first one comes from the pages of *Punch*. Wooler, who misdates it to 1845, quotes only the opening, deadpan section, as a completely serious proposal:

'The Smoking Saloon on the Eastern Counties is only the first which it is intended to bestow upon travellers by railway. It is in contemplation to run a refreshment room with every train...'[32]

In fact, though, it is a satirical spoof – though that by no means invalidates its importance as an early evocation of the possibility of on-train dining – and it is its reference to the Eastern Counties Railway that gives it away. (And it is that which gives away Wooler's date, because the Smoking Saloon that occasioned the spoof did not appear until September 1846.)

The passage has its origins in an almost weekly running battle that *Punch* was waging against the abuses that characterised the railway industry during the middle 1840s, among them the poor treatment of passengers at the 'refreshment stops' on early railways. These stops were modelled on the stops made by stagecoaches while changing horses, but whereas stagecoaches carried only 12 to 16 passengers, the provisioning of a trainload of around 100 was next to impossible in the time allowed – just 10 minutes at Swindon refreshment rooms – even with the new 'bar counter' as a means of speeding up service. How could one consume the food in so short a time?

One problem was that coffee, tea and soup could not be cooled enough to be ingested before the departure bell summoned everyone back to their coaches. This was annoying enough, but the situation was compounded by the 'great refreshment stop scam'. The hot liquid left unimbibed on the bar counter, to thrifty Victorian businessmen, represented a potential for additional sales. After all, it had not been consumed, so why could it not be sold again? Back went the coffee in the urns, the tea in the pots, and the soup in the cauldrons, ready for the next trainload of unwary punters. This probably did not happen everywhere – it pretty certainly did *not* happen at the LNWR's refreshment stop at Wolverton, for example – but it certainly *did* happen at Tonbridge, where an unexpected delay in the train departure meant that customers saw their recently abandoned refreshment being made over – and one of them, the writer F. S. Williams, publicised the fact.[33]

One particular company that *Punch* had its knife into around this time was the Eastern Counties Railway. To Mr Punch, the ECR was a classic example of mismanagement, with high fares, poor services, bad punctuality and a disastrous safety record. *Punch* singled out the line by name for a number of spoof news reports, usually quite short and tucked away at the bottom of a page somewhere. A typical example comes from 1846:

'Railway Curiosity

The papers inform us that not a single accident has occurred on the Jamaica Railway during the last quarter! The Directors of the Eastern Counties have sent out agents to Jamaica to look at this story, as they will not believe there exists such a phenomenon.'[34]

By 1846 the Directors of the Eastern Counties had realised that they needed to do something to improve their public image, and introduced smoking saloons for First Class passengers on the fastest trains on their most 'up-market' line, that to Cambridge and Newmarket. Smoking at that time was not usually permitted on railway trains – and smoking cigars was a gentleman's hobby, as distinct from the 'common herd', who smoked pipes.

The saloons were of considerable opulence, and almost immediately made the news. They set new standards of comfort for travel on the Eastern Counties and for their time were outstandingly opulent vehicles. The Eastern Counties Railway was very proud of the fact that the saloons had been designed and built entirely in its own works, and made considerable play with the similarities between that design and the Royal Saloon for Queen Victoria.

To Mr Punch, however, it appeared merely to offer a 'faddish' additional comfort to a particular, rather

A RAILWAY SMOKING SALOON
(From the Bristol Gazette *report
for 10 September 1846)*

Its extreme length is 49 feet, the body being 30 feet, the ends being converted to a kind of open lounge. It runs upon six wheels, which are fitted with Adams patent bow springs. The internal decorations are of the most *recherché* (sic) description. The seats extend the full length of the side, and are handsomely covered with Morocco leather. A highly polished mahogany table occupies the centre, the entire fitted with self-balancing lamps. The sides are lighted by eight plate-glass windows of unusual size, while the ends are fitted up with four plates of looking-glass. Its drapery is composed of bright crimson silk framed in very graceful design. The roof presents an exceedingly chaste appearance. The groundwork is painted white, the mouldings being gilt. The general furniture is of richly carved polished mahogany. The exterior is painted a deep marone (sic) colour, ornamented with gold etchings and emblazoned with the company's ciphers... They will be attached to all the fast trains to and from Cambridge, passengers using them paying First Class fare.[35]

rakish group within the élite minority of First Class ticket-holders. It did nothing whatever to amend the real discomforts of travel, the breakdowns and general unpunctuality, the poor safety record, or the twin 'scams' of refreshment stop food and company travel insurance.

The campaign opened with one of *Punch*'s brief 'news announcements':

'RAILWAY LUXURIES
THE Railway Smoking Saloon having given such great satisfaction in the Eastern Counties, the spirited directors intend to start a billiard room on the same line.'[37]

Billiard rooms, if anything, were even more rakish than smoking rooms, because of potential gambling on the results of billiard matches, and the resulting possible cheating by 'billiard sharks'. By implication, then, this fake news item puts the real innovation in its social and moral place – mere pandering to the preferences of young upper-class rakehells.

A second brief announcement made use of part of

the ECR's actual original press release. Here, the satire lay in Mr Punch's comment:

'Railway Smoking
IT is announced that the smoking saloons are only to be attached to the fast trains of the Eastern Counties Railway. We presume that the fast trains on this line are those which are stuck fast in consequence of stoppages. It is certainly desirable to allow the passengers, under such circumstances, the opportunity of smoking, instead of leaving them to fume, as they have done hitherto.'[38]

This brings us to the real nub of Mr Punch's objections – the smoking saloons are merely cosmetic. Putting smoking saloons on the fast trains does nothing to cure the Eastern Counties' chronic unpunctuality and proneness to locomotive breakdown. We may chuckle at the bilingual pun of 'smoke' and 'fume', or groan at the pun on 'fast', but the point goes home: '*It could be so much better*' – and the Eastern Counties' 'spirited directors' are improving the *wrong thing*.

At this point *Punch* decides to produce a piece that will address the entire sorry mess of discomfort, scams, and cosmetic improvements and, actually on the facing page to 'Railway Smoking' above, prints the superb spoof article reproduced here. Both the spoof itself and its connection with the development of the ideas behind on-train dining are worth examination, so let us look at them in more detail.

The title and the opening statement between them make the basic point: it is perfectly possible to give a railway journey the comfort and luxury of a gentleman's club. But there are much more important elements of comfort, affecting many more passengers, than mere smoking rooms. Clubs, after all, serve refreshments, so why not run a 'refreshment room with every train' rather than a smoking saloon? At this point, *Punch*'s bête noir, the refreshment stop scam, is introduced, complete with comic exaggeration. Starting with M Chabert's fireproofing preparation, alternative 'solutions' to the problem are then given, in declining order of ridiculousness, with the travelling refreshment room being suggested as the least impractical.

Travelling refreshment rooms, however, imply to Mr Punch travelling soup, and the question of where to store this leads on to a fanfare of splendid nonsense that enables the writers to bring in most of *Punch*'s other bêtes noirs about the Eastern Counties Railway. The thick steam rising from the over-hot soup is much more visible than that rising from simple hot water, so it should logically have more power, and Eastern Counties engines are notoriously underpowered. So let's store the soup in the boiler, and run the engine on it – and if it is *pea* soup, so much the better, because we all know Eastern

---

Railway Luxuries

(*From* Punch *for September 1846*)

The Smoking Saloon on the Eastern Counties is only the first of a series of luxuries which it is intended to bestow upon travellers by railway. It is in contemplation to run a refreshment room with every train, so that people will have time allowed them to eat the articles sold, instead of being restricted as at present to the privilege of payment. Various plans have been suggested to enable passengers to swallow a cup of boiling hot tea or coffee, or a basin of hot soup in a minute and a half, but it has been proved that the period specified is quite insufficient for such a purpose. [*] It has been suggested that there might be kept and sold at all the refreshment rooms a preparation similar to that which enabled a certain MONSIEUR CHABERT some years ago to swallow melted lead without any inconvenience. Others have proposed that parties should be allowed to take soup or tea into the carriage with them, and send back the cup or basin by the up or down train, with a return ticket fastened to the piece of crockery as proof of its contents having been paid for. [*]

The most feasible scheme is, however, a portable refreshment-room, one of which should travel with every train; [**] and it might be advisable to have the boiler of the engine supplied with soup instead of plain water. It has been calculated that the steam produced by the former liquid, would have much greater force than the vapour arising from the latter, and the power of the pea in pea soup would have a wonderful influence on the speed of the locomotive.

A circulating library and reading-room will also shortly be placed on the Eastern Counties, and passengers will be at liberty to subscribe by the mile, or by the whole journey. There will be a Mechanics Institute for the Third Class, and the secretary has kindly undertaken to deliver a course of lectures on Anatomy, Life Insurance, and other subjects likely to prove useful to passengers travelling on this railway.[38]

Counties trains are notoriously late-running, and 'the power of the pea ['pee'?] would have a wonderful influence on the speed of the locomotive.'

The theme of slowness and late running reappears in the final paragraph too, along with another 'genteel' suggestion for an on-train comfort, the circulating library (reading on trains had become a national habit by this time, W. H. Smith's station bookstall franchises having started only two years later[39]) – but charging 'by the mile, or by the whole journey' rather than by the day, or by the week! And if a library, why not that other improving social scheme of the period, a Mechanics Institute? This enables Mr Punch to remind us of two or three more themes – the need to improve Third Class travel as well, and through the choice of lecture topics the Eastern Counties' poor safety record and the travel insurance scam.

The passage is certainly splendid mockery, but can we claim it has any serious currency in the history of the idea of 'dining at speed'? I believe we can, for several reasons. First, *Punch* in this period commonly combines a mixture of satire and perfectly serious suggestion in just this way; its characteristic satirical method at the time depends on putting ridicule and serious comment together and leaving the reader to reflect. Second, *Punch* was very widely read, often by influential people. Its general political stance in these early years was reformist. Ideas aired in its columns, therefore, even when expressed in a far-fetched form, are likely to find later consideration. And although the satirical point of the article is not merely on-train dining so much as a general insistence on the need for more comfortable provision for railway travellers, the satire may well have gained topicality from the fact that, according to the *Norwich Mercury*, three years earlier a party of 'ladies and gentlemen from the metropolis' actually had enjoyed a 'portable refreshment room' – or at least a cold luncheon collation – on one ECR train, on their way back from an excursion to Colchester![40]

And finally, the piece includes several interesting technical notions. It is the earliest UK piece of writing to clearly envision on-train catering provision in the form of a *saloon* carriage. It is also the first British piece of writing clearly to associate on-train dining with 'railway luxury' and the notion of club quality. Even the apparently dotty notion of taking crockery containing food on board and returning it later can be viewed as a pointer to the refreshment basket service pioneered in the 1870s – and also illustrates that there were possible alternative ideas of comfort travel available, apart from that of the dining car. Above all, however, the piece is important as showing yet again the genesis of ideas of comfortable travel in the feeling that 'it could be so much better'.

The third early British example of the idea of on-train dining is the most mysterious. In the same passage in which he quotes *Punch*, Wooler also quotes an extract that he claims is from the *Bristol Gazette*. The (untitled) extract is quite short, and I repeat it in full below:

'The invention consists in the construction of some newly-formed carriages, so as to constitute a sort of travelling caffe (sic) or railway restaurant, to be placed in the rear of the carriages, which are to be so constructed as to open into one another to an extent, enabling waiters to travel along the train and relieve the *ennui*, so inseparable from railway travelling, by supplies from a locomotive larder at the other end.

A bill of fare, showing what the refectory contains, is to be provided in each carriage, so that passengers, first, second, and third, may at any time stay the rage of hunger. Bells are to be at the command of the passengers to announce their wants to the waiter, who will travel to them along a narrow passage alongside the interior of the carriages constructed for the purpose. Should the proposed plan be adopted, railway travelling may be ranked among the beatitudes.'[32]

Wooler talks of this as repeating the ideas contained in the *Punch* passage, but clearly that can't be correct. The technical details of the passage are very different from the *Punch* spoof. That referred clearly to a refreshment *saloon*, in which passengers would sit to be served. This passage describes equally clearly at-seat waiter service of passengers *in their compartments*, of the sort envisaged 50 years later on the Great Central's London extension[19], but never really satisfactorily provided until refreshment trolleys came in in 1948 and open stock in 1960.[41]

Other of the ideas in the passage are ahead of their time too. The travellers call the waiter by a bell, and this too antedates the earliest non-emergency passenger-train staff communication between separate parts of the train by 50 years – to the Great Central's London Extension stock, again – and predates even internal within-carriage electric bell communication (first encountered in the GNR Pullman dining car of 1879) by around 30 years.

Perhaps even more remarkable, though, is the fairly detailed description of proposals for corridor coaches with through connections. The side corridor coach is generally attributed to Heussinger von Waldegg, who developed it between 1863 and 1870, in response to two notorious railway compartment murders in the early 1860s[42], while vestibule connections are normally ascribed to Pullman and came into use in the UK even later.

The passage also explicitly offers the comfort benefits of on-train food to all classes of traveller, 'first, second and third', which is again ahead of its time, the treatment of Third Class passengers in comparable terms to the other classes otherwise dating from Allport's Midland Railway reforms of 1872-5.[43] It also differs in this respect from the *Punch* passage, which consigns Third Class passengers to the travelling Mechanics Institute rather than allowing them into the refreshment saloon with the other classes.

Where then do the ideas contained in this passage originate? Wooler gives the passage as being from the *Bristol Gazette* for 1846, but no such passage occurs anywhere in that paper for that year. Given that Wooler believes it is later than the *Punch* article, it seems possible that the passage could come from 1847, but again no such passage occurs in any of the numbers for either that year or 1848. Thus either Wooler's date is completely wrong, or the passage comes not from the *Gazette*, but from one of its contemporaries – the *Bristol Mercury*, perhaps, or the *Railway Times*.

Similar problems surround the question of the piece's authorship. Stylistically it could well be from the Editor's own pen, but the ideas are technically highly original, and other original items from the Editor himself around this time tend to be social and political. Further, the opening as it stands – 'The invention consists…' – suggests that another's work is being editorially reported. But whose? The suggestion of forming a corridor 'alongside the interior of the carriages' suggests the inventor has broad gauge carriages in mind. The breadth and sweep of the originality, and its detail, put one in mind of Brunel, but by this time Brunel had already signed the Swindon refreshment room contract and was busy on the SS *Great Britain*.

One other possibility, however, is that the item could be a report of a suggestion from a correspondent, reproduced editorially rather than in the form of a letter. During this period, individuals did periodically write in to the paper to suggest possible improvements to railway travel comfort or safety arrangements, and these were sometimes printed in editorial comment format. It is therefore entirely possible that the suggestion of the 'locomotive larder' could have originated as a correspondent's response to journey inconvenience. The journey from London to Bristol around this time took about 4 hours, and Brunel's deal meant that the Great Western's only refreshment stop was at Swindon – just 1hr 10min out of London. If this was indeed the origin, then this proposal too may be said to be rooted in the notion that 'things could be so much better'.

I want to end this series of early occurrences of the idea of on-train dining and related ideas of travel in comfort with two more examples from the USA. Both of them will be discussed again later on in the book, but their importance here is to show increasingly common dissatisfaction with the way things were in US travel too, rather than any theoretical analysis such as Dearborn's, as the spur to ideas of comfort and improvement.

The first case is that of George Mortimer Pullman. Pullman's connections with on-train dining, for which he is best remembered in the UK, do not occur until 1868, and will be discussed in Chapter 3, but the germ of his ideas about travel comfort date from much earlier – from 1853, in fact. At that point Pullman was still working as a commercial traveller for his cabinet-maker brother in Albion, NY, and the journey was undertaken as part of a sales promotion tour. The journey was overnight, from Buffalo to Westfield, a distance of 58 miles, in a contemporary primitive sleeping car of a type that had been running on US railroads since 1836, and in winter. Behrend describes it like this:

> 'Such a vehicle could be described today as a *couchette* without any of its modern refinements, blankets, pillows [or] heating... The journey was 58 miles long. It was extremely cold. There was no heating of any kind; lighting was by candles'[44]

Pullman himself seems to have ascribed his interest in developing comfortable railroad travel to the trauma of that particular journey. Morel even claims that his vision of a luxurious day/sleeper convertible began actually during the journey:

> 'Dissatisfied with the crude accommodation and unable to sleep, Pullman spent the night thinking how the vehicle in which they were travelling could be improved.'[45]

The second case is of Fred Harvey, well into the 20th century a legend of railroad catering in the American West. We met Fred's ideas on customer care and service earlier in this chapter, but where did his notions of the supremacy of quality service come from?

Born in London in 1835, by 1856 Fred Harvey was working in the restaurant business in St Louis. By 1870 he had become general western freight agent for the Chicago Burlington & Quincy RR, and his business took him all over the Midwest. It was these journeys that were the key stimulus to develop his concepts of quality eating later demonstrated in his famous chain of refreshment stop depots and fleet of dining cars for the Atchison, Topeka & Santa Fé. Harvey was by nature a 'foodie', and back at his home his wife was also an excellent cook. But during his travels for the CB&Q he had to endure:

> '...terrible food [served] in a slovenly manner ... rancid bacon, canned beans, or ... eggs from the East aged and preserved in lime... The soda biscuits served with the eggs were known as "sinkers"... The diners could choose either cold tea or bitter black coffee... The tables lacked napkins and were covered by dirty cloths ... many times the trains would whistle [ie to signal departure] just as the food arrived.'[46]

Bryant in fact records that Harvey even tried to set up a company to do something about the situation while still working as freight agent for the CB&Q: it was only when these two hats proved too difficult to wear simultaneously that he approached the AT&SF, through contacts made in the freight agency business, to propose the highly successful catering business that still bears his name. Mitchell goes even further, and claims that 'ulcers caused by the poor food Harvey ate while working on the railroad was what inspired the idea for the Harvey Houses'.[47]

Alternatives to 'Dining at Speed'

The case of Fred Harvey is important to this account in another way. One frequent defining characteristic of an 'historical idea' is that it is one of several competing concepts or explanations in the same area. There are a number of such alternative conceptual solutions to the problem of refreshment discomfort while travelling, apart from the notion of the dining car, and the work and career of Fred Harvey demonstrates one of them. The *Punch* satire of 1846 had indicated the basic problem: the then normal method of railway catering provision – by short stops at refreshment rooms at intervals during the journey – had been inherited from the stagecoach, where it had worked reasonably well. On the railways, however, it clearly was not working, sometimes through business venality but more often simply through lack of organisation and time to serve the larger numbers involved. Put down like this, the problem suggests a number of possible responses:

1 Do nothing: This was not an acceptable solution, particularly as the number of travellers, their disposable income, and their expectations of comfort all steadily increased as the century wore on. *Punch*'s strictures make this very clear.

2 Allow travellers to purchase refreshments off-train, but take them on the train and consume them during the journey: This solution was attempted in the UK from about 1871 by Spiers and Pond[48] in the form of the railway refreshment hamper, sold at major stations to be handed in at journey's end, and enjoyed a considerable vogue in parallel to the dining car for many years.

3 Provide a means whereby travellers can be served with good-quality food on-train, which they can consume at will and in comfort: This is the classic 'dining at speed' solution. As *Punch* puts it, 'a portable refreshment room … should travel with every train.' This solution proved by far the most simple and complete – and additionally, as railway companies and travellers alike came to realise, it provided elements of an exotic experience that had in itself substantial drawing power.

4 Enable the travellers to consume the food comfortably in the time allowed at the refreshment stops: Although he eventually also operated a fleet of dining cars for the AT&SF, this last solution to providing refreshment comfort for rail travellers was initially what Fred Harvey developed.

When Harvey began operation for the AT&SF in 1876, no dining cars worked west of Kansas City. Indeed, until the 1880s there was a cartel agreement between the major Pacific-bound railroads not to operate such cars on any of their tracks.[49] Thus Harvey concentrated on what modifications to depot design and management would be needed to provide travellers with the opportunity at refreshment stops to consume quality food in comfort.

From Harvey's point of view, there were four main things wrong with the refreshment he had experienced on the road: the food quality was poor; the surroundings were unpleasant and insanitary; the service was slovenly; and the travellers were not given sufficient time to consume their food in a civilised manner. As an added problem, eating under such conditions brought out the worst in the customer, but Harvey realised that he could not enforce standards of customer behaviour unless his own establishments were decent. By addressing the problem in terms of its specific variables in this way, Harvey was able to provide a package of management decisions and quality standards, applied across all his establishments.

Food quality was improved by hiring professional and experienced chefs, by insisting on buying only first-class fresh provisions, and by ensuring a supply of good, potable water for drinking and cooking. In many Western railroad stops the local water supply was highly alkaline, so Harvey had the AT&SF freight in spring water from 'back East' in tanker cars.

Surroundings were often makeshift near the 'end of the line'. Nevertheless, even in the most extempore surroundings, the interiors were tastefully decorated, and the tables furnished with clean linen; whenever possible, Harvey built his own premises. Periodic, unscheduled inspections ensured cleanliness and decorum – Harvey would arrive wearing gloves, and run his fingers along the tops of doors and windows. Cracked or chipped crockery was thrown on the floor and broken: mis-set or dirty tables were overturned on the spot.

Improving the service similarly involved a complete re-think. Carefully selected waitresses – the famous 'Harvey Girls' – replaced the 'hash slingers'. Harvey advertised in newspapers and young women's magazines for 'young women of good character, attractive and intelligent, 18 to 30'.[47] The successful applicants had to sign a contract not to marry for a year, and lived in dormitories under the strictly regulated supervision of a matron. They wore a uniform of a clean white apron over a long-sleeved black dress. Harvey also paid his 'girls' well by contemporary standards – $17.50 per month[50], plus room and board, which equates to £3 10s 0d. per month, or £42 per annum – the upper end of Mrs

Beeton's 1869 scale for a housekeeper, and within her range for a 'professed cook'.[51]

Only the problem of ensuring that the customers had sufficient time to finish their meals now remained: crucially, this depended on how long it took the customer from arriving to being served. Harvey's solution made use of the now standard electric telegraph. As the train approached the last station before the refreshment stop, a conductor went through each car counting up how many wanted the standard set dinner in the restaurant, and how many wanted to order a light meal at the lunch counter. The numbers were telegraphed ahead at the stop, allowing the Harvey House manager to arrange the relevant number of settings and amounts of food in each category. When the train was around one mile from the refreshment stop, a warning gong sounded, and the table settings were checked and the starters put in place ready for the diners immediately they came in. As they began their first course, their main course and drinks order was taken, and by the time they had finished the starter, these were in process of being served to them.[45] Careful menu scheduling ensured that no refreshment stop on the line repeated any table d'hôte menu within four days.[47]

The Harvey House alternative solution to the problem of providing comfortable dining while travelling was elegant and ingenious, and found a great deal of favour with the travelling public in the American West. In the end, however, it was almost inevitable that it would lose out to actual 'dining at speed', for two reasons. First, however comfortable the dining and however good the food, one could only dine at fixed points and within a fixed time limit. And second, *one had to leave the train to do it.* Railway travel in comfort carries within it elements of dreamlike fantasy: the traveller is in a closed world, insulated from reality. But once the forward rolling motion stops and one comes down from the train, one is back in touch with reality: the dream is shattered, and it takes time for the mood to be rebuilt. Once one company decided to break the cartel ban on running dining cars, therefore, it was inevitable that eventually the others would follow suit.

And finally...

At the start of this chapter I suggested that there was one more characteristic of a historical 'idea' that we have not yet discussed – that it should have *explanatory power*. We have already seen that treating on-train dining as a historical idea begins to enable one to offer a consistent explanation of how the idea originated, and also to demonstrate its psychological and marketing force and suggest why this particular way of dealing with the problem of dining comfortably while on a railway journey should find greater favour than alternative solutions to the problem such as the Harvey House or the refreshment basket. In the next chapter, we shall explore another puzzling question: *Why did it take so long?*

2
WHY DID IT TAKE SO LONG?

The earliest ideas of on-train dining originate mainly from dissatisfaction with the existing state of railway travel comfort on both sides of the Atlantic.[1] By the mid-1840s these ideas are already invested with an aura of glamour: *Punch* talks of 'luxury' and the *Bristol Gazette* of making 'railway travel among the beatitudes'. Yet on-train dining does not become a reality in Britain until 1879. Even in the USA, George Pullman's first dining car is not built till 1868 – and dining cars do not operate west of Kansas City until an astonishing 1892.

So what took it so long? Previous accounts seem either to answer the question with a fatalistic 'History was to let more than three decades roll by'[2], to point to the lack of technical advances[3], or to give credit for the development to particular innovators, such as Pullman[4] – which again begs the question, why did those men address the problem when they did? Mitchell suggests that the American Civil War may have retarded the development of on-train dining in USA[5], but Pullman had started working on his luxury day and sleeping cars before that conflict began, and did not add dining facilities until three years after it had finished. Thus, none of the existing explanations provides an adequate account for the delay.

Waiting for technical advances?

We can be fairly sure that the delay in implementing on-train dining was *not* caused by a lack of technology. The essential requirements for on-train catering were:

1 **A saloon coach**, in which diners could sit at table
2 **Sufficient carriage size** to incorporate a kitchen and a dining area
3 **Sufficiently smooth riding** to enable passengers to dine in comfort, and food and drink to be served without spilling

4 **Bogie suspension** to contribute to both 2 and 3 above
5 **A means of cooking** suitable for use on a moving vehicle
6 **Vestibule connections** between the dining car and the rest of the train

Early US cars were even shorter than their British counterparts.[6] However, within a year of the invention of **bogie suspension** in 1834, **open saloon stock** was developed on the Baltimore & Ohio RR, and by the early 1840s the design had become general. Saloon coaches existed in England from an early date also, witness Brunel's 'grand saloon' of 1838 and the Eastern Counties smoking saloon of 1846, and Joseph Wright of Birmingham, founder of Metropolitan Cammell, took out a patent in 1844 for 'carriages with four, six, or eight wheeled bogies'[7]. On the straighter British track, however, coaches up to 40 feet long could be carried on six wheels, so that Wright's patent went largely unused until the 1870s.

As early as 1835, the Philadelphia & Columbia RR introduced a car with a food service counter at one end.[1] It was not successful, however, and the experiment was not repeated until 1863 on the Philadelphia, Wilmington & Baltimore, when two cars were fitted with a bar counter and steam-box. The experiment, again unsuccessful, was terminated after three years.[5] These abortive early US attempts demonstrate that simply having the technology available does not guarantee successful innovation in this area, and, together with the ECR's smoking saloons, they indicate that both **sufficient overall length** and adequately **smooth riding** were available by the middle 1840s.

That leaves just two supposed technological prerequisites for on-train dining: **a portable means of cooking** and **vestibule connections**. Although the early American attempts at on-train meals served food prepared off-train, cooking ranges for use 'unfixed' in a wide variety of settings were available by the late 1850s. Mrs Beeton's *Book of Household Management*, first published in 1861, describes three main types of 'unfixed' range. Two of them burn anthracite: the 'Treasure' range, from Constantine & Co (a London firm), which 'do their work well wherever they may be placed', and the 'Mistress' range from Smith & Welland, British agents for an American design, whose products 'are portable, and therefore tenants' fixtures'. The third, Fletcher's No 4 Range, cooks by gas, a process that 'has been much on the increase in late years'.[8]

Thus the only technical 'prerequisite' for on-train dining not already in existence by the 1850s was the through vestibule connection. But although connections between the dining car and the rest of the train are desirable for increased trade, they are not absolutely necessary, and the dining cars of both the original GNR Leeds-London service of 1879 and the Midland's slightly later Liverpool-Manchester-London service were self-contained. A prospective diner on the Leeds-London service could 'enter or quit the Pullman Car at any station where the train stops, but should give notice beforehand of his intention, lest the train be full'[9], while dining car passengers joining the up Liverpool-London service at Manchester were asked to book in advance so that their reservations could be telegraphed ahead to Liverpool.[10]

Thus all the essential technical elements needed to make on-train dining possible existed, both in the USA and in Britain, at least 20 years before such dining became a reality.

Attitudes to railway travel – public ambivalence?

The mechanisation and speed of railway travel shocked the people who first encountered them. In an early chapter of *The Railway Journey*, Wolfgang Schivelbusch quotes an anonymous piece of 1839 that encapsulates the strangeness of the new mechanised travel:

'When we are travelling by stage-coach at the rate of eight or ten miles an hour, we can understand the nature of the force which sets the vehicle in motion... But, when proceeding on a journey by the rail-road, we are seldom allowed to get a sight of the wondrous power which draws us so rapidly along... The traveller then wonders, not only at the rapidity of his journey, but often wishes to ... comprehend the means by which it was effected.'[11]

One favourite early Victorian metaphor for railway travel was flight[12]: another was the projectile or cannonball[13], with its overtones of death and destruction, borne out in alarmingly frequent railway accidents. And this new form of travel came at what has been described as 'the grimmest period in the history of the nineteenth century'[14]. Rail journeys brought urban deprivation into the direct vision of the middle-class traveller, and if the Government could use railway speed to move troops to put down insurrection[15], rioters from Wigan and Chorley could use it to reach Preston[16].

It is thus not surprising that early attitudes to railway travel should have been characterised by severe uncertainty, and while under mild stress people have a tendency to want to nibble, the last thing people who are really *seriously* stressed want to do is relax over a meal. They will either eat first, or they will wait until the stressful situation is over, then celebrate their release. Ruskin, writing in 1849, sums the situation up like this:

'The whole system of railway travel is addressed to people who, being in a hurry, are therefore ... miserable. No one would travel in that manner who could help it.'[17]

Thus it would hardly be surprising if interest in dining while travelling needed to wait on the emergence of a new generation, for whom railways were a normal means of conveyance. This scenario requires individuals born after the railway network had largely been completed to be the ones who would grow up to be the dining-car patrons we are looking for – and the time-lag involved would put our start date for an interest in on-train dining to the 1870s – just where we find it occurring in reality.

This is all very well as theory, but can we be sure that railways were *really* viewed in such stressful terms? And can we be sure there weren't other factors at work? The answers seem to be 'Yes, railways were often viewed like that', but 'No, we can't exclude other causes too.' Several examples of ambivalent attitudes towards railway travel corroborate this general argument. Brunel, for instance, reacts to his first train journey with a mixture of exhilaration at the overall experience and of irritation at its current limitations. Brunel is an enthusiast already in tune with the coming railway world, yet even he feels that railway travel is not yet all it should be. So what about his contemporaries?

Another relatively sanguine scientific early traveller was Charles Darwin, who in late 1838 and early 1839 travelled between London and his fiancée Emma Wedgwood's family home in Maer, Shropshire, on three occasions, the first of these seemingly also his first rail journey. Clearly he found the shortening of the journey important, but even so, he had serious reservations about the activity. Of the first of his three journeys he wrote to Emma:

> 'My journey up was dull enough – I was altogether disappointed with the railroad – it was so rough and so much plagued with the many changes. – At Birmingham, I heard a head-man scolding furiously at a guard for something he had done – he ended with the remark – not particularly consolatory to me, who had no very clear idea, where they had hurried my luggage, – "& that is the reason, we lose so many things every day." – It was raining hard, when we reached London, & the scramble for luggage was glorious, – two or three poor old ladies, I suspect, died broken hearted that same night. – poor old souls they appeared greatly agitated.'[18]

Like Brunel, he finds the train ride 'rough', but the stresses for Darwin go far beyond that. He feels 'plagued' (disoriented) by the series of rapid changes of train, pressed for time, unsure of what is going on around him ('no very clear idea, where they had hurried my luggage'), and not sure of the trustworthiness or competence of those in whose charge he had put himself. Even ending the journey is stressful – 'the scramble for luggage was glorious … two or three poor old ladies … died broken hearted'.

Darwin's second train journey between Maer and London (in November 1838) was even more of a disaster: Darwin himself records that it was extremely unpleasant. The train into Birmingham was delayed by high winds, and the London connection was not held. However, since Darwin's earlier journey the Royal Station Hotel had been opened, so that he was able to obtain his steak and a bed while waiting for the Manchester-Birmingham-London night train. Darwin shows no surprise at this facility, and is quite cool about his unusual retiring hours and waking instruction: he is treating the whole episode exactly like a similar problem at a

---

Darwin's second train journey

My dear Emma

I have been writing letters all morning, & before I go to the Geolog Soc. I shall amuse myself by giving you an account of my travels. – The train was retarded by the high winds, & a rumour passed from one carriage to the other, that we possibly should miss the London train. – Accordingly as we entered the station-yard at Birmingham, we saw the London train start, & they would not wait even the five minutes necessary just to jump into the carriages. – The indignation of all us unfortunates was immense. – I can laugh now, though I could not then, at the expression of all faces, as each group turned out of its carriage, like bees out of a hive. – nothing could be heard, but 'infamous, scandalous conduct – directors, parliament rascals.' &c. – One high-minded passenger avenged himself, there being nobody to abuse excepting porters, by going to London in a night horse coach, much to his inconvenience. –

I took another line, & comforted myself with a beefsteak & tea, & then went to bed at 5 o'clock with orders, which greatly amused the chamber maids, to be called at ¼ before eleven to go by ½ past 11 night train. I did [not] sleep, but enjoyed a nice quiet cogitation over the last few days, & the prospect of the long future & the realization of my day dreams. – At the proper time I got into the London train, with my temper somewhat soured by the cold and wet night, & found for my companions three Manchester hogs, who passed the whole night playing whist on one of the cushions, drinking huge quantities of brandy & water & singing half-blasphemous songs. I was right glad to escape out of such a hogsty & reach my lodging at half past six in the morning…'[19]

---

coaching inn. This point further underpins the notion of eating accompanying the *relief* of stress: Darwin feels himself to be back on well-known territory.

In novels and other literary works of the period, and in journalism, the same perceptions of rail travel as a turbulent and alarming upheaval again find wide acknowledgement across the general period 1835-55. Mrs Gaskell's *Cranford*, for example, finds the railway a dangerous intrusion. Although it only appears three times in the novel, all three occasions are malevolent. It first appears on the very first page, as the main factor that has depopulated Cranford of its menfolk:

> 'If a married couple comes to settle in the town, somehow the gentleman disappears; he is … accounted for by being with his regiment, his ship, or closely engaged in business all the week in the great neighbouring commercial town of Drumble, distant only twenty miles on a railroad.'[20]

And this state of affairs is contrasted with the older, more natural and organic order that the railway, by changing the location of business, has disturbed, represented by the local surgeon:

> 'In short, whatever has become of the gentlemen, they are not at Cranford. What could they do if they were there? The surgeon has his round of thirty miles, and sleeps at Cranford; but every man cannot be a surgeon.'

The second reference occurs a few pages later:

> 'He was a half-pay captain, and had obtained some situation on a neighbouring railroad, which had been vehemently petitioned against by the little town.'[21]

This time the railway introduces a new character – Captain Brown. Captain Brown's attitudes represent a different set of mores from those of the genteel inhabitants of Cranford, and one they initially find difficult to come to terms with. He freely admits he is poor (instead of dressing it up as 'elegant economy') and he is an enthusiastic follower of the works of 'Mr Boz' (Charles Dickens). The 'obnoxious railroad' is introducing notions of modernity and openness into an older, more closed society: the Cranford folk are unnerved by this, and though they eventually come to accept, and even like, Captain Brown, the railway remains an Indian giver. Its third intrusion into the novel is to cause the death of the Captain in saving the life of an innocent child, and in so doing to characterise 'them nasty cruel railroads' as a whole.[22]

It was Charles Dickens's journal *Household Words* that serialised *Cranford*, and Dickens remains our largest single literary source of attitudes towards railways and railway journeys, especially in *Dombey and Son* (1846-48). Dickens, too, sees railway building as displacing the older way of life, but to him the subject is much more complex – and much more

frightening. For Dickens, railway building releases an immense source of uncontrolled energy, likened in the early chapters of *Dombey* to 'the shock of a great earthquake'[23]. There are elements of natural disaster in his description of the works in Camden Town to complete Euston terminus, mixed with nightmare ('unintelligible as a dream') and apocalyptic vision. In the end the new world triumphs over the old, and brings apparent prosperity in its wake, but there is a restlessness in the piling up of the 'railway goods' on show in the windows, a suggestion that the new externally provided prosperity has broken something profound in the natural world – 'as if the sun itself had given in'[24].

The construction and arrival of the railway, then, brings energy, economic prosperity, new ideas, and freedom of expression, but it also disturbs and destroys the older, quieter way of life, rooted in the pastoral, the country town or the urban village, and substitutes a man-made external regulation for natural order. And this ambivalence is made the more threatening by the association of the 'nasty cruel railroad' with violent upheaval, explosions, and accidents.

The individual railway journey is invested with a similar ambivalence. Here is the young Coningsby, in Disraeli's 1844 novel of the same name, arriving in Manchester:

> 'He had travelled the whole day through the great district of labour, his mind excited by strange sights, and at length wearied by their multiplication. He had passed over the plains where iron and coal supersede turf and corn, dingy as the entrance of Hades, and flaming with furnaces; and now he was among illumined factories with more windows than Italian palaces, and smoking chimneys taller than Egyptian obelisks. Alone in the great metropolis of machinery itself, sitting down in a solitary coffee-room glaring with gas, with no appetite, a whirling head, and not a plan or purpose for the morrow, why was he there?'[25]

In Disraeli's novel, the very rapidity of railway travel dislocates the senses and causes weariness and stress. It carries the traveller in a single day from the old familiar world of 'turf and corn' to the new industrial world of glaring light and shadow, engendering a pervading sense of anomie. The description of the factories and chimneys deliberately recalls the great buildings of the Renaissance and of antiquity, but only to efface them and substitute glare and smoke for beauty and reason. The end-product is astonishingly uncomfortable: we would be hard put to it to recognise that Coningsby was actually sitting in Manchester's most prestigious and comfortable hotel – the Adelphi – had we not been told so in the preceding paragraph.

For Dickens, in a passage of *Dombey* first published during 1847, the journey has become equally rapid, equally industrial, but now even wilder and more terrifying. Mr Dombey's railway journey, after the death of Paul, with Major Bagshot to Birmingham, on their visit to Leamington, is described thus:

'He found no pleasure or relief in the journey. The power that forced itself upon its iron way – its own – defiant of all paths and roads, piercing through the heart of every obstacle, and dragging every living creature of all classes, ages and degrees behind it, was a type of the triumphant monster, Death…

Louder and louder yet, it shrieks and cries as it comes tearing on resistless to the goal: and now its way … is strewn with ashes thickly. Everything around is blackened. There are dark pools of water, muddy lanes, and miserable habitations far below. There are jagged walls and falling houses close at hand, and through the battered roofs and broken windows, wretched rooms are seen, where want and fever hide themselves… As Mr Dombey looks out of his carriage window, it is never in his thoughts that the monster who has brought him there has let the light of day in on these things, not made or caused them. It was the journey's fitting end.'[26]

The journey, like Coningsby's, leaves the traveller enervated and nervous, but Dombey's journey into Hades reveals two things that Coningsby's does not: first, that the scene is merely dreadful, not dreadful-but-triumphant (there are no comparisons of factories here with palaces or obelisks), and second, that the scene is populated – it has wretched inhabitants, about whom we are invited to feel guilt and pity. Dickens is of course well aware, as he points out, that the railway 'let the light of day in' on these social evils, rather than caused them, but Dombey clearly doesn't understand the difference, and many real-life Victorians would have harboured similar feelings of guilt and concern.[27]

Mrs Gaskell's novel associated 'them nasty cruel railroads' with motiveless and unjustified fatal accidents, and of course at the climax to *Dombey and Son* itself the villain is mown down by 'the express, [which] don't stop', while attempting to evade his pursuers, who have arrived on 'the short train'[28]. Because of their spectacular nature, railway accidents were very much in the public consciousness, so much so, for example, that *Punch* repeatedly harped on them:

'Smashery, mashery, crash!
Into the "Goods" we dash:
The "Express", we find,
Is just behind –
Smashery, mashery, crash!'[29]

The public was not entirely silly in being worried about early railway journeys. Before the electric telegraph block system, when trains were despatched on a 'time interval' system and travelled at very uneven speeds, accidents like the one mocked in *Punch*'s parody of 'Hickory Dickory Dock' were all too common. During 1844 and 1845, the *Bristol Gazette* averages between one and two reports of fatal railway accidents somewhere in the country per week – three or four in bad weeks – and by 14 August 1845 was sufficiently concerned to devote an editorial to the topic. By the late 1850s, though, attitudes to railway travel had begun to change, with the coming of a generation of travellers for whom railways were part of the normal landscape. By 1858, when Trollope wrote *Doctor Thorne*, he could present his younger characters as taking a railway journey of between five and six hours from 'Barchester' to London with sufficient equanimity for one of them to quietly go to sleep:

'"Do you know, Oriel, I was never so sleepy in my life. What with all that fuss of Gazebee's, and one thing and another, I could not get to bed till one o'clock; and then I couldn't sleep. I'll take a snooze now, if you won't think it uncivil." And then, putting his feet upon the opposite seat, he settled himself comfortably to his rest.'[30]

And by six years later, as shown by the list of the 'Wonders of Modern Travel' from *Punch* for 1864 (reproduced overleaf), the fears of the railway journey had degenerated into a set of relatively minor anxieties, chiefly about time and luggage, among which interestingly enough figure 'Wonder if I've got time for a sandwich and a glass of sherry' and 'Wonder that they don't keep nice sandwiches and glasses of sherry.'[31]

THE WONDERS OF MODERN TRAVEL.

TO THE STATION.

WONDER if my watch is right, or slow, or fast.
Wonder if that church clock is right.
Wonder if the cabman will take eighteenpence from my house to the Station.

THE STATION.

Wonder if the porter understood what I said to him about the luggage.
Wonder if I shall see him again.
Wonder if I shall know him when I *do* see him again.
Wonder if I gave my writing-case to the porter, or left it in the cab.
Wonder where I take my ticket.
Wonder in which pocket I put my gold.
Wonder where I got that bad half-crown which the clerk won't take.
Wonder if that's another that I've just put down.
Wonder where the porter is who took my luggage.
Wonder where my luggage is.
Wonder again whether I gave my writing-case to the porter, or left it in the cab.
Wonder which is my train.
Wonder if the guard knows anything about that porter with the writing-case.
Wonder if it *will* be "all right" as the guard says it will be.
Wonder if my luggage, being now labelled, will be put into the proper van.
Wonder if I've got time to get a sandwich and a glass of Sherry.
Wonder if they've got the *Times* of the day before yesterday, which I haven't seen.
Wonder if *Punch* of this week is out yet.
Wonder why they don't keep nice sandwiches and Sherry.
Wonder if there's time for a cup of coffee instead.
Wonder if that's our bell for starting.
Wonder which is the carriage where I left my rug and umbrella, so as to know it again.
Wonder where the guard is to whom I gave a shilling to keep a carriage for me.
Wonder why he didn't keep it; by "it," I mean the carriage.
Wonder where they've put my luggage.

THE JOURNEY.

Wonder if my change is all right.
Wonder for the second time in which pocket I put my gold.
Wonder if I gave the cabman a sovereign for a shilling.
Wonder if that was the reason why he grumbled less than usual and drove off rapidly.
Wonder if any one objects to smoking.
Wonder that nobody does.
Wonder where I put my lights.
Wonder whether I put them in my writing-case.
Wonder for the third time whether I gave my writing-case to the porter or left it in the cab.
Wonder if anybody in the carriage has got any lights.
Wonder that nobody has.
Wonder when we can get some.
Wonder if there's anything in the paper.
Wonder why they don't cut it.
Wonder if I put my knife in my writing-case.
Wonder for the fourth time whether I gave, &c.
Wonder if I can cut the paper with my ticket.
Wonder where I put my ticket.
Wonder where I *could* have put my ticket.
Wonder where the deuce I put my ticket.

A satirical list of passengers' concerns. *Reproduced from Punch for 26 November 1864, Vol XLVII, p217*

Corporate attitudes – what are railways for?

Contemporary railway company attitudes also played a part in delaying on-train catering. Directors of early railways thought of themselves as movers of goods, not passengers; the evidence to Parliament for the Liverpool & Manchester Railway, for example, concentrates on the advantages to Manchester merchants of 'a safe and cheap mode of transit for merchandise'[32], and the historian Roy Williams comments of the Leicester & Swannington:

'We now take it for granted that railways have stations for the convenience of passengers. Not so on the Leicester & Swannington. *Passengers were not really encouraged anyway* [my italics], so they just followed the happy coaching habit of using the inns near the (ungated) road crossings.'[33]

However, it was obvious from its opening that passengers wanted to travel on the Liverpool & Manchester, and by 1845 the passenger receipts of many lines outweighed their goods traffic receipts. For example, in January 1845 the *Bristol Gazette* reported the weekly receipts of the Bristol & Gloucester Railway to be £678 11s 0d for passengers, as against £372 13s 0d for goods. Clearly, by 1845 it made good business sense to carry passengers!

But even so, acceptance of passenger traffic was somewhat grudging. Passenger demand was there, and First and Second Class passenger receipts certainly seemed to pay. Third Class passengers, though, were a different matter: both economically and socially their conveyance was felt much more dubious, and adequate provision for them had to wait several decades. In fact their economic importance depended on the industrialisation of the area served by the company – by 1850 they produced a majority of passenger receipts on the Lancashire & Yorkshire, but their contribution on the Great Western was barely half that.[34] Initially the Liverpool & Manchester made no provision for them at all, and the dreaded Eastern Counties provided 'truck platforms, with eight open seats fixed thereon transversely'[35] – a far cry from the opulence of its Smoking Saloon!

But providing anything more than spartan facilities even for First and Second Class passengers created problems for the early companies. To service capital outlays on infrastructure, early railways needed an operating ratio of no more than 50%, but operating passenger services caused substantial additional labour expenses.[36] Providing on-train amenities also increased carriage weight, which led to extra coal used per journey, and new, more powerful locomotives to pull the heavier trains. Thus, for example, Patrick Stirling and Charles Sacré, the CMEs of the Great Northern and the Manchester, Sheffield & Lincolnshire respectively, wrote to the directors of the latter concern, as late as October 1875, opposing the introduction of bogie saloons to give smoother running on their joint Sheffield-London business services, in terms of both maintenance and operating costs.

On-train amenities also increased opportunity costs, because they took up space that could be used to carry additional fare-paying passengers. Providing such amenities thus not only increased the running costs, but also reduced the number of passenger fare receipts with which to pay for them. The result was that the average passenger train operating ratio had increased from 50% to 64% by 1914. Worst of all were dining cars, which from the passenger receipt point of view were completely 'dead weight'. And this was not merely a British railway concern: McKenzie points out that American railroads felt it too:

'American railroad managers thought of themselves as people movers, not caterers … railroad managers were … unconvinced that the investment was worth it. Concerned directors, and the shareholders who elected them, both watched the bottom line. The problems were as simple as the rules of supply and demand.'[37]

But the 'rules of supply and demand' also meant that a company providing a passenger train service of any length had to take *some* account of the need for passenger refreshment. Coaching firms had catered for such demands by providing refreshment at the posting inns, and by allowing hawkers to offer their wares to passengers at stops. From the beginning of passenger railway travel, customers and purveyors alike had assumed that the same would apply:

'At Eccles, trays were "poked" at the passengers filled with the cakes then famous and at Newton, where an hotel of note was situated near the line, the same attention was paid; "home-brewed" and sandwiches were carried by waiters along the length of the train, in imitation of the stage-coach custom.'[38]

However, railway trains conveyed many more people at a time than coaches, were much more dangerous objects for anyone who slipped under the wheels, and were crucially dependent for service punctuality and safety on keeping to precise timings, to the minute. The only way to solve this problem was by banning hawkers altogether, and strictly licensing what hotels might be permitted to serve arriving and departing passengers 'on the Line', and by 1837 several railways had already enacted such rules.

But that didn't stop passenger demand for refreshment facilities. By 1840, accordingly, most companies had instituted refreshment rooms with stops of around 20 minutes at journey midway points. Usually, the premises were railway-owned, but their management and operation was contracted out. Again, this was true on both sides of the Atlantic; as McKenzie observed, railways were 'people movers, not caterers'. Thus, during the early part of the railway age, travellers find the actual journey so stressful that it is improbable they would have had much appetite for dining *while on a moving train*, but they *do* need to dine *somewhere*, before setting out, on arrival, or during a break in the journey. It is in the financial interests of the railway companies to meet this demand by providing refreshments at breaks of journey, but to eschew any on-train refinements that would add serious 'dead weight' to the operating cost equations.

Eating while travelling – happy coaching habits rule OK?

Early railway passengers carried over attitudes or practices from the world of the stagecoach into their rail journeys. Although we tend to talk about 'the railway age' superseding 'the age of the stagecoach', the two forms of public conveyance co-existed overall for around a generation (1825-50) while the railway network was being built – and in some more remote parts of Britain (and in the American West) for a good deal longer. Further, people tend to stick to existing paradigms for as long as possible, even when circumstances change.

Coach operation was closely linked with inns and livery stables: coaches started from and terminated at major inns, while others were interchange points. The coach operators were often also the proprietors of these inns, and the operating profit from them provided the initial capital for their coaching businesses. It was therefore in the interests of coaching operators to provide refreshments at their inns for their travellers: the business practice had been basic to coaching since 1720. Departures from the main coaching inns seem to have been block timed, with timings designed to fit in between mealtimes: the common 8am departure allowed for an early breakfast before boarding, while an arrival at somewhere between 3pm (Oxford-London) and 5pm (Banbury-Oxford) likewise fitted in well with the usual timings (3.30 to 5.45) for dinner at the period.[39]

These coaching breakfasters and diners, booking at around 4d a mile inside or 2d a mile outside, ate from the 'ordinary' or host's table menu.[40] Socially this group is very wide, from the son of a country squire going away to public school (as in *Tom Brown's Schooldays*) to the medical student son of a stable liveryman (John Keats, who despite his consumptive cough travelled 'outside' to save money). The coaching passages in *Tom Brown's Schooldays* afford us good examples of stagecoach travel and refreshment during the 1830s.[41]

Tom and his father, Squire Brown, travel up to London on one day, and Tom travels down to Rugby on the next by an 'early coach' (his own words). As a result of this schedule, Tom needs a breakfast 'on the road' while on the way to Rugby. The substantial quantity of this breakfast is not particularly surprising – breakfasts in contemporary literature are frequently massive affairs, and we have every reason to suppose the reality was similar to the fiction.[42] What is perhaps surprising, though, is the unhurried nature of the whole affair. The coach arrives, and is clearly expected. The passengers enter the inn's front room, assemble round, and are served at, a common table – literally the 'table d'hôte'. They eat, pay, have time for a stroll, while the horses are being changed 'leisurely and in a highly-finished manner', all in the space of 20 minutes. Of course, there would only have been around 12-15 of them, even if the 'Tally-Ho' were full.

The passage also sheds some interesting light on social gradations among the passengers and staff. The passengers are collectively described as 'gentlemen' and Tom, despite his youth, is addressed as 'sir'. It is tacitly assumed that all the long-distance passengers on the coach fall into this category, though we are less sure about one character, the 'sportsman', a short-distance fare picked up from 'a lodge' within the stage immediately before breakfast; indeed, we are not even altogether sure of his name.

The social gradations among the passengers and coaching staff are also indicated by where they breakfast and what they eat (and smoke). The 'gentlemen' breakfast in the front room, and consume a mixture of hot and cold viands and tea or coffee. The Coachman, who has a status in between that of a servant and a gentleman, breakfasts there too, but 'eschews hot potations', eating cold beef and drinking ale: he is served not by the head waiter but by the barmaid. The 'sportsman' gives further indication of his ambiguous social standing by joining him (and they later share a cigar, at a time when gentlemen did not usually smoke in public). The Guard, who is subordinate to the Coachman, does not enter the front room at all, but breakfasts in the Tap: we are not told what he ate or drank, but he

is given a cheroot to smoke – even less gentrified than the sportsman's cigars.

In real life, stagecoach passenger social gradations could be even more complex. Hughes chooses not to show us any marked distinction between 'inside' and 'outside' passengers – but such distinctions certainly existed in reality. In September 1847 our old friend the *Bristol Gazette* printed in its 'VARIETIES' column a reminiscence of a stagecoach journey a few years earlier made by a young lady going north to take up a position as a governess to a titled family, and travelling 'inside', where she happened to be the only passenger. The account continues as follows:

‘At midday the coach stopped at an inn, at which dinner was provided, and she alighted and sat down at the table. An elderly man followed and sat down also. The young lady rang the bell and, addressing the waiter, said "This is an outside passenger. I cannot dine with an outside passenger"…’[43]

The story has a moral ending: the gentleman, who good-naturedly offers to move to a different room, turns out to be the noble Lord to whose residence she is travelling, and the young lady is duly mortified about her snobbery. The importance for us lies in the clear sense of social segregation between 'inside' and 'outside' passengers implied by the tale, and its direct ancestry of the railway notion of separate First and Second Class refreshment rooms.

The company of stagecoach travellers did *not*, however, include the labouring classes. If these people travelled at all, they travelled by market cart or by canal barge, very much more slowly and at rates of between ½d and 1¼d a mile[44]; they took food with them or bought snacks and beer from hawkers or potboys along the way. Thus we can already see the beginnings of the distinction between First or Second Class travellers and Third Class, travelling in much slower and cruder conveyances, sometimes together with goods, and excluded from railway refreshment facilities for much of the 19th century. It was not, after all, as Freeman suggests[45], that the coming of the railways led directly to class segregation among the travelling public: they may certainly have coined the term, but the phenomenon was already there in the days of the stagecoach and carrier's cart.

The early railways took over this refreshment paradigm of eating at an associated inn: the London & Birmingham opened its Royal Station Hotel at its Curzon Street terminus, at which Darwin consumed his beefsteak after having missed his connection, as early as 1838. Facilities such as the Royal Station were used almost exactly as their equivalents were used by travellers by stagecoach. Eating 'on the road', however, was less easy to replicate on a rail journey, since trains did not stop long enough at intermediate stations; but once through services commenced the pattern developed of refreshment breaks at designated stations – Wolverton, Normanton, York – which were roughly midway in the journey. From the description in *Tom Brown's Schooldays* it would even seem that the standard stopping time of 20 minutes at these points was directly derived from the old stagecoach practice.

Arrangements at terminal stations worked reasonably well, but it was not long before unexpected problems arose with eating at a refreshment break and at a changing point. The 20-minute refreshment stop, leisurely when only 12-15 people had to be served and everything could be prepared on time, simply could not be adjusted to feeding trainloads of 150 people or more. (Even Fred Harvey found that each of his 'Harvey Girls' could only serve 16 people in that time.[46]) In an attempt to bring some order into the British railway refreshment room chaos, the 'bar counter' was invented, but even this could not solve the problem. There was also a problem of quality control, with so much food being prepared for such fast service with an unknown actual number of consumers, even leaving aside the 'soup scam' described in the previous chapter. Brunel, as we have already seen, abominated Swindon coffee and said so, and as late as 1868 Trollope was remarking 'The real disgrace of England is the railway sandwich.'[47]

The logistical problems of eating while waiting for connecting trains were analogous. Here, the vagaries of early railway travel made it impossible to predict if there would be time at all. Sometimes the problem lay in the early railways' ticketing regulations, which might require the traveller to re-book at each connection, as in this account given to the Parliamentary Select Committee on Railways of a journey from Preston to London in January 1839:

'I came up to London in the middle of January and was very desirous … to come through in one carriage… I found that there was no chance of it, and I could only book to Parkside, and from Parkside I had to book again to Birmingham, and the inconvenience was so great at Birmingham that I had no time to get refreshment properly, having to look after my luggage.'[48]

Clearly the incensed traveller had expected to use the change of trains at Birmingham as a coaching-style 'on the road' refreshment stop, and was angry at being unable to do so.

A second cause of difficulty lay in the much shorter connecting times that had come along with the general increase in speed from coach to train, coupled with the uncertainty of early trains, with their lightly powered locomotives, keeping time. We have already seen one such contretemps described by Charles Darwin. As a result of that experience, Darwin had intended to arrange the timings of his next journey in such a way as to take maximum advantage of the break at Curzon Street as a potential dinner stop – but fate was to take a hand. The result is described in his third 'railway letter' to Emma Wedgwood.

Darwin's third 'railway letter'

To Emma Wedgwood [20 January 1839]
Athenaeum
Sunday Night

My dear Emma,
I suspect I have to thank you, that I am a living man, for if you had not given me the sandwiches I should have died from starvation in one of the rail road carriages. We only got to Birmingham, five minutes before the London train started, so that by the time I had got my luggage all safe and a ticket, the bell rang to be off. – I drank a glass of water preparatory & eat my luncheon in the coach; nevertheless I was awesomely hungry by 9 o'clock when, I reached *home*, good dear home in Gower St[t]. [sic] – There is something good in all bad things: in the first place I had no dinner to pay for; the doing of which to the amount of half a crown had considerably ruffled my companion's temper without apparently having filled his stomach; & secondly they had no time to weigh my luggage, which they did at Whitmore and made me pay three shillings for – I vow, during our journeys to & fro, we will buy a basket and take dinner with us, & a bottle of water; my inward man shall not be so maltreated another time…'[49]

The letter then continues with domestic news.

Darwin had intended to leave himself enough time between trains to both rebook and also use the hotel coffee room as a dinner stop. What upset his plan was not the rebooking arrangements, but the late running yet again of the train on the Whitmore branch – arriving on this occasion only just in time for his connection. He jokes about 'saving half a crown' and suggests that the dinner would not in fact have been very good – but it is clear that he was more than a little angry, at the disappointment to his plans as much as at the resultant privation – 'my inward man shall not be so maltreated another time'.

'Luncheon is for wimps'

If on-train dining facilities had been provided earlier than they were, then what meals could have been served? In this final section of the chapter I shall argue that the most likely meal to be needed during most of this period would have been lunch, that at this time men of business dined comparatively early and either did not eat lunch, or ate only a snack at their desks, and that the introduction of dining cars coincides with the point in Victorian society when this ceased to be true.

At the beginning of the period, times and journey timings on most railways had a restricted pattern. Darwin's letters show that if one missed the 5pm departure from Birmingham for London, there was not another train until 11.30, and the equivalent down train would have left London at about 3pm, arriving at Birmingham at around 6pm.[50] Further north, the main trains per day on the Manchester–Bolton line were two only, those from Manchester leaving at 7.25am and 3.15pm (described as 'a late train').[51] For the journey from Birmingham to Bristol, the information is very similar. All of this points to early rail travel continuing the timings of the stagecoaches, with the main timings involving either departure after breakfast or arrival in time for dinner.

It follows, then, that the meal most likely to have been required en route by travellers at this time would have been what we would today call 'lunch'. But did such a meal actually exist, as a regular set meal, at this period? The answer to this question is far from simple, but I will try and précis the main lines of historical argument about it. At the opening of our period, the usual hour for breakfast for the upper and middle classes was 10am[52], with dinner occurring, according to local fashion and personal whim, at a range of times between 3.45 and 6pm.[53] However, it is clear from Palmer's groundbreaking book *Movable Feasts*

that throughout the 19th century breakfast became steadily earlier, and dinner steadily later. The question that arises is thus 'what did people do when the interval between these two meals started to reach or exceed eight hours?' A brief general answer is given in Gerard Brett's *Dinner Is Served*:

'As the pressure of daily work combined with other forces to push the breakfast hour back and the dinner hour forward, and thus lengthen the day between them to perhaps ten or eleven hours, other meals had to be invented to fill in the time. The first of these is lunch, ... [also] ... known as Nunchin, defined in Johnson's *Dictionary* of 1753 as a 'piece of victuals eaten between meals'... Lunch long retained the incidental character of its earlier days, and not until far into the nineteenth century was it recognised as a regular feature of daily life. It interfered with the day's work, and when admitted at all it was in many cases kept to a minimum.'[54]

Darwin is thus keeping to an old tradition when he refers above to the sandwiches provided by Emma Wedgwood for him to eat in the initial coach journey as 'my lunch'. Mrs Beeton provides similar evidence for Brett's analysis:

'Luncheon, as a word of comprehensive meaning, may fairly take a high place, signifying as it does such a grand variety of meals, ranging from the simple "glass of wine and a biscuit" or the more humble "crust of bread and cheese and a glass of ale" to an elaborate meal that is in all but name a dinner.'[55]

Indeed, even her most elaborate production – a gargantuan affair for a large public event – turns out from the table diagram to be entirely composed of a range of cold buffet dishes.[56]

Both documentary and fictional evidence suggests that Palmer and Brett are right in claiming that a large proportion of 'men of affairs' did not eat lunch as a regular meal. Thomas Love Peacock, working for the East India Company in London in the 1820s and 1830s, recorded his contempt for the bureaucratic day in doggerel verse:

'From ten to eleven, ate a breakfast for seven:
From eleven to noon, to begin 'twas too soon;
From twelve to one, asked "What's to be done?"
From one to two, found nothing to do;
From two to three, began to foresee

Table plan for a 'public luncheon for a large party', c1860, from Mrs Beeton's *Book of Household Management*, 1869 edition, p1327 Note the totally cold buffet, the game pies and the large quantities of jellies and the like. (Compare with the passage from *Coningsby* referred to at note 59 below.) *Author's collection*

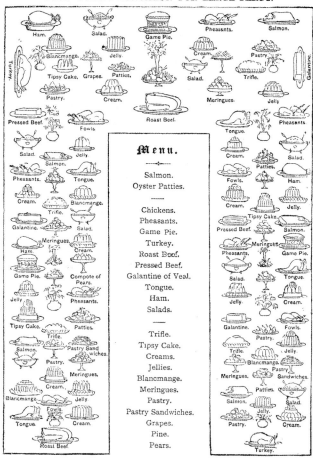

3023.—PUBLIC LUNCHEON FOR LARGE PARTY.

Menu.

Salmon.
Oyster Patties.

Chickens.
Pheasants.
Game Pie.
Turkey.
Roast Beef.
Pressed Beef.
Galantine of Veal.
Tongue.
Ham.
Salads.

Trifle.
Tipsy Cake.
Creams.
Jellies.
Blancmange.
Meringues.
Pastry.
Pastry Sandwiches.
Grapes.
Pine.
Pears.

Note.—The above illustration shows the shape of a table very commonly used for large parties. Sometimes, for a still larger one, a third table is put from the upper and chief one, thus making the whole into the form of an M.

That from three to four would be a damned bore.'[57]

That is, Peacock breakfasted at ten, dined some time after four, and took no lunch in between, even on a day when he 'found nothing to do'. By 1864 Mr Podsnap, in Dickens's *Our Mutual Friend*, is still working a similar one-shift day at the office, even though he 'breakfasted at nine, went to the City at ten, came home at half-past five, and dined at seven'[58], giving a time between meals of some ten hours, still without lunch. But there is a difference of tone between the two passages. For Peacock, the description of his day is in part a joke. For Podsnap, it is deadly serious: any departure from it is social and moral anathema. What happened, in the intervening 35 years, to produce such an astonishing change?

The answer appears to be that taking lunch as a sit-down meal had been feminised, so that *not* taking lunch became part of the gender-definition of the Victorian businessman. Taking lunch was the sort of thing that 'the ladies' did, together with flirting, idle gossip, morning calls and shopping; to admit to it would therefore be neither manly nor demonstrable of moral fibre. It is Disraeli who gives the game away, once again in *Coningsby*, at the point (Book I, Chapters IV and V) where the young hero is introduced to the ladies of his ancestral home. Chapter IV shows us a luncheon scene among the ladies of Lord Monmouth's house, deliberately designed to resemble a flirtatious rococo interior, while Chapter V contrasts it with the utterly serious scene of a crisis of affairs in His Lordship's political offices.[59]

Like most of the examples quoted so far, the lunch at Lord Monmouth's is entirely cold. Disraeli himself summarises it as a 'pasty and glass of sherry' – a turn of phrase remarkably similar to several others used of even lighter lunches during this period. And significantly, Coningsby's 'luncheoning' is exonerated by circumstance: he has driven up from Eton, and it is a common convention that driving makes you hungry. Indeed, even as late as 1861 Mrs Beeton lists the need to offer hospitality to those paying calls as one of the circumstances that legitimate the provision of luncheon in a household:

'In a high class house … it is usual to serve a good repast, not alone for the family, but for the reason that, at an informal meal, chance guests have to be provided for.'[55]

To take luncheon, at this period, then, is to be weak and somehow unmanly. The weakness may be excusable when it is merely a need to stave off the pangs of hunger, as a note in *The Family Friend* for 1853 remarks:

'This meal is admissible only when the interval between the breakfast and dinner is very prolonged, or the quantity of food taken at breakfast is very small.'[60]

But the weakness of hunger can all too easily tip over into the moral weakness of greed or gluttony, and this most certainly is not excusable, even when one is on a journey.

Dickens again furnishes us with several good examples of luncheon as an indicator of moral turpitude. In *Nicholas Nickleby*, published in 1839, Ralph Nickleby, the villain of the piece, eats lunch, but the Cheeryble brothers, protagonists of good, do not.[61] In the section of *A Christmas Carol*, first published in 1843, devoted to the visit of the Ghost of Christmas Yet To Come, Scrooge is shown a 'little knot of business men' discussing the funeral arrangements for a colleague (who turns out to be himself). One says, 'I don't mind going if a lunch is provided, but I must be fed.' To which another replies, 'I never wear black gloves, and I never eat lunch. But I'll offer to go, if anybody else will.'[62] None of his colleagues cares a fig for Ebenezer Scrooge, but the reference to lunch serves to define their shortcomings in detail. The respondent is pompous and self-righteous; the initial speaker is, simply, greedy.

It is a bold Victorian businessman, then, during this period, who will admit to either needing or taking lunch on a regular basis, and even for those who do, the meal is usually little more than a quick

snack – Darwin's 'sandwiches', Mrs Beeton's 'glass of wine and a biscuit' and 'crust of bread and cheese and a glass of ale', the 'glass of sherry with a rock-cake or a couple of biscuits' taken by the City gentlemen 'standing at Birch's counter'[63], or the 'nice sandwich and a glass of sherry' sought in vain by the traveller in *Punch*'s 'The Wonders of Modern Travel'. Even then, some of the references seem more than a little apologetic: for example, in George Measom's *Illustrated Guide to the Great Western Railway* (1852), the section on Swindon Refreshment Rooms is introduced by:

'*Pleading a weakness* towards banbury cakes and sherry cobbler, we shall bend our steps towards the refreshment rooms…'[64] (The italics are mine.)

It seems, then, that the delay between the earliest appearances of the idea of 'dining at speed' and its actual implementation was due to a combination of several factors. Early railway travellers found the experience unexpectedly stressful. The railway companies did not initially think of themselves as passenger-carriers, and when they did, the financial requirements of the mid-Victorian railway business meant that maximum passenger revenue needed to be extracted per train, and any on-train services implying greater weight or fewer fares per journey were to be avoided. Passengers demanded the type of catering with which they were already familiar, and the railway companies adopted that paradigm, although the increased numbers to be served meant that it gave rise to problems of logistics and quality control. And finally, masculine society saw lunching as an unmanly, almost immoral thing to do, even on a journey.

But from the mid-point of the century things began to change. Passengers began to feel reasonably at ease with travelling from about 1858 onwards, and from the end of the 1860s a number of other attitudes begin to alter also. Lunch became more respectable and comfort in general more acceptable. Attitudes on the part of the railway companies changed too, as competition for passengers became more intense. The development of on-train dining itself, however, seems to have been very much dependent on a small group of individual men – George Pullman, Georges Nagelmackers, James Allport and Henry Villard. The background changes that made this possible, and the part these men played in bringing it about, will form the subject of the next chapter, together with the first dining car services that they engendered.

3
'DINING AT SPEED' FINALLY ARRIVES

But why did it happen when it did?

By 1870 an entire generation had come to adulthood regarding railways as a normal means of transport. As early as 1858 Trollope had one of his characters go happily to sleep during a journey from 'Barchester' to London, and ten years later children's tales could even describe the train as going 'uncommonly slow' when you wanted to get to a desired destination quickly.[1] The possibility of such a reaction being credible to either the readers or their parents implies a comfortable familiarity with railway travel it would have been hard to find a generation earlier. Also, three further factors came together during this period: a change in eating habits, an increasing emphasis on comfort, and a growing need by the railway companies to consolidate passenger travel market share. In turn, four major innovators responded to these changes – Pullman and Villard in the USA, Allport in the UK, and Nagelmackers in mainland Europe.

The change in eating habits – luncheon restored

During the later 19th century, the time between breakfast and dinner went on getting longer. By around 1880 the normal space between a British middle-class breakfast and dinner had lengthened to almost 12 hours (though the lower middle and working classes still ate their main meal around midday[2]). Even with a large breakfast at one end and a gigantic dinner at the other, a between-meals stretch of this length was becoming hard to bear; as the *Illustrated London News* put it:

> 'Irregular dining hours, beyond all doubt, have shortened the lives of many prosperous and active men of business who were little past middle age.'[3]

Something obviously had to give.

What gave was the attitude towards taking lunch, and with it the gender divide between the masculine and feminine day. In 1861 the first edition of Mrs Beeton's *Book of Household Management* had given only 8½ lines to the subject of lunch[4], and had made it very clear that it was essentially associated with female domesticity and the nursery. In the second edition of 1869, however, although the text continues to warn against spoiling one's appetite for dinner by eating lunch, the tone of the entry is now completely different. The opening analysis, while admitting that 'many are the arguments for and against luncheon, some right, some wrong, no doubt', concludes that 'but for all that, we have luncheon fully installed amongst our list of meals'. The entry is then expanded from the original 8½ lines to six pages, including the 'gargantuan buffet' public luncheon, a section on luncheon beverages, summer and winter sample luncheon party menus, a section on picnics, and particularly important, a page devoted entirely to weekly menus for *family* lunches.

The illustration that forms the heading for her chapter is titled 'Luncheon At Home', and four people are at the lunch-table, the master and lady of the house, together with a grown-up son and daughter. By 1869, then, lunch is a meal that at least part of the time the businessman shares with his wife. The same year also provides us with a good example from contemporary fiction of the changed attitude to luncheon. In Mrs Henry Wood's *Roland Yorke* the author

> '…shows us a solicitor of good standing who daily, at 1 o'clock, mounted the stairs from his office to his home above and joined his family at luncheon. At that hour his clerks, too, went out, but to eat dinner, since it was the principal meal of their day.'[5]

One o'clock seems to have remained the usual hour for luncheon for the next 20 years, and the meal seems also to have remained a family fixture rather than an occasion for social entertaining, though by the late 1890s luncheon parties became a little more frequent, and there was also a tendency to time the meal a little later.[6]

What did people eat at these lunches? Mrs Beeton talks of the upper end of the spectrum of lunch being 'an elaborate meal that is, in all but name, a dinner'. Her actual lunch menus do not quite reach the massive length of her dinner menus, and are mainly made up of cold dishes, but even so they would have been quite substantial. Here is her suggestion for a family luncheon for a Tuesday in summer:

'TUESDAY – Salmon mayonnaise, rissoles made of cold chicken, brawn, tapioca pudding, fruit, bread, butter, cheese, biscuits, claret and sherry'[7]

Ten years later, the relationship between lunch and dinner in the first British dining car, the Pullman 'Prince of Wales', was similar. *The Engineer* for 24 October 1879 reports:

'The Pullman Palace Car Company, under arrangements with the Great Northern Railway Company, will on the 1st November begin to run one of their dining-room carriages between Leeds and King's-cross [sic] station, London. As this will be attached to a fast train, leaving Leeds at ten in the morning, the manufacturers and merchants of that town will be able to get a substantial luncheon in comfort on the way up … and, leaving King's-cross on the return journey … they will be able to dine at their leisure with a choice of dishes from a bill of fare including soups, fish, *entrées*, roast joints, puddings, and fruit for dessert.'[8]

Perhaps the most telling illustration of the changed attitude, however, is the engraving accompanying the *Illustrated London News* account of the first British dining car, the Pullman 'Prince of Wales', on that same Leeds–London businessmen's service. The picture, reproduced here, shows the steward James Bowyer and the 'boy of the smoking room' serving a meal on the inaugural run. Four of the ten tables are shown, with six passengers: two are men dining alone, but the other four are two couples. Some commentators assume the meal shown must be dinner, and caption the picture accordingly.[9] But A. J. Bower's memoir states that for the 5.30pm start from King's Cross on that November evening, there was darkness outside the windows:

'…the blinds were lowered and the lighted lamps gave a cosy "London Club" atmosphere to the car.'[10]

By contrast, the *Illustrated London News* plate shows no blinds down and light coming in. Clearly, the meal illustrated must be lunch, and two at least of the businessmen have their wives with them.

Changes in attitudes to comfort – an end to 'muscular Christianity'?

This change in attitudes to lunch forms part of a wider change of attitudes, the replacement of

This plate forms the illustration to the *Illustrated London News* report of the first British dining service, on the GNR Leeds-London businessmen's train. The illustration shows a meal being served in the Pullman car 'Prince of Wales' on the inaugural run. Note that two of the diners are women, and also that it appears to be light outside the carriage windows. *Reproduced from the* Illustrated London News *for 22 November 1879, p481*

Arnoldian 'muscular Christianity' by a gentler, more relaxed set of mores, paying a good deal more attention to pleasure and comfort. People begin to expect more ease, and put up with less difficulty, in a precursor of modern consumerism. The change is gradual, but as Palmer puts it:

'Something – I am not sure what – on some unidentifiable date – perhaps about 1870 – had happened. No doubt it was not so sudden as to impress itself upon the notice of people living at the time, and even now it is difficult to describe it more precisely than as a certain loosening, and lightening, and splitting up; and among possible causes the choice is embarrassingly wide, from ever-mounting wealth … to the late Georgian traits exhibited by the Heir to the Throne.'[11]

The change manifested itself in everyday life in many ways. People began to dine out more[12]: half of the London clubs listed in 1914 were founded after 1875. Restaurants were beginning to open – the Café Royal in 1863, Pagani's in 1871, the Monico in 1876 – and one could now dine at one of the new luxury hotels such as the Savoy (1889) – themselves a testament to the demand for increased comfort – without being a resident.

At home, increased desire for comfort had led to the introduction of early morning tea – brought up on a tray to be consumed in bed or while getting up, and accompanied ideally by thinly sliced bread and butter or, failing that, by a Marie biscuit.[13] This little piece of initial daily luxury was added on to the beginning of the day, usually timed around 7.45am. By 1880 English society had become comfortable (and comfort-loving) in a way that had been largely missing since Peacock.

When people travelled they now expected levels of comfort commensurate with those they were accustomed to at home, or at the Savoy. In railway travel, riding quality was improved, by the use from the late 1860s of radial axle systems, then, from 1874, bogie carriages. Seat comfort also increased during this period. Jenkinson comments:

'Typical first class materials, in addition to the familiar blue cloth, could now embrace velvet, morocco and buffalo leather, moquette and sometimes even brocade.'[14]

And in 1873 the Midland provided upholstered seats even in Third Class[15], though it was the rival Great Northern that first tackled the problem of winter warmth by providing foot-warmers.

Corridors and gangway connections also date from late in this period. Saloon coaches had already been in use for some years for family parties and special activities such as smoking, but despite the development of corridor coaches by Waldegg in 1863-70[16], they were slow in catching on in Britain. Gangway connections in regular service date from 1882, and the first all-corridor train was run by the GWR on its Paddington-Birkenhead service only as late as 1892[17].

On-train toilet provision did not have to wait quite so long. Although as late as 1855 Bedonnet's handbook on railway construction remarked 'especially on the arrival platform we have to install urinals of large dimensions'[18], the Webb radial carriages of 1870 onwards had toilet accommodation, and toilets were also provided in the Midland Pullman saloons of 1874, which also featured hot-water heating from an on-board stove[19]. By the time of the Paris Exhibition of 1889, British railway carriage design had reached such excellence of comfort and style that the Grand Prix was won by one of Clayton's bogie carriages for the Midland Railway, No 916, described by Roy Williams in the following terms:

'It had three first class and three third class compartments, with lavatory accommodation for each class. The first class compartment for ladies had brown plush, cased in walnut relieved by gold chasings and mouldings. The first class smoking compartment had crimson morocco décor, while the non-smokers enjoyed blue woollen cloth upholstery with sycamore casing, maple and walnut mouldings. The third class passengers were content with the standard plush.'[20]

Anyone who had come to expect these standards of travel comfort would want something better in the way of refreshment on their journey than congested 20-minute refreshment stops; indeed, we have already seen Darwin, as early as 1839, determine to 'buy a basket and take dinner with us'. The Railway Traveller's Handybook [sic] of 1862 advised travellers to take their own refreshments in order to avoid the problem at these stops of 'some two or three hundred persons requiring refreshments, and only about a dozen hands to supply them'[21], and in the USA Susan Coolidge similarly advised packing lunch baskets with Albert biscuit, orange marmalade, fresh rolls and cold roasted chicken 'which could be obtained at Omaha and Ogden'[22].

Responding to this, the earliest British attempts to provide on-train refreshments were by the provision of ready-made refreshment baskets. The earliest were the brainchild of Spiers & Pond[23], who in 1863 opened an up-market refreshment room on Farringdon station. The following year they opened similar rooms for the London, Chatham & Dover at Victoria station, and by 1871 they were managing refreshment rooms for the Midland at Leicester and Trent, from which they began the new service.

In 1875 the Midland began its own basket service based on Derby. These baskets were advertised as 'luncheon' baskets, and came in two 'classes', one at the Spiers & Pond price of 3 shillings and a cheaper version at 2 shillings.[26] By the following year the LNWR was following suit from Chester station, with its more expensive basket, 'The Aristocrat', going

still further up-market, with a price of 5 shillings. Baskets containing hot meals seem to have first been added in 1884, again by the Midland: passenger orders could be telegraphed ahead and small boys called 'nippers' called out passengers' names as the trains came in and delivered their baskets to them.

Other meals were catered for by basket also: the Highland Railway provided a particularly splendid breakfast basket called the 'Kingussie', while several railways offered Tea Baskets priced at around 1 shilling. That of the LNWR featured a pot of tea (with milk, sugar and hot water), two thin slices of bread and butter, two rounds of plum cake and a small bar of chocolate; the GNR provided 'a pretty basket of chocolate biscuits' instead of the cake and choc bar; and Spiers & Pond's Dover refreshment rooms on the SER specialised in tea baskets for travellers disembarking from cross-Channel ferries, with Oxo as an alternative beverage choice.

The basket trade reached its peak around 1906, with the LNWR offering the basic service from 22 stations, and 'hot lunch baskets' from five, including Preston, its main refreshment stop for the Scottish services. Thereafter it seems to have fallen off as restaurant cars became more widely available, but, even after the subsequent arrival of the buffet car, it and its post-war successors never completely died out.

Refreshment baskets cost on average the same as an equivalent meal in the dining car. The LNWR's 'Aristocrat' basket by these standards may even be seen as over-priced, and by 1912 the price for that basket had come down to 3s 6d. They also suffered from some of the same problems of logistics and quality control as the refreshment rooms, and were cumbersome to handle if the train was crowded. A particular problem with the hot luncheon and tea baskets was keeping the food properly warm, especially if the train's arrival was delayed. There were also logistic problems of ensuring the right baskets were returned to the right stations, and problems of breakage and theft.

Nevertheless, refreshment baskets were popular for some considerable period. The companies liked them because they solved the problem of on-train refreshment without loss of passenger-seat revenue or extra hauled weight on the train. To the passengers they provided an immediate labour-saving device; and since the commonest meal taken while travelling was lunch, they also appealed to the long-standing connections of 'lunch' with the idea of a picnic. It is difficult to say if they delayed the introduction of dining cars, or whether the ongoing

---

Some late-19th-century refreshment basket menus

Spiers & Pond, Trent, 1871 – Cost 3/-[24]
Half a Chicken
Ham
Bread
Butter
Cheese
Half a pint of claret or stout

LNWR, Chester, 1876[25]
'The Aristocrat' – Cost 5/-
Chicken
Ham or tongue
Bread
Cheese
Full pint of claret or half pint of sherry

'The Democrat' – Cost 2/6
Cold meat or pie
Bread and cheese
Pint bottle of ale or stout

Midland, Derby and Leicester, 1884[25]
'Hot Basket' [cost not given]
Steak or chop with vegetables
Cheese
Bread
Half bottle of claret, stout, apollinaris or
    aerated water

popularity of the baskets is simply evidence of unfilled demand for on-train dining proper. It is perhaps significant, though, that dining cars developed in America, where there were no refreshment baskets, some ten years earlier than they did in Britain, where there were, although the longer train journeys involved must also have played a part.

Dining as commercial warfare: the companies' fight for market share

These trends had created the conditions for an acceptance of on-train dining by the travelling public. But the railway companies themselves still regarded with extreme suspicion any additional services that would have a knock-on effect on operating costs or lead to a reduction in potential passenger revenue, and providing dining car services potentially does both those things. For companies to be willing to move from the refreshment basket to the refreshment car needed a particular incentive that would make it worth their while despite the operating and opportunity costs. That incentive can be summed up in two words – 'Territoriality' and 'Competition'.

Railways were always fiercely competitive, but acquiring maximum market share of the available traffic and defending the integrity of their physical catchment area became particularly important from around 1870 onwards. Railway maps of England and Wales for 1845 showed just a few widely separated lines. By 1852 all the major elements of the finished network were visible, but there were still substantial clear areas within and between the main trunk lines, potential catchments for goods and passengers that remained to be exploited. By the end of the century, however, that had all changed:

'By the death of Queen Victoria in 1901, the total route mileage had grown to … nearly three times the figure of 1852… The 1860s witnessed a burst of railway promotion and building which vied … with the manias of the formative years.'[27]

This second promotional burst filled in almost all the remaining catchment areas, so that there were no new markets to exploit, and for the first time UK railways found themselves competing in a market that was no longer capable of geographical expansion. In North America, the pattern of railroad development was similar, though the larger area to be covered meant that the 'infilling' phase did not really start in earnest until the 1880s, and the fact that the western interior of the continent was still being settled up to the end of the century meant, particularly given the Land Grant system of the Enabling Act of 1862[28], that the new railroads sometimes actually created towns as well as linking existing ones.

Initially, competition between rival lines in Britain concentrated on three areas – speed, cheapness, and attempts to 'infill' each other's territory so as to gain access to major rivals' terminus towns, and to secure traffic to their own main line from 'feeders' within their rivals' catchment area. However, because in Britain every new railway proposal required a separate Act of Parliament, 'infilling' attempts frequently took on a complex political dimension.

In the USA, competition by speed was harder to create, but the other two strategies were certainly practiced, as Bryant points out:

'The prevailing philosophy of the 1880s was to meet competition not only by cutting rates but also by invading the "territories" of rivals.'

The absence in the USA of the British Parliamentary approval system meant that this was easier to do in that country, with the result that

'In the process of expansion, the railroads overbuilt, giving some states … far more rail mileage than could be operated profitably.'[29]

But despite the Parliamentary system, something not too dissimilar eventually also happened in Britain. In both countries, therefore, the 'infilling' strategy proved by 1900 at the latest to be a self-limiting option.

Rate-cutting similarly turned out to be fairly rapidly self-limiting. In a situation where the ideal operating ratio of any rail company was 50%, and where operators blanched at the thought of any changes likely to reduce potential passenger revenue per car or increase operating costs, scope for fare reductions was limited. In Britain, this limit was effectively reached around the time of the Great Exhibition of 1851, as Roy Williams points out:

'The Great Northern managed to open its superb direct line from Leeds and York to London in time to attract most of the huge 1851

Exhibition traffic away from the Midland and the London & North Western … the Midland and the LNWR cut fares, the GN followed, and so on until the excursion fare … was only five shillings from Leeds.'[30]

That fare worked out at roughly one-third of a penny per mile, and was clearly about as far as any railway company could go without seriously losing money. Rates eventually stabilised in 1868 at around one penny per mile, led by the Midland under James Allport.

Similar self-limitation applied to cut rates on goods, and the limiting effects were felt both in Britain and in the USA. Writing of the period around 1880, Tayler comments on the US scene:

'The struggle for traffic forced down rates to a point where none but the strongest roads could earn a profit. Although there were agreements to maintain rates, these were just pieces of paper and there was practically no limit to the rebates extorted by the shippers and their agents under threat of diverting traffic to other carriers… While many large industries prospered by these practices, the railroads suffered.'[31]

American railroads also went in for passenger fare rate-cutting, but again, as in Britain, the net end effect was simply to stabilise fares. The initial effects of rate-cutting had been more dramatic in the USA than in Britain, because initially American railroads had less Government regulation, but in 1887 the Interstate Commerce Act effectively outlawed the practice of competitive rate-cutting to specific customers.[32]

Reducing journey times turned out to be self-limiting, too, for both safety and economic reasons. Many of the initial slow timings were due to the need to rebook or change trains and to the indirect nature of the early routes, and much of the initial acceleration therefore was the result of cutting out the need for changes of train or locomotive stops, and opening direct 'cut-off' routes. The Great Northern's new direct line of 1851, for example, immediately cut the journey time between York and London from 10¾ hours to 5, while the provision of water troughs enabled London to be reached in 5 hours from Holyhead in 1862.[33] After that, further cuts in timing involved substantial costs in increased fuel consumption and the provision of new, more powerful locomotives. As Jack Simmons has remarked:

'The aerodynamic drag of a vehicle increases with the square of its speed, and the energy cost, as well as the ability to deploy the power required, has always been important.'[34]

By the 1880s, therefore, timings had stabilised at, for example, 4¼ hours to London from Liverpool[35] and 4 hours from Manchester[36], by whichever competing company one cared to use.

Reducing journey time by faster running had limited results in the USA also, although it produced some spectacular initial effects. American railways at this period had a much poorer safety record than their British counterparts[37] and the more cavalier attitudes behind this difference also showed themselves in railway races of a much more literal sort than in Britain, aided by the fact that competing lines often either departed from the same station and ran parallel for some miles, or crossed each other on the level. Eventually, a fatal accident led to the general introduction of laws requiring all trains to stop at such 'grade crossings' and check that the opposing track was clear, and, by 1870, to the adoption of centralised signalling with interlocking levers. Even so, however, the more harmless practice of racing on competing lines that ran parallel but did not cross still continued until after the end of this period[38], though the effects were more those of passenger spectacle than of real difference in journey time.

True, on 10 May 1893 the famous NY Central 'high wheeler' 4-4-0 No 999 was claimed to have reached 112.5mph over a slightly downhill measured mile with a light train, and during 1896 a pair of Atlantic City RR specially built 'camelback' 4-4-2s regularly ran between Atlantic City and Camden NJ at a published start-to-stop speed of 70mph[39]. But in terms of acceleration of general journey times, the overall effects were slight. Despite the publicity antics of No 999, the 24-hour Chicago-New York journey was reduced by just 4 hours[38], although the Santa Fé did eventually manage to cut 9 hours off the regular 72-hour Chicago-Los Angeles timings[40].

By around 1880, therefore, railway operators in both Britain and the USA were faced with something of an impasse, just as territorial traffic competition became fiercest. In Britain, from 1876, there were three directly competing routes between London and each of Edinburgh, Glasgow, and Manchester, and two between London and each of Liverpool/Birkenhead, Birmingham, Leeds and Sheffield. In the USA there were two major directly competing routes between New York and Chicago,

This is not a photograph of No 999 covering her record-breaking measured mile, but it does show her at work on the 'regular' 'Empire State Express' – and a very fine machine she was! *Courtesy of California State Railroad Museum*

and by 1883 four between Chicago and the Pacific Coast. The only remaining inducement competing lines could offer was a higher standard of comfort and service, and it was out of this that the major adoption of dining cars was born. The prime movers in this revolution were particularly innovative and entrepreneurial senior managers of companies at a disadvantage over route length and overall speed – Allport on the Midland (UK) and Villard on the Northern Pacific (USA). But neither would have produced precisely the innovations they did had it not been for George Mortimer Pullman.

George Mortimer Pullman: luxury travel as a niche market business

Born in 1831, by 1848 Pullman was working as a salesman in his elder brother's cabinet-making business.[41] During 1853 he moved to Chicago, and went into business as a building contractor, specialising in jacking up and even moving buildings without causing any ruffle in the everyday activities going on inside them.[42] It was also during 1853 that he took the famously uncomfortable sleeper ride from Buffalo to Westfield that caused him to germinate the notion of the Pullman car, though as a luxurious alternative to *sleeping car* design, not a diner.

Pullman brought to this aim of improving the standard of railroad comfort all the attention to detail that had led to his business success in the building removal field. Significantly perhaps, both were niche markets. First, however, he had to convince a suitable railroad to back his ideas. Playing on the favourable publicity of one of his most spectacular building jobs

– jacking up the four-storey Chicago Tremont Hotel 'without breaking a pane of glass, spilling a drop of beer, or causing the chambermaids to drop any crockery'[42] – Pullman approached the Chicago & Alton Railroad in late 1858.

The C&A was initially reluctant to back Pullman's proposals with its own money[43], but was willing to have him convert one or two of its older cars at his own expense. The cars were C&A standard 44-foot open-ended saloon-type passenger day cars: Pullman converted them to superior seating with plush upholstery, and convertible to beds for night travel according to his patented 'Pullman section' system, described by Behrend as follows:

'This comprised two seats set parallel to the sides of the cars, facing each other. For night use the seats slid together and the backs let down to form the lower berth. The upper berth let down on ropes and during the day was slung against the roof of the car... Only curtains separated [the beds] from each other and from the central corridor.'[44]

However, in the initial 1859 conversions the upper berths were raised and lowered on floor-to-ceiling guide rods rather than ropes. The cars had 20 berths equipped with pillows and blankets, a washroom at each end, and oil-lamp lighting. Each car had a 'conductor' to see to passengers' needs: J. L. Barnes, the conductor on the first car, simply wore a badge[43], but later conductors wore uniform. The railway kept the train fare, and paid Pullman a supplement for use of the facilities, the so-called 'Pullman contract'[41]: they charged $2 for use of the Pullman sleepers, against $1.50 for use of their own, older models, but

This photograph of an 1897 replica of Chicago & Alton car No 9 as converted by Pullman in 1859 shows a view of the interior in process of being arranged for sleeping accommodation. The day seats have been converted into beds, but the upper berths are not yet lowered. *Pullman-Standard Car Mfg Co, Chicago, courtesy J. B. Radford*

it is unclear whether Pullman received the entire $2 per head for his cars, or just the 50c difference.

Pullman now wanted to build new coaches to his specification rather than upgrading existing designs, but the Civil War broke out in April 1861, and the entire C&A rolling-stock was commandeered by the US Government for the duration. Pullman spent the next years running a supply store for California gold-rush miners, and returned to Chicago with an amassed capital of $20,000, which he used to finance the construction of 'Pioneer', the first all-Pullman-designed car; the C&A supplied him with an old repair shed in which to do it.[45]

'Pioneer' was intended to be a display platform for all Pullman's skills in creating comfort and luxury-making. Radford describes it like this:

'It incorporated Pullman's by now perfected swinging berths, which were raised to fit up

against the roof when not in use, the lower bunk ... being produced by adapting the day seats ... into a comfortable bed. Pure linen bedding was provided. Heating was by grilles fed with hot air from a furnace beneath the floor and lighting was by candles set in elaborate chandeliers. The interior finish was in polished black walnut and washstands of marble were provided in the lavatory compartments. The floor was covered with rich red carpet, the seats upholstered with brocaded fabric, and the walls were hung with gilt-edged mirrors... "Pioneer" was provided with two four-wheeled bogies, having much improved springing and solid rubber shock absorbers... "Never before," wrote Joseph Husband, "had such a car been seen. Never had the wildest flights of fancy imagined such magnificence."'[46]

As fully completed, the car cost five times the cost of a 'normal' contemporary sleeping car, a total of a little over Pullman's entire working capital of $20,000. But the finished car was 12 inches higher and 2ft 6in wider than any car in service with the C&A, and fouled a number of platform edges and some low bridges. The C&A refused to run it, and throughout the winter of 1864/5 it stood resplendent but unused. Then, on 14 April 1865 President Abraham Lincoln was assassinated, and his body taken by rail back to his home town of Springfield for burial. By the time the cortège reached Chicago, Mrs Lincoln was in a state of near nervous exhaustion. Pullman offered her the use of 'Pioneer' for the rest of the journey; the offer was accepted, the C&A rapidly altered the necessary parts of its lineside structures, and on the funeral journey of 2 May 1865 Pullman's magnificent vehicle received the most massive publicity he could have hoped for.

Lincoln's successor as President also used the car to return via Chicago to his home town of Detroit, and Pullman's reputation and future were assured. In the same year, the C&A gave him a contract to build a further six cars similar to 'Pioneer'[47]; by the following year he also had contracts with the Michigan Central and the Great Western of Canada, and by 1867 he had contracts with seven roads, and had built and was operating a total of 48 cars[48]. Around this time he coined the slogan 'Improvement is our Watchword'. On 22 February 1867 the Pullman Palace Car Company was incorporated, with a capital of $100,000 and the backing of Andrew Carnegie.

No one seems to know precisely how Pullman

came to take the step of moving into on-train dining provision. It may simply have been that meals provision was a further revenue stream. It may also have been the result of the noticeable dissonance between his on-train luxury and the 'undignified scramble' on coming down from the train at meal stops. It could equally have been simply a logical extension of Pullman's own service concept, or a wish to better the pioneering 1863 experimental Philadelphia & Baltimore meals service, which used steam boxes to keep hot the food 'prepared at the terminal and put aboard the cars just before they left'[49]. In any case, in 1867 Pullman introduced his first cars serving refreshments.

This first group of cars differed from subsequent Pullman diners. Built in late 1867 and early 1868, and described as 'hotel cars', they consisted of a standard day/night convertible Pullman design with the addition of removable tables between the seats, together with a kitchen area, and the passengers rode in the same cars throughout the journey, using them for sitting, sleeping and eating alike. The first of these cars, 'President', was built for the Great Western of Canada, and was the first Pullman vehicle to operate outside the United States.[50] It catered for 32 passengers, 16 either side of the central kitchen area. Its opening Bill of Fare, as recorded by the Newcomen Society of North America, is reproduced alongside: note the abundance of game, the remarkable cheapness of lobster, and the lack of any dessert or cheese course.

Despite its luxury, 'President' received customer complaints at the persistence of cooking and food aromas in the car. Pullman redesigned the cars with end kitchens fitted with an exhaust system, but the complaints persisted. The cars were also extremely expensive to operate, and it was clear that passengers objected to remaining in the same vehicle throughout the entire multi-day journey. Pullman had not miscalculated his concept of an entire hotel service on a train – but he had miscalculated the acceptability of putting it all in one coach![52]

Pullman thought again, and in 1868 came up with the first true dining car, named 'Delmonico' after the famous New York restaurant. Like 'President', its kitchen was in the central section, but this time there were 24 places on either side. Most importantly, its service was not restricted to those who had booked seats in it; it was intended to provide meals also for travellers from other parts of the train, made possible by Pullman's second major patented invention after the 'Pullman section' swinging berth – the vestibule connection.

Bill of fare of the hotel car 'President', 1867[51]	
Prairie Chicken	$1.00
Woodcock	$1.00
Pheasant	$1.00
Snipe, Quail, Golden Plover, Blue Winged Teal, Each	.75
Cold Tongue, Ham & Corned Beef	.30
Venison	.60
Chicken, Whole	.75
Half Chicken	.50
Sirloin Steak	.50
Sardines, Lobster & Broiled Ham or Bacon	.40

On such cars the 'Pullman contract' described above did not apply. Instead, Pullman contracted with the railroad to operate them on a 'cost-plus-profit' basis (which meant that any losses made on the catering were subsidised by the operating railroad). After trials on various roads, the car was leased by the C&A, which operated it between Chicago and Kansas City. Any risk of loss was more than matched by the increase in revenue from traffic drawn from the competing roads; by 1872 the company was operating four additional Pullman dining cars as well as 'Delmonico' herself.[53]

By 1878 virtually every long-haul railroad out of Chicago had the cars in service, and Pullman had designed and was operating a standard menu and pricing structure as shown alongside. There was still no dessert, unless you count Omelette with Rum, or Welsh Rarebit as a savoury, or just possibly Chow Chow Pickles, but the bill of fare was nevertheless somewhat closer to a modern menu. The presence of Pullman diners on a train had by now become as much a publicity draw as Pullman sleepers or parlour cars, as the contemporary poster for the Chicago-Toronto service reproduced overleaf demonstrates.

By the time Allport met him, therefore, Pullman had become established as a designer and operator of luxury sleepers, day or 'parlour' cars, and dining vehicles, the latter operation centred on Chicago. Pullman's concept of a total service package dedicated to on-board comfort, and his constant attention to customer response and detailed improvement, was aimed at a niche market of the rich and discerning traveller, and was priced accordingly via the fare supplement system. It was this total concept that initially attracted Allport.

This 1884 poster for the Chicago-Toronto Michigan Central/Canadian Pacific joint service gives equal large-type emphasis to the new 'Palace Sleeping Car' and the 'Dining Cars'. *Canadian Pacific Archives, Image No A6413*

Standard Pullman bill of fare, 1868 onwards[50]	
MENU	
OYSTERS	
Raw	.50
Fried or Roast	.60
COLD	
Beef, Tongue, Sugar-Cured Ham	.40
Pressed Corn Beef, Sardines	.40
Chicken Salad, Lobster Salad	.40
BROILED	
Beefsteak, with Potatoes	.60
Mutton Chop, with Potatoes	.60
Ham, with Potatoes	.40
EGGS	
Boiled, Fried, Scrambled,	
Omelette Plain	.40
Omelette with Rum	.50
CHOW CHOW PICKLES	
Welsh Rarebit	.50
French Coffee	.25
Tea	.25
Note: Prices are in American cents	

James Allport and Henry Oakley: travel comfort as a competitive strategy

In 1853 James Joseph Allport was appointed General Manager of the Midland Railway, serving an area from Leeds, Sheffield and Manchester to Birmingham, Rugby and Leicester, with its headquarters at Derby. It was bounded to the west and north-west by the LNWR and to the east and north-east by the Great Northern and North Eastern. Within its heartland it had a major competitor also, the Manchester, Sheffield & Lincolnshire (later the Great Central).

The Midland's principal source of goods revenue came from the haulage of iron and coal and their finished products. But the principal market for much of this production was the London area, to which the goods had to be transhipped over other lines. The business passenger traffic of the area was likewise to

London, which again it could reach a great deal more easily by the competing lines; and a businessman who found it more convenient to travel to London by LNWR would be likely to consign his factory's products by LNWR also. Similarly, the Midland served plenty of landed families and wealthy industrialists who would be glad to follow the fashion for a Scottish vacation. But lacking any direct northern link or way of capturing any London-Scottish traffic, it could not cater for this market either.

The Midland thus urgently needed both a direct route to London and an end-on connection with one or more major Scottish railways. Of the two, building the direct London line was the more urgent – problems resulting from its lack had bedevilled both goods delivery schedules and passenger choice, and during 1848-50 had very nearly cost the line its independent existence. In 1853, therefore, John Ellis, the Midland's Chairman, appointed James Allport with the brief to do precisely that.

Although concentrating initially on the direct London extension, Allport never lost sight of a strategic vision for the line that would make it one of the premier railway lines in Britain. This strategy, among other things, aimed to create a quality through Anglo-Scottish passenger service to compete with, and ideally surpass, the West Coast and East Coast routes. The London extension was duly completed throughout by 1867, and the Settle and Carlisle route opened for through Anglo-Scottish services in 1876. But the developments that particularly concern us are Allport's upgrading of the northern and Anglo-Scottish service quality.

Because the possibility of cutting journey times was strictly limited, Allport had to concentrate his main competitive strategy on journey quality. His genius lay in the fact that he had realised two things fractionally ahead of his competitors. The first was that, as the LNWR's General Manager put it a little later,

'It requires but a trifling inducement to influence the travelling public in the choice of route, so that there is a constant temptation to the competing companies to make fresh concessions so as to attract the business from their rivals'[54]

and the second was that, with the growth in disposable income for all classes, there was now for the first time a substantial long-haul market in Third Class travel. These two concepts formed the core of Allport's 'comfort revolution'.

Allport began by persuading the Midland Board, in April 1872, to admit Third Class passengers to all trains. In his brief to this proposal he justified it on social and humanitarian grounds:

'When a poor man travels, he has not only to pay his fare but to sink his capital, for his time is his capital; and if he now consumes only five hours instead of ten in making his journey, he has saved five hours of time for useful labour – useful to himself, to his family, and to society.'[55]

Such social reformist arguments, particularly if they also included elements of political economy, enabled the Board to take the moral high ground over the reforms. But it is likely that both Allport and his colleagues were primarily swayed by the possibility of obtaining increased revenue from expenditure on fewer trains if Third Class trains no longer had to run separately. (They were right, too: between 1874 and 1888 Third Class passengers increased by around 14 per cent.[56])

This, however, was simply the first of a suite of strategic improvements. In 1873 Allport created a new post of Carriage & Wagon Superintendent to which he appointed James Clayton, specially headhunted from the GWR, with a brief to upgrade carriage design. Interior upgrades were started immediately, by putting seats upholstered to Second Class standard into the Third Class carriages for the new all-class fast trains Then, in 1875, Allport pulled his master-stroke: he persuaded the Board to simultaneously abolish Second Class, upgrade existing Second Class stock to First Class standards and reclassify it, and drop First Class fare levels to those of the former Second Class. Third Class on the Midland was now the equivalent in comfort of Second Class anywhere else, and First Class was available at Second Class prices.

The impact of these changes cascaded through the other companies, but Allport seems to have realised, even while planning this suite of changes, both that others would soon copy them and that he had left the Premium First market uncatered for. Accordingly, he obtained permission from the Board in autumn 1872 to carry out a fact-finding visit to America[57], to examine their carriage practice, and in particular that of George Pullman, who addressed the shareholders' meeting for February 1873.

It was not on-train dining *per se* that interested Allport so much as the general idea of luxury travel. It is not clear whether asking Pullman to address a full shareholders' meeting implied some reservations within the Board about Allport's ideas (Banderali, in his *Notes* of 1874, believed the question of the extra cost of Pullman haulage still remained controversial[58]) or was simply a public relations exercise – but in either case it paid off. Behrend describes the result thus:

'It was agreed that [Pullman] should build and operate, at a supplementary fare for his own profit, as many sleeping cars, dining cars, and parlour or drawing room cars as demand warranted, with exclusive rights to the provision of these facilities for fifteen years… The principal condition was that he … built and supplied for the Midland Railway, which immediately became owners of them, cars of the same exterior form, containing ordinary seats for the use of passengers of all three classes who did not wish to pay a supplement…

The arrangements made between the Midland Railway and Pullman included the provision of two sheds at Derby in which to erect the cars, and allowed him to do so in respect of Pullman-owned cars for use on other lines.'[59]

This account suggests that from the outset the agreement envisaged the construction and operation of Pullman dining cars, although in practice the initial services involved sleeper and parlour cars only. The 'principal condition' is also interesting. Allport did not want to risk operating a complete super-train at a supplementary fare, and he wanted to maintain the new policy of admitting Third Class on all services; but he wanted the publicity value of having a spanking new train that *looked* all in one piece. Third, while the Midland got its cars built at Pullman's expense, Pullman got somewhere to build them, and the right to build there for other companies too; like Allport he was a strategic thinker. This provision was to be crucial to the start of dining car services in the UK.

The new service took about a year to materialise. On 21 March 1874, two sleepers, 'Midland' and 'Excelsior', together with the parlour car 'Victoria'[60], were exhibited at a publicity run from London to Bedford and back, displaying the cars' range of uses, including serving cold refreshments, which *The Times* seems to have taken as a signal that on-train dining facilities actually *were* on the way in regular service.

The Times's prediction, however, did not immediately come true. Allport was given to introducing his innovations in succession rather than all at once, and the concerns that led him to avoid running an entire train of Pullmans turned out

to be justified. The travelling public seem to have taken against the day cars, and throughout the later 1870s Allport was fighting a rearguard action with his own Board simply to keep what he had already put in operation. By 1878 it was even proposed to take two Pullman parlour cars out of service.[61]

Meanwhile, in late 1875 Pullman signed an agreement with Henry Oakley of the GNR to supply and operate two cars, the sleeping car 'Ocean' and the parlour car 'Ohio'[62], on its route to Manchester via Sheffield. Oakley was not really a ground-breaking innovator, but the Midland's Pullman sleepers were proving popular and the Great Northern needed to make some response on its routes to the northern industrial towns the Midland's cars were covering. Pullman then offered to supply the GNR with

'a day car for our ten o'clock Scotch express, which they will fit up, if we like, with accommodation for refreshments so that travellers can obtain foods [sic] etc, on the journey after the fashion of the dining-room saloons on the American Railways.'[63]

Accordingly, in 1878 Oakley and his Board sent 'Ohio' back to Derby for alteration to a dining saloon, whence it emerged in late summer 1879 as the first British dining car, with the new name 'Prince of Wales'. Like Allport, Oakley organised a publicity run, from London to Peterborough and back, on 18 October 1879. Following this successful run, the car was placed in regular service on the Leeds-London business trains (10am up, 5.30pm down) from 1 November 1879. The service was reviewed in *The Illustrated London News* issue for 22 November, occasioning the famous illustration already discussed earlier in this chapter.

The Illustrated London News article also included three other illustrations, the smoking saloon, the car's US-style open-ended scullery, and a view into the kitchen proper, showing a fairly small stove. We know from the correspondence with Henry Oakley that this was a coal-burning range[64] 'capable of cooking all sorts of food for 20 persons'. Bower describes it as being 'a "kitchener" about the size of a writing desk, with two rings, an oven, and a plate warmer … the box for fuel also formed part of the stove', and says that the kitchen also contained a 'Steinberger double water filter' (a type of coffee percolator).[65] The illustration also shows what appears to be an assistant to the cook not listed among the staff mentioned in the article – Radford[66] suggests it may be his son. The smoking saloon area was deliberately designed, as *The Engineer* pointed out, so that 'after dining the passenger may walk into the smoking area to take his coffee and cigar'. When the car was full, both areas could be used for dining purposes, which was why the kitchen range had been sized to cook for 20.

There were sound commercial reasons for changing the diner from the Scottish to the Leeds service. The GNR's Scotch service timing included a dining stop at York, profits from which went into the Company coffers, so that any replacement by dining car would have the effect of moving net income from the Company to the Pullman organisation. The Leeds trains, however, had no access to this stop. And the Leeds service's direct competitor, the Midland's Bradford service, included a 5-minute stop at Trent, from where refreshment baskets could be ordered in advance and delivered by 'nipper'; the GNR had no such basket station on its route.

Most important, however, was the particular innovation the Great Northern was offering. The Bradford Pullman train of 1874 came up to London in the morning, arriving at around 2pm; the return journey took place by sleeper, which the returning businessman could board from 10pm, or, as *The Times* put it, 'after the theatres have closed'. Thus the itinerary the Bradford businessman was being offered was a morning journey up after breakfast, an afternoon's business in the City, dinner and a theatre in London, and a sleeper back to Bradford. The Great Northern's proposal speeded this process up, so that the Bradford man's Leeds colleague could do the same amount of business in London *and still get home in time to sleep in his own bed*. But there was little competitive advantage to be gained if this involved starving him till 10 o'clock at night! Thus on-train dining was essential to the success of the Great Northern offer.

The Midland did not respond immediately. On 3 December 1879 E. S. Ellis (who had taken over from his father as Chairman) died, and his replacement was not appointed until 17 February 1880[67]; Allport also retired, and his place was taken by John Noble. But on 3 August 1881 the Midland converted its two oldest parlour cars, 'Britannia' and 'Leo', for dining, renaming them 'Windsor' and 'Delmonico'. The cars were ready in April and July 1882 respectively.[68] Noble, too, provided a publicity run, between London and Leicester, with the diner coupled to the parlour car 'Venus'. The *Railway Review* reported the trip in terms that suggested that it believed the Midland's cars had everything the Great Northern's had, and then some!

The cars went into service on the London-Manchester-Liverpool evening business services, one in each direction. In 1883 the Midland bought them outright from Pullman, and for the first time passengers in Britain could dine on-train without having to pay a Pullman supplement. The Great Northern followed suit two years later, purchasing 'Prince of Wales' in 1885, modifying the kitchen to cook by gas, and also enclosing the kitchen end[69] 'saving walk [sic] round on deck outside in wind, hail, snow or rain, making the service of dinner more expeditious and better for it'.[70] By 1889, the *Hotel Guide & Caterer's Journal* is quoting typical menus as:

'**18 January 1889**
Julienne Soup, Codfish, Stewed Rabbit, Roast Loin of Mutton
Apple Tart, Cheese
21 January 1889
Mock Turtle, Turbot, Poulet Sauté, Roast Beef
Apple Tart, Cheese'

By 1895 'Prince of Wales' had been superseded by the GNR's own later designs, and was used 'on Sunday trains, Hull boat trains, and as a spare'. It was scrapped in 1901.

Henry Villard and the Northern Pacific: a US parallel case-study

The introduction of dining cars in Britain involved a change in public attitudes to dining, increasing demand for comfort on journeys, increasing competition between railway companies, and the combination of a senior manager committed to passenger comfort with a company otherwise at a disadvantage *vis-à-vis* its rivals. Evidence from American railroads suggests that similar circumstances produced similar results there too. Of these parallel cases, none is more compelling than the Northern Pacific and its President from 1881, Henry Villard, who seems once again in part to have been motivated by the feeling that 'things could be so much better'.[71]

Both the NP and the Midland faced intense competition on their major routes. Both were relative latecomers on the long-haul scene. Both were 'hemmed in' by rival companies. Both had suffered financial reverses that had brought them almost to ruin. Lastly, both had routes that ran through terrain where speeding up journey times was not practicable.

Villard's responses were also strikingly reminiscent of those of Allport. He concentrated on a mixture of strategic construction, management change, and comfort innovations, including contracts specifying 'head and shoulder rests' on seats in the First Class coaches 'in view of the long runs to be made', upgrading Third Class coaches to Second Class, introducing 'emigrant sleepers' for settlers at special rates, and beginning an internal dialogue about the introduction of dining cars.

There had been no regular on-train dining service on the NP's scheduled trains prior to Villard's arrival, and the NP's rivals – the Burlington, the AT&SF and the Union Pacific – operated an agreement that none of them would operate dining cars 'regularly on its trains [west of] the Missouri River'[72], on the grounds that dining car operation over such long distances was bound to lose money. The Northern Pacific, however, was not a member of this cartel, and Villard and Haupt, his new General Manager, could hardly have failed to be aware of the success of Pullman's dining cars in attracting custom to the Chicago & Alton; but the NP's Transportation Superintendent, George W. Cross, was very much inclined to follow the received wisdom of the cartel lines, opting for refreshment stops and hotels/dining-halls. Villard, Oakes and Haupt, however, believed otherwise, and an order for ten dining cars was placed with Pullman in December 1882, for delivery in mid-1883, to coincide with the completion of the through line. The first one was ready by 16 April 1883, and on the 17th Villard and Oakes mounted a press run in considerable style.

The intention of Villard and Oakes was for the dining cars to be one of the main planks in a suite of comfort upgrades, to come into force from the beginning of the through Pacific Coast services, that would attract custom from the cartel lines. In this they were undoubtedly successful. By 1890/91, the NP carried 45% of the westbound transcontinental passenger traffic and 39½% of the eastbound – more than double the percentage carried by the Union Pacific. The dining cars made an operating loss when accounted separately, but this was steadily reduced from around 20% in 1885/86 to a mere 9% in 1893/94 as passenger usage rose – and most of those amounts were actually from the provision of subsidised meals to company employees[73]. The cartel lines' policy lingered on for a few years, but from 1887 onwards the loss of First Class passenger business to the NP became so marked that they began to reconsider. The Union Pacific initiated dining cars in December 1889, and the Santa Fé finally followed suit in 1891 from Chicago and 1892 from Denver.

Tailpiece: Nagelmackers, Mann and a Chatham curiosity

During this period, Georges Nagelmackers of Belgium felt similar concerns to those of James Allport at the fragmented nature of rail travel in mainland Europe, and likewise visited America in 1868-69[74] to trawl for ideas. Nagelmackers, however, opted to team up not with Pullman but with Colonel William D'Alton Mann (who had served with some honour under Custer but had subsequently had a somewhat chequered business career) because Mann's 'boudoir' carriages were smaller than Pullman's 'palace cars' and more amenable to design round compartments, which the Europeans generally preferred.

Nagelmackers's plans for European cross-border through trains under one ownership, complete with sleeping convertability and on-train dining facilities, were severely set back by the Franco-Prussian War, and he was unable to re-start his company (Compagnie Internationale des Wagons-Lits et des Grands Express Européens – CIWL for short) until 1873, and only then with financial support from Mann and the King of the Belgians. His most famous train, the 'Orient Express', began operating in 1883. Thus his work really falls into the period covered by the next chapter.

He did, however, briefly operate two vehicles in the UK during the 1870s. One was an experimental sleeping car on the East Coast route, the other a 'boudoir car' operated on the London, Chatham & Dover's Victoria-Dover expresses from 1875 to around 1882. Design details are sparse, but judging from early photographs of other Mann boudoir cars[75] and German line drawings[76] of Nagelmackers's earliest official dining car (hastily introduced for the Marseille-Nice service, in response to Pullman's first French venture[77]), it was probably a radial six-wheeler. Behrend describes it as having 'a pantry, drawing-room, smoking-room and honeymoon compartment'[78] (a half-compartment, with seats on one side only). There seems to be no indication of what was served from the 'pantry' (which judging by the German drawings was probably amidships), though it may well have been food prepared off-train by Spiers & Pond, who since 1864 had held the catering contract for Victoria Station[79]. It is thus unlikely that the service offered could ever have qualified it to replace 'Prince of Wales' as the UK's first dining car.

4
THE IDEA CATCHES ON

'Dining at Speed' in the 'Golden Age' of railways, 1880-1914

By around 1880 there were First Class-only dining car services on the Great Northern and the Midland between London and Leeds, Manchester and Liverpool. Initially both services charged a Pullman supplement, though the Midland had bought this out by 1883. In America, the key date for the start of dining services from Chicago was 1868 eastward and 1883 westward. In continental Europe, by 1880 Nagelmackers's suite of on-train comfort reforms was only just getting under way, due to the Franco-Prussian War, and no effective dining car services yet existed.

By 1914, however, this had utterly changed. In Britain, apart from the Highland Railway[1], there was no main-line company without regular scheduled dining car services for all classes, and the Great Central[2] and the SECR[3] had both pioneered a buffet car service. Several famous 'named trains', such as the 'Cornish Riviera'[4] and the 'Flying Scotsman'[5], were already running. In America prestigious high-comfort flyers criss-crossed the country; the western 'cartel' ban on dining cars was long since dead[6]. In mainland Europe, CIWL spanned the continent with a series of 'Grands Trains de Luxe', the most famous undoubtedly the 'Orient Express'. Clearly, the 'idea' of on-train dining had caught on in a big way.

This spread of dining-car services in Britain and Europe flowed as a series of 'domino effects' from the two initial competitive stimuli of the Midland-Great Northern rivalry and Pullman's interest in European operations. American developments have different origins but a similar structure.

London, the North and Scotland

The 'domino effect' seems to have been triggered by the Midland's decision in 1883 to buy out its diners

from Pullman and make them available without any supplement. On routes from London to the industrial North and Scotland, the Midland and the GN were both in competition with the LNWR. That line desired no truck with Pullman supplements, but providing dining in one's own stock was different.

The LNWR, however, wanted to be sure that on-train dining was not just a passing fad before committing money to a service involving extra expense, loss of revenue opportunity and increase in train weight. It also had contractual obligations at its designated refreshment stops that had to be sorted out.[7] Thus its response did not come until 1889, when it took the form of modifying existing carriages built around 1875 for the Holyhead and Liverpool routes. Facilities at the Euston carriage traverser meant that they had to be restricted to 34 feet overall length, and thus were of Webb radial six-wheel construction. Initially the design was used for sleepers, but from about 1880 also for First Class day saloons, and in 1882 a few pairs of these were built specifically coupled together by means of an off-centre gangway, one saloon for gentlemen, the other for ladies, but separate from the rest of the train.[8]

Two pairs of these saloons were converted to form the LNWR's first dining cars. One car contained the kitchen plus eight seats, and the other car contained 14 seats[7]: cooking and lighting were both by gas[9]. They were put into service during spring 1889, one pair each separately to Manchester and Liverpool, thus giving the LNWR a competitive advantage over the Midland. Initially the cars did not ride well as diners, and by 1890 they had been rebuilt with bogies. Rogers suggests that 'they were not highly regarded as vehicles', but they were elegantly and sumptuously furnished and laid out, and Jenkinson remarks that 'they lacked nothing in opulence and splendour'. A further pair of diners, lengthened to 42 feet, was added in 1892.

Once again there were several economic reasons for initially preferring these routes. They were of suitable length and timing for a single-meal service in each direction. They did not call at the company's main refreshment stop. And they were primarily business routes – the business community was seen as a market desirable to woo with added value, since if a Victorian business manufacturer was impressed with your passenger service, he was all the more liable to consign his goods via your company.

Both Rogers[9] and Wooler[10] quote evidence suggesting that the economics of the initial LNWR dining car operation were somewhat shaky. During

This 1898 GNR St Valentine's Day luncheon menu shows how competition standardised prices on the competing northern companies. First Class luncheon cost 2s 6d: there was also an à la carte menu. The 2s 0d Third Class lunch menu was identical except for omitting the grilled turbot and replacing the à la carte salmon with boiled cod and oyster sauce.[11] *Courtesy Harpenden Railway Museum*

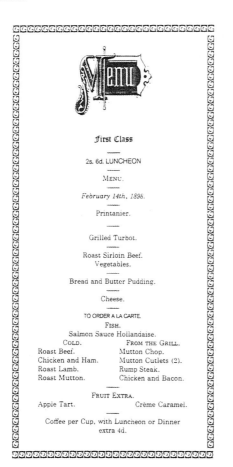

the six months July-December 1890, for example, the service made a small operating loss: dining car receipts totalled £2,787, but costs – including provisions and wages, but excluding construction, maintenance and fuel – totalled £2,817. Some 8,815 diners used the cars, but this worked out at an average of only 24 meals sold per trip. The LNWR was learning the hard way how sensitive on-train catering is to customer numbers.

Dealing with this shortfall by putting up prices was not an option: any attempt at a price increase was likely to result in loss of business to other companies who had not raised their menu charge. Even at the end of the decade First Class lunches on all the northern companies were still being offered at the standard price of 2s 6d, as demonstrated by the Great Northern's 1898 menu reproduced alongside. What was needed to make the service viable was to serve more meals.

This increase in meals served could be brought about in four ways. Increasing the size of dining cars or connecting a kitchen-diner to an open saloon could enlarge the number of seats available. Dining facilities could be extended to other trains, particularly the Anglo-Scottish routes. Gangway connections could be added to join the diner to corridor coaches in the rest of the train. Finally, dining could be offered to other classes of traveller. The competing companies tried all four methods.

All three companies increased the size of their dining coaches, eventually reaching lengths of 59 feet to 65ft 6in, carried on two six-wheel bogies.[12] However, the longest of these cars only seated 30-35 diners[13] against the 22 seats initially available. The Midland, on finding in September 1895 that, even when coupled to an open saloon for overflow, its 59-foot diners could not satisfy the demand for seats, toyed with the idea of making the coaches longer and wider still: it even fitted up a sample dining car with wooden templates to the new sizes. But tight tunnel clearances knocked off the templates[14], so there was no further seating increase to be gained in that way.

The next alternative for increasing dining seats to be put into effect was the extension of dining facilities to Second and Third Class passengers. This innovation started with an unexpected line – the Great Eastern – which operated boat trains from Harwich, one to London and another to Doncaster and York, connecting with the ECJS services and carrying through coaches for Birmingham and Liverpool.[15] Harwich-London was a short journey (less than 1½ hours), but at over 5¼ hours Harwich-York was not. Thus in 1891 the Great Eastern chose to introduce its first restaurant cars on the 7am from Harwich off the morning boat arrival, returning from York at 3.50pm to connect with the overnight sailing to Hook.[16] Since the ferries catered for all three classes of passenger, the Great Eastern decided to provide restaurant accommodation for all three classes too, using *three* linked six-wheel saloons.

Both Rogers[17] and Wooler[18] describe the design of this three-car set. The lead carriage was a composite side-corridor coach with two Second and two First Class compartments, plus a lavatory between them. This was gangwayed to the centre carriage, a First/Second dining saloon with 18 seats arranged in a 2+1 format; at the opposite end of this carriage was the kitchen, only 6 feet long but extending the full width of the coach, thus blocking access from the Third Class carriage that followed. The cooking range (which used gas) was in the centre of the kitchen. A gangway connection beyond led to the dining end of the semi-open Third Class coach. Nearest to the kitchen was a small dining saloon, with a single table for six passengers. Beyond this, a side corridor led to three Third Class compartments. Finally came a Third Class Ladies' compartment, non-corridor and thus with access to the rest of the set only at stations.

This set presaged many later standard features of dining car service – the end-kitchen kitchen-diner coupled to a saloon and serving meals to different classes of traveller on each side; the 'semi-open' carriage; and the gangwaying together of dining and non-dining stock, with fluid dining. None of the passengers needed to travel all the way in the dining section, and the dining seating provided could be used several times during the 6 hours, though the scanty provision for Third Class suggests that the GER was uncertain about how effective Third Class take-up would be. In 1892 a second set was constructed for the London-Harwich service[17], and a further set was added to the 'Norfolk Coast Express' to Cromer in 1899.[19] This began a long-lasting reputation for fine catering on the Great Eastern; indeed, by the end of our period the 'Harwich Continental' also carried a Pullman dining car, giving four different levels of dining.[20]

The notion of serving diners of several classes was speedily adopted by the competing northern companies. By 1893 all of them were making use of it, and had begun to extend dining service to their afternoon Anglo-Scottish trains.[21] The LNWR had also 'scooped' its competitors by providing Britain's first completely through-gangwayed dining car service, the 2.00pm Euston departure for Glasgow

and Edinburgh, known as a result for many years as 'The Corridor'[18]. The other main Anglo-Scottish expresses followed suit, with increasing production of corridor stock after 1897; all were using gangwayed stock by 1901, the Midland being the last to convert.[22, 23, 24]

At first, only one train each way per day – the 'Corridor', the 1.30pm ex-St Pancras and the 2.20pm ex-Kings' Cross – featured dining cars, but the West Coast morning expresses received dining cars also in 1897 and 1898[25], and the 'Flying Scotsman' in 1900[26]. By 1903 a restaurant car was being attached to the Midland's London-Glasgow sleeper express north of Carlisle, serving breakfasts, and in the same year the 7.30pm for Edinburgh, Perth and Inverness and 8.30pm for Glasgow and Stranraer both had dining cars as far as Leeds.[27]

There were several reasons why this coverage was phased in across a decade. One was the cost of dining cars and gangwayed corridor stock, and the time it took to produce them; even Wolverton Works going flat-out could manage only one diner every five weeks.[28] The cost and time involved in producing more powerful locomotives was also no minor matter. And offering this level of service involved logistic problems: the Midland's Anglo-Scottish services, for example, involved the serving of three meals – lunch, afternoon tea, and dinner – together with 'Other viands at Buffet charges'. And demand meant that the leisurely serving of a single group of passengers was replaced by 'fluid dining', complete with tickets, attendant calls, and two, three or even four meal sittings.[29] The meals served were not light affairs either: seven courses were normal for dinner, and breakfast and lunch were equally substantial.

As demand continued to rise, dining was extended to cross-country expresses. In 1905 the Midland included a restaurant car on its 10.55am Leeds-Bristol service[30], and in 1907 the LYR introduced First Class diners on its Newcastle-Liverpool and Leeds-Fleetwood trains, adding open Second/Third composites from 1908.[31] From 1902 the North Eastern operated a breakfast car on its morning Scarborough-Leeds train, which returned as a tea car on the afternoon working.[32] And from 1906 the LNWR built a dozen tea cars for routes whose journey timings were outside main meal times. These last were not saloons but corridor coaches with two middle compartments converted into a kitchen and pantry[33]: they had some cooking facilities, and so could serve light hot snacks as well as teas[34]. Food was served in the individual compartments, with some elegance, as the photograph overleaf shows.

This view of the attendant's compartment to the tea car on the 2.30pm Birmingham express, taken about 1912, shows the pantry boy holding a dark wooden portable afternoon tea sandwich/cake stand, of a type common in 'up-market' tea rooms then and later. (Although the photographic quality of this print is poor, it is so far as I know the only LNWR tea car interior photo to survive, and would be of historical value for that alone!) *Courtesy National Railway Museum/Science & Society*

Carriages, kitchens, menus and food

The dining cars of this period were their companies' flagship vehicles, designed as experiences of 'train magic'[35]. David Jenkinson describes what they were like:

> '…at all times the use of decorative finishes was high on the priority list, whether it be inlaid veneer, marquetry panels, flamboyant Lincrusta panelling or superb quality upholstery… Polished and carved wood detail was common, associated with delicate mouldings and decorative light fittings. Built-in bottle holders, courtesy lights and push-buttons to call the attendant were all commonly to be found and … there was much less difference between First and Third Class than in most other carriages. Most Third Class diners were literally First Class in their provisioning, and it was often difficult … to tell the difference … save, perhaps, for a slight reduction in the length of each seating bay in the Third Class section.'[36]

Often leading furniture designers were employed to create the cars' interior fittings. For example, Waring of London was involved in the décor of the initial Great Northern Pullman diner of 1879[37], and Gillow of Lancaster was responsible for the interior of Midland diner 361 of 1896, featured in the accompanying illustration.

To build dining carriages of this quality for both First and Third Class passengers implied that the general service stock, at any rate on the principal trains, needed to be commensurate. The companies were aware of this: dining carriages were marketed as part of a suite of attractions, including sleepers, through coaches, corridor trains, and even lavatories. Sometimes, as on the 1895 East Coast Route poster

This illustration shows the interior of Midland Dining Car 361 of 1896, which was specially furnished by Gillow of Lancaster. Although unfortunately the view does not show the car laid out for a meal, the fine quality of the interior decoration is clearly visible. *Courtesy National Railway Museum/Science & Society*

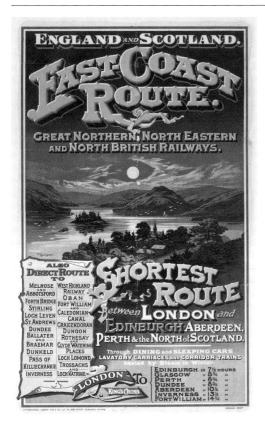

This 1895 poster for the East Coast Route to Scotland advertises the whole suite of on-train comfort upgrades available at the time, but is also clearly intended to appeal to the romantic holidaymaker. (Note, incidentally, the rubric 'Heated by Steam in Winter'.) *Courtesy National Railway Museum/Science & Society*

reproduced here, which combines this list of goodies with a romantic moonlit view of Loch Lomond, the advertising is aimed at least in part at a tourist market. At other times, it is much more clearly aimed at the business market. But in all cases, it is a suite of virtues that is being praised – 'Swiftest, Shortest, Smoothest Route', 'Comfort, Speed and Punctuality' or 'The Business Line – Luxury Vestibuled Lavatory Carriages, Through Services, Dining Car Trains'.

This close similarity of the dining car appointments and menus in First and Third Class, however, was a complete reversal of the attitudes of the mid-19th century, when Third Class passengers were relegated to miserable open accommodation, not even admitted to most long-distance expresses, and confined to their own separate and decidedly inferior station facilities, far removed from the First

and Second Class refreshment rooms. What are we to make of such a change?

Some people argue that attitudes had not really changed at all. Smith, for example, in *The Railway and Its Passengers*, argues that

'...the gap between the two main classes of travel remained considerable ... the railways of the pre-First World War period continued to shower the latest innovations and comforts on the First Class traveller long before they filtered down to Third Class.'[38]

The evidence from carriage design and building programmes, however, does not support this view. The companies offered the latest improvements in First Class first, but where main-line expresses were concerned the 'filtering down' of on-train comforts to Third Class happened much faster than Smith's argument suggests. And that the railway managements were conscious of this is shown by a comment by the LNWR's general manager, Sir Frank Ree:

'...the companies have spent and are spending large sums of money in providing the most luxurious accommodation ... for the benefit of the superior classes, but ... it is the humble and once despised Third Class traveller who furnishes the sinews of war.'

The 'humble Third Class travellers' are now to be valued: their money provides 91 per cent of all passenger receipts as against only 9 per cent in First Class. Further, during the period 1890-1914, the range of people travelling in Third Class got wider as Second Class vanished. The Third Class traveller was no longer just a rough working man: he had money to spend on his journey and a taste for 'joint luncheons'.

But what of the kitchens that could be called on to produce up to four sittings of lunch? Again, Jenkinson furnishes the best description:

'...they were veritable masterpieces of ingenuity. They normally used compressed oil gas for fuel and literally every nook and cranny was pressed, cleverly, into service. This did, of course, lead to some particularly odd-shaped cupboards and storage areas, but space was at a premium and none was wasted. Thus, for example, in a kitchen not much more than 10 feet by 6 feet, one might regularly expect to find

This photograph of the kitchen of Great Northern First Class diner 3251, built in 1912, shows the care with which much was packed into a little space, including the stove and hot plates. *Courtesy National Railway Museum/ Science & Society*

West Coast Dining Saloon.

LUNCHEON, 2/6

Soles au Chablis.
Roast Beef.
Pressed Beef.   Ham
Chicken.
Vegetables.
Salad.
Gooseberry Pie and Custard.

Biscuits Cheese, Radishes, Butter, etc

Cup of Tea or Coffee, 4d

23rd April, 1906.

Despite being a luncheon menu for only 2s 6d, this WCJS menu from 1906 features sole cooked in Chablis, as well as the more down-to-earth gooseberry pie and custard. *Author's collection*

anything between six and twelve burner rings and at least two ovens, each capable of holding a 30lb turkey.'[39]

The working drawings show even more remarkable things. The kitchen for the 1906 Edinburgh WCJS stock[40] contains oven, hot plate and grill, nine burner rings, a refrigerator and two sinks, while the butler's pantry contains a sink, an icebox, and four sets of cupboards and drawers, one with a plate-rack over. The 1908 Midland First Class end-kitchen diner design[41] shows pantries either side of the kitchen, the rear one for service into an open Third. The accompanying illustration shows such a kitchen in a Great Northern dining car.

What was the food produced in these kitchens like? The meals were substantial (up to eight courses), but the individual dishes were also frequently sophisticated and intricate. The WCJS lunch menu reproduced here, for example, features sole cooked in Chablis, as well as the more traditionally English gooseberry pie and custard.

But how good was this food? In July 1902 Austin Brereton reviewed British dining car services for

Transport magazine, in 1903 a second review appeared in *The Tourist*, and on 7 November 1904 the *Manchester Evening Chronicle* described a return trip from Euston to Manchester by dining car express. Brereton's article indicates that main-line services into and out of London were much better covered by restaurant facilities than cross-country services, and that meal prices, at 2s 6d for lunch in all classes and 3s 6d for dinner in First and 3 shillings in Third, were standard across all companies.[42] Where quality was concerned, he handed the palm to the Midland:

'In every respect – selection of food, its quality and cooking, and the charge made for it – the Midland Railway have left nothing to be desired: the Midland wine list is very extensive, and the prices asked are very reasonable indeed

… you can obtain, when ordinary meals are not being served, other refreshments; varying from tea and coffee with toast and butter for 9d up to the chop or steak with fried potatoes, bread, butter, etc, and tea or coffee for half-a-crown.'[43]

Cross-country, Brereton warmly praised the Scarborough-Leeds breakfast car service, the LYR's Fleetwood boat trains, and the 11-hour Newcastle-Bournemouth service.

The article in *The Tourist* was much more critical. Of a lunch on the LNWR, it grumbled that the fish course, boiled haddock and parsley sauce, was 'full of bones, small and watery'. For the main course, the writer's party ordered ham with vegetables, which they 'regretted insulting our gastric juices with: the vegetables were so beautifully messed up that we passed the dish'. Salad, while on the menu, was not actually available. The sweet, apple pie and custard, was, however, 'passable'. Dinner on the Midland fared better – the soup, fish and sweet were all of good quality, though the chicken curry was 'skin and grief' and the vegetables were 'imperfectly drained' – but the complaint throughout was of excessively small portions, needing 'the conspicuous and questionable taste of a double go all round' for satisfaction.[44]

The *Manchester Evening Chronicle*, however, presents a rosier picture of a restaurant car dinner:

'The waiter, who appears with soup, says that we are doing sixty miles an hour, though it is difficult to realise it. In the best West-end restaurant style, fish, joint, poultry, sweets, cheese, coffee and liqueurs are produced in a magic kind of way from an absurdly small room at the end of the carriage…'[45]

Likewise, of one of the LNWR's six-course breakfasts it says:

'The little table before us is laid for breakfast, and as we glide through the suburbs of the Metropolis, waiters in neat uniforms appear with coffee, fish, eggs, bacon, cutlets, toast, and so on. We are travelling at certainly fifty miles an hour, but … not a drop of coffee splashes over into the saucer. When the marmalade stage is reached, we are racing through open country…'

At its best, then, the quality of restaurant car food at this period seems to have been very high, but given the pressures of cooking for so many in such a small space, we may perhaps not be too surprised to find evidence that the standard could vary.

The Great Western – losing the Swindon albatross

The LNWR was in competition with the Great Western to Merseyside and for the highly profitable Birmingham-London business traffic. The Great Western, however, at the beginning of our period, was under two major disadvantages, the Swindon Refreshment Room contract, which precluded the GWR from setting up 'any rival establishment along the line that might abstract from business at Swindon'[46], and the fact that initially its Birmingham and Merseyside services travelled via the London and Bristol line, adding substantially to journey time. Not until the Bicester cut-off for Birmingham was completed in July 1910[47], therefore, could the Great Western compete with its northern neighbour on timing.

But it could compete on comfort and on-train services. It operated the UK's first through-gangwayed corridor train, between Paddington and Birkenhead, in 1892, and also systematically made up for its less attractive end-to-end journey timings by arranging for its trains to serve many more places than those of its rivals by means of 'slip coaches'. Once the Swindon contract had been bought out, dining cars followed within a year, initially to South Wales and the West Country.[47] These were all results of a strategic Board decision, taken in the middle 1890s, to speed up GWR services considerably by reducing the number of stops made by express trains. From this flowed operating decisions to buy out the Swindon contract, to intensify the slip coach operations, and to offer refreshment on trains. As Griffin commented in 1909: 'Non-stop services have necessitated the provision of well-equipped dining-cars on all long-distance trains…'[48]

The initial three cars introduced in 1896 were fairly small affairs, with an end kitchen and seats for 16 First Class diners. One was rostered on the 9.18am Cardiff-London express, returning on the 6.10pm from Paddington to Cardiff; the other two were rostered on the 'Cornishman'.[49] Seats could be reserved throughout the journey. A fourth car joined them in 1897, and worked between Bristol and London, up on the 6.55am ex-Weston-super-Mare and back on the 6.00pm to Plymouth.[50]

The succeeding designs, however, at 68 and 70 feet long, were both longer and heavier than anything on the northern railways. The 1904 'Dreadnoughts' were centre-kitchen composite diners, and seated 18 at the First Class end, and 32 at the Second.[51] Their successors, the 1906/7-type H.15 'Concertinas' were an end-kitchen design seating 42.[52] The 1906 batch were built for First Class use, and had individual dining chairs[53]; the diagram for the 1907 batch shows them as 'unclassed' and as having fixed seating. Twelve of this version were built in all; they were very long-lived, some surviving in main-line service till as late as 1961. The kitchens and pantries of both types included two refrigerators positioned on the angles of the corridor, a cellar sunk beneath the kitchen floor, cupboards over the pantry doorway and a removable-flap table across the kitchen doorway, and a wine bin under one of the pantry tables. Cooking was by gas, lighting by electricity.

The 'Dreadnought' stock was used on the new 'Cornish Riviera Limited', inaugurated in July 1904. By 1905 five West Country services had restaurant cars, together with two each to South Wales and to Birmingham (extended to five from 1910). By 1913 the Third Class Falmouth holiday express also had a restaurant car, and the 11.50am to Torquay had *two* cars, one on the main train and the other on the Taunton slip portion for Ilfracombe.[47] By summer 1914 the GWR restaurant car total came to 72 – 56 diners, eight buffet cars, and eight 'tea kitchen brake thirds', operating across the entire system, together with cross-country through trains with other systems.

The LSWR held out till 1901 before likewise introducing dining facilities, initially on its 'North Cornwall Express'.[54] Initially these took the form of open coaches with meals served from a Kitchen Brake[55], but eight conventional diners followed in 1904, which Weddell describes as 'quite outstanding vehicles'[56]. They had central kitchens able to provide 60 luncheons, with 11 First Class seats forward and 17 Second and Third Class aft. First Class was upholstered in blue buffalo hide and Second/Third in moquette. Six more followed in 1913, but with end kitchens and panelled in mahogany and satinwood.[57] The LSWR leased its on-train catering out to Spiers & Pond; by May 1910 they were providing catering on five West Country and two Bournemouth services, and demand at times became so great that the kitchens, sized for 60 meals, had to provide 100. Typical Spiers & Pond menus for May 1910 are shown below[58]:

Luncheon 2s 6d
Soup
Consommé Fermière Purée Parmentier
Fish
Boiled Turbot in Sauce Cardinal
Joint
Roast Sirloin of Beef
Vegetables
Brussels Sprouts, Potatoes
Sweets
Apple Tart and Devonshire Cream

Dinner 3s 6d
Soup
Consommé Julienne Mulligatawny
Fish
Fried Fillet of Sole with Tartare Sauce
Entrée
Chicken Sauté Paysanne
Joint
Roast Leg of Mutton
Vegetables
Cauliflower, Potatoes
Sweets
Rhubarb Tart and Devonshire Cream
Cheese Dessert

The Great Central and the Metropolitan: the effects of competition

The Great Central began as a regional concern, in competition with both the Midland and the LNWR in the western part of its area. It had initially responded to the Midland's series of upgrades in much the same way as the other northern companies, and by 1885 was running an elegant 12-wheeler bogie First Class kitchen-dining car with eight smoking and 12 non-smoking seats on its 11am joint service with the GNR from Manchester to London, returning on the 6.15pm departure from King's Cross.[59] However, it had one characteristic its fellow northern companies did not have: its Chairman from 1864 to 1894 was Edward Watkin.

Watkin was a mix of strategic thinker, Eurocentric visionary and megalomaniac. In 1866 he also became Chairman of the South Eastern, in 1872 of the Metropolitan, and in 1875 of one of the three companies working on the Channel Tunnel.[60] Always a fierce opponent of the Midland, Watkin decided to build his own London extension, engineered to mainland European loading gauge, and via 'his' Metropolitan and South Eastern railways and the Channel Tunnel to link Manchester directly with Paris.[61] However, when the London Extension was finally opened, in 1899, Watkin had retired from all his chairmanships, and the company was left with a beautifully engineered line, well over budget, almost every town on which was already linked with London by another existing, well-tried and speedy route.[62]

This left the Great Central with an ongoing financial problem regarding passenger receipts; in 1910 Robinson, the line's CME, calculated that express service revenue yielded only 2s 2d per mile, while express running expenses came to 3s 6d.[63] The company had built up a profitable market in express freight, particularly fish from Grimsby and Immingham and perishable imports from Germany and Holland, which it moved on to the new line. But because the Victorian entrepreneur tended to place his goods contracts with lines whose passenger services pleased him, the Great Central dared not economise on its loss-making express passenger services. It needed to run regular, frequent, high-quality, high-speed, high-comfort services, in order to maintain the support of its business customers.

This was well realised by both William Pollitt, General Manager when the London Extension opened, and his successor, Sam Fay. From the outset, Pollitt planned a service of short, frequent, fast trains, with rapid start-to-stop timings, highly competitive overall journey times, all-corridor through-gangwayed stock, and refreshment facilities on every train. Fay continued and consolidated this policy, introducing slip coaches for such places as Bradford and Huddersfield and a range of high-quality, fast cross-country services, including the Newcastle-Bournemouth service whose food was praised by Brereton. All the trains were finished to a very high standard of comfort; George Dow's description of the dining cars has already been quoted in Chapter 1.

But the Great Central's major contribution to on-train dining was the Buffet Car. Initially, it was intended to build kitchen cars only and cater for passengers' refreshment needs at their seats; removable tables, to be set up in the individual compartments, were stacked at the corridor ends when not in use. In practice, however, problems arose over passengers entering and leaving compartments at intermediate stops if the tables were up. The problem could be fairly easily resolved for those services that operated across the time of a main meal, by providing open dining cars with the kitchen car serving them. But what was to be done about services such as the 2.15pm up from Manchester, which started their journey too late for one main meal and arrived at their destination too

early for the next one? It was for these services that the initial buffet cars were devised.

Dow describes these pioneering buffet cars as follows,

'The buffet cars ... were the first of their kind in this country. They contained a spacious buffet, a kitchen with a gas range, an attendant's compartment, a lavatory, three Third Class compartments and internal decoration similar to that of the Third Class corridor coaches. But they were years before their time. Why should one think of snacks when a five-course lunch could be enjoyed, comfortably seated in the diner, for half-a-crown?'

and Wooler describes the buffet area thus:

'The inside of these buffet cars looked every inch a miniature pub on wheels ... they sported appropriate pictures ... on the walls while across the corner stood an elegant and very substantial [curved] mahogany bar.'[64]

Wooler also confirms that the buffet cars were not very successful, and notes that they were converted into 'orthodox restaurant cars' in 1907-8. He offers a different reason, however, that First Class passengers disliked their resemblance to pubs, and that the fact they were open to all made both classes of passenger feel uncomfortable – a reason which has also been put forward by Kitchenside:

'...the buffet car with bar ... conjured up visions of the public house, then more associated with working men. Moreover, titled country families from the Shires would have to rub shoulders with heaven knows who, for the buffet car was available to all.'[65]

Some of these statements need some qualification, though. The cars *were* the first British buffet cars to be railway-owned, the first to serve passengers from other parts of the train, and the first to be open to all classes. But they were *not* the first to bear the title 'buffet cars', nor were they the first to provide a continuous service of hot and cold drinks and light snacks. Both those features had existed on the Brighton line since 1881[66], though the early Brighton Pullmans were available to First Class only, and passengers were served at their seats.

There is also some doubt about the reasons for the cars' lack of success. Dow's suggestion that snacks did not represent good value for money ignores the fact that the buffet cars were run on trains that did not provide formal dining facilities. And while fear of 'mutually embarrassing mixing of the classes'[67] may have kept some people away, the notion that the GC catered primarily for 'titled families from the Shires' is just not true. The reason for lack of success may have been much simpler: hitherto, on-train dining had involved *being served* with food at table. By comparison, going to a buffet counter for food or drink would be perceived very much as 'slumming it'.

Although five of the 1899 kitchen cars were re-designed as buffet cars, serving at-seat was not completely abandoned. Jenkinson prints diagrams of two GC train sets of 1915, a four-car London-Manchester-Bradford set and a five-car set for London-Manchester. The four-car set has no restaurant car, but has a kitchen car lying second, with two Third Class compartments in front of the kitchen and two First Class behind it; the remaining First Class seats are close by, in car 3. The five-car set's kitchen car lies third, with the First Class seating ahead of it, in car 2. Car 4 is a 48-seater Third Class dining car, but there is no First Class dining car, and every car except the diner has shelving for portable tables. It is hard to resist the conclusion that on both trains passengers were served with refreshments at-seat in their compartments.[68]

The Metropolitan Railway's Pullman buffet cars

'Mayflower' and 'Galatea', though, commissioned in 1910, were much more successful. The GC and the Metropolitan Railway saw themselves as competitors; both companies competed for the affluent outer-suburban traffic, with slogans such as 'Live In Metroland'[69] and 'The Great Central – The Line of Health'[70].

The Metropolitan saw the Great Central as a major threat. Several of its expresses made stops at stations such as Aylesbury at peak business hours.[71] The Metropolitan could run its services direct into the City, but the GC had its 'buffet car on every express', and much superior carriage stock, described by Robotham as 'some of the most luxurious ever built for suburban trains'. In 1909, Dalziel approached the Great Central with a proposal to run Pullman 'trains-de-luxe' for 15 years from 1910.[72] The Metropolitan's general manager, Robert H. Selbie, was determined to scotch these plans, and while the GC's Board was considering Dalziel's proposal, he negotiated for two Pullman cars to run on selected outer-suburban trains on the

This picture of one of the Metropolitan's 1910 Pullman buffet cars shows the bar end of the car and typical 1+1 seating. Note the division into small open saloon compartments – much more like the interior of a gentlemen's club than the pub bar of the competing Great Central! *Courtesy London's Transport Museum*

Metropolitan itself, and from July 1910 the Metropolitan ran two specially constructed Pullman buffet cars in selected rakes of normal stock.

The cars were finished in full Pullman livery with 18th-century-style interiors.[73] Each seated 19 First Class passengers in a 1+1 format, in three glass-partitioned saloons, with a toilet at one end and a bar counter at the other, with a small kitchen behind. One car was upholstered in green and panelled in mahogany with satinwood inlay; the other had crimson upholstery, and oak and holly panelling. Both had connecting gangway doors, but these were always kept locked, as the remainder of each train was non-corridor stock.[74] The cars had a handsome, airy appearance, and Fryer's description of them in use, quoted in Chapter 1, illustrates the glamour they gave to their occupants' journeys.

Selbie deployed his Pullmans in a highly strategic manner. Morning services to the City from Aylesbury and Chesham were matched by evening services to Aylesbury and Verney Junction, replaced on Saturdays by lunchtime journeys. Intermediate workings included a shoppers' train at 1.35pm from Aylesbury to Baker Street, and a theatregoers' train at 4.15pm. The timings were all carefully chosen to maximise profit – even the 9.15pm up journey from Verney Junction, needed to work the afternoon business car back to London for the always well loaded late-night theatre train. The cars, both stabled at Aylesbury, were worked extremely hard, logging up totals of 6½ hours' and 9½ hours' revenue-earning service per day, and at least some of those services were deliberately timed to 'cut out' Great Central expresses.

Although described on the Pullman list as 'buffet' cars, the cars certainly served more than simply 'tea on the Underground' or gins and tonics. Both the up morning business trains were noted as serving breakfast, and the two Saturday down journeys from the City were noted 'Pullman Luncheon Car Attached'; the 11.35pm after-theatre train was similarly noted as serving Suppers.[75]

Other Pullman developments

From the major northern companies' decision to operate dining cars themselves, without charging any supplement, until the end of the First World War, Pullman diners had only a toe-hold in Britain.[76] Nevertheless, two developments during this period had a significant effect on the growth of on-train dining overall.

The first occurred in 1881 when the LBSCR instituted the 'Pullman Limited Express', using four former Midland Railway cars specially renamed and rebuilt. One of the four – 'Adonis', now renamed 'Victoria' – was fitted up to serve refreshments; Fryer refers to it as serving 'tea and freshly prepared sandwiches on request', in true buffet car style[77], but Radford's Pullman Car Table shows the conversion as being from a simple parlour car to a 'kitchen car'[78]. The four Pullman cars were included in a rake of ordinary carriages, and the train made two trips a day in each direction.

At first, the appeal of extra comfort was offset by the open saloon coaches, the supplementary fare, and an ill-conceived attempt to run it on Sundays (which earned it the nickname of 'The Sabbath-Breaker'). However, patronage gradually improved, till by 1888 a second suite of Pullmans was being employed. The catering vehicle of this second set, 'Prince', definitely *was* a 'buffet car' in the modern sense: Fryer describes it as having 'a pantry that supplied light refreshments'. Patronage continued to rise through the 1890s, and by 1898 it proved possible to re-instate the Sunday journeys. The weekday journeys, too, had acquired some prestige: the 8.45am up Pullman made a special City stop at London Bridge, and the 9.20am terminated there. Coming back, Pullmans departed from London Bridge at 4, 5 and 6pm, and hot meals could be obtained 'in certain Trains … on Weekdays'[79].

The final development came in 1908, when the all-Pullman format became used every day, and the special train so created was named the 'Southern Belle'. New stock was provided, including a kitchen-parlour car 'Grosvenor', one of the first Pullmans to include a bar, and an elegant parlour car 'Belgravia', a picture of which is included here. The whole suite was advertised as radiating luxury and 'train magic':

'Upon entering the Southern Belle we leave London behind … we have come into a place of enchantment, of beauty and exquisite comfort. The spirit of a cultured man or woman is uplifted at once by this palace of elegance and refinement. Watch some pretty, well-dressed woman making her choice of seat for this short journey. She gives a little cry of delight upon entering the first carriage … her eyes are filled with admiration as she looks at the beautiful mahogany panelling inlaid with satinwood, at the delicate moulding of the frieze and cornices, at the fluted pillars, at the carpet with its soft

The interior of 'Belgravia', from a contemporary painting, radiates all the ambience of an aristocratic Edwardian drawing-room on wheels. Note particularly the 'pretty, well-dressed young lady' in the foreground, penning an elegant missive. *Courtesy National Railway Museum/Science & Society*

shade of green with its *fleur de lys* pattern, at the damask silk blinds, and at the cosy chairs and settees in a restful shade of green morocco…'[80]

A crucial aspect of the 'Southern Belle' was its emphasis on at-seat catering. Dalziel deliberately made the UK Pullman hallmark courteous, attentive meal or refreshment service at seat in luxurious surroundings, without the need to go to the dining car.[81] He also realised that there was a market for a slightly less luxurious version for Third Class passengers, and in 1915 introduced this too.[82] The 'Southern Belle' was the test-bed on which he proved these concepts, and they worked well throughout the next half-century. Of the food served on these Pullmans, we know of the tea and freshly made sandwiches on the 1881 cars, and of cold luncheon on the 1.20pm Saturdays-only businessman's train from London Bridge, and cold supper on the 12.05 midnight from Victoria, both at 2s 6d, but no menus for the 'hot meals on certain trains' survive.

The second Pullman development occurred on the LSWR, starting with a trial of the parlour car 'Alexandra' during 1880. It proved as unpopular as its fellow parlour cars on the Midland, and was withdrawn after a few months[83], but from 1889 the South Western acquired further Pullman buffet cars, which it ran on the London-Bournemouth route. By 1893 four cars were in use, described by Weddell as

'finished in vermilion wood, whilst the smoking compartments, passages and buffets were mahogany. The swing seats and stools were covered in old-gold velour velvet and the curtains were crushed-strawberry-coloured damask.'[84]

However, when in 1905 the South Western included its own diners, offering a full meal service, on two of its principal Bournemouth expresses, Pullman traffic declined seriously, and the company even had passengers petition for access from the Pullmans to the dining cars. The number of cars was gradually reduced across the following years, and the LSWR Pullman service ended in 1911/12.[85] But the LSWR experiment is still of importance to our story: first, its failure in direct competition with a full-meal dining service provided further support for Dalziel's reforms, and second it seems to have led to Nagelmackers's first European dining car initiative.

In 1879 Nagelmackers obtained the contract for the lucrative P&O Brindisi 'Indian Mail' traffic, using the Dover-Calais route, then onwards through Paris, but Pullman's Italian contract blocked the southern end, forcing passengers to change trains at Bologna.[86] Thus, when Nagelmackers learned first that Pullman was operating in 1880 on the LSWR, in trains that served the rival Southampton-Le Havre crossing, then, early in 1881, that a French Pullman dining car contract had been signed to operate on the Paris-Le Havre line[87], he must have felt that Pullman was preparing to cut off traffic from his prized route at both ends.

The idea catches on in Europe – Nagelmackers and Wagons-Lits

Georges Nagelmackers's initial emphasis, like Pullman's, had been on long-distance overnight luxury travel, with on-train dining as an adjunct only. Between 1881 and 1883, though, that changed, following Pullman's securing of the Paris-Le Havre dining car contract in 1881, though CIWL had already experimented with a service during the summer of 1880, converting two day saloons on the Berlin-Frankfurt service into a kitchen car and a dining saloon.[88]

Nagelmackers's response was decisive. Wagons-Lits saloon No 107, a standard six-wheeler, was rebuilt as kitchen-dining saloon D107. This is the car featured in the German line-drawings mentioned at the end of the previous chapter, and thus it may have been either one of the cars converted for the 1880 Berlin-Frankfurt summer service or a design based on that conversion. It had a centre kitchen a mere 1.97m by 2m (just over 6 feet square); this did not even go all the way across the car, since opposite it in the drawings is a section labelled 'Toilett Cabinet'. Into this tiny kitchen space were packed an oven, two washing-up tubs, two tables, a sideboard and a coal-box, and various racks for plates and utensils. The wine cellar was 'embedded in the floor'[89]. The chef must have been a contortionist!

On either side of the kitchen section were 12-seater First Class saloons with seats in a 2+1 formation, for smokers and non-smokers. Décor was in velvet and Cordoba leather. D107 went into initial service on the Nice-Marseille route in late 1881[87], and was an immediate success. Nagelmackers then featured it on a special run of his Paris-Vienna service, publicised as 'Train éclair de luxe', on 10 October 1882, which was similarly successful.

Nagelmackers was now able to proceed with unveiling his flagship international service – the 'Orient Express'. Conceived from the start as a super-luxury train, it was designed to link the capitals of pre-1914 central Europe with Paris and London at one end and the Ottoman Empire at the other. It obtained substantial revenue from the carriage of official and diplomatic mail[90] and its passenger accommodation was aimed especially at senior government figures. By 1914 it was the flagship of an entire suite of 'trains de luxe' aimed at this area of the international travel market, with prices and service levels set accordingly.

It was crucial to Nagelmackers's plans that the 'Orient Express' was a success from the outset, and a carefully prepared exhibition run by invitation only was mounted for the inaugural journey of 4 October 1883, including in particular three of the most influential journalists in Paris – Georges Boyer of Le Figaro, the novelist and editor Edmond About, and Henri Opper de Blowitz, the Paris correspondent of

The Times. The three men were seated well apart in the dining car, and Nagelmackers appears to have taken considerable trouble to talk carefully to each of them separately.[91]

Considerable excitement was aroused by the then brand-new bogie dining car D151 used on this inaugural service – a vehicle almost double the size of the groundbreaking D107. D151 had an aft end-kitchen and three saloon compartments, with two, one and four pairs of tables respectively.

Nagelmackers realised that the chef is a key quality element of any luxury dining service. Because CIWL's headquarters were in Paris, and because his careful publicity had created an unprecedented level of prestige for his trains, he was able to attract and retain the best chefs in France. And aware that chefs of this quality were in high demand and liable to be 'poached' by leading hotels and restaurants, he took care of them too. Many people tried to seduce Wagons-Lits chefs away from their trains – including King Edward VII – but none succeeded.[92]

The 'Orient Express' was the first of a fleet of luxury European expresses. In 1889 Italian railways were unified and Nagelmackers finally succeeded in obtaining the contract for the entire 'Indian Mail' right through to Brindisi; in 1890 it was upgraded to a passengers-only 'train de luxe' limited to 60 places, with new Wagons-Lits carriages and a restaurant car advertised as follows:[93]

'Breakfasts, Luncheons, and Dinners are served in the Dining Car at the following times and prices:

From 6.30am to 10am, Tea or coffee with rolls and butter	2s 6d
At 11am Luncheon (wine not included)	4s 0d
From 4.0pm to 5.30pm, Tea or coffee with rolls and butter	2s 6d
At 7.0pm Dinner (wine not included)	7s 0d'

The service was restricted to First Class passengers holding P&O steamship tickets. Other passengers could join at intermediate stations, but only if complete vacant compartments were available for them to sit in.

Other 'trains de luxe' followed. From 1896 the 'Nord Express' linked London, via Ostend, with Paris, Berlin, St Petersburg and Moscow; then, in 1897, the Calais-Paris-Rome express was upgraded to 'train de luxe' status similar to the 'Indian Mail'. Dalziel continued the suite of trains: once the Simplon Tunnel was completed in 1906 the 'Simplon' express was introduced, running Calais-

---

**A typical Wagons-Lits menu
of the 'Golden Age'**[96]

Ostend-Vienna Express, 14 November 1910

Menu

Hors d'oeuvres varies

Huitres royales d'Ostend

Omelette au Fromages
Patés-frites
Chateaubriand – Sauce Béarnaise
Céléris braise au jus

Fromages
Fruits

Paris-Lausanne-Milan-Venice-Trieste – not yet the 'Simplon-*Orient*', since it did not serve Vienna[94] – and in 1910 the Ostend-Vienna express.

All the CIWL 'trains de luxe' were operated to high standards, with updated rolling-stock the latest technological advances, continually improved services, the highest level of attention to commissariat organisation and fine cuisine, as in the typical menu printed in the panel alongside. All, too, intentionally catered for a limited market, admitting First Class only with restricted numbers (even by 1909 the 'Orient' only mustered four passenger coaches including the restaurant car[95]) and a high price-tag supplement.

Thus Nagelmackers developed the idea of on-train dining in a different direction from that which it had taken in Britain. In Britain, the key feature of the idea as it developed had been the promotion of moderate comfort for an ever-widening range of passengers. Along with this went for the most part (Pullman excepted) cuisine and service standards typical of the period rather than outstanding. The object was to make the travellers feel in something like their own drawing-room, and to feed them accordingly. Hence menus that can include sophisticated dishes, sole in Chablis for example, but also include roast leg of mutton or rhubarb tart; hence, too, the sort of 'boiled cod' fiascos that can occur when things go wrong. Nagelmackers, on the other hand, deliberately aimed to provide outright luxury for a restricted clientèle. His trains were exclusive; his accoutrements were of the very finest (the 'Orient Express' table glasses were of Baccarat crystal); and the food and wines were the acme of haut cuisine, with 'boiled cod fiascos' non-

existent. The two concepts were socially and ideologically quite different.

But all this luxury did not mean that there was no dining car provision for the ordinary European traveller. From around 1882 national railway systems too began to offer 'ordinary' restaurant car facilities, and also Midland-style refreshment baskets, particularly in Germany, which had always mistrusted CIWL. Indeed, by 1898 CIWL found it necessary to start its own rather more mundane German operation, the Deutsche Eisenbahn Speisewagen Gesellschaft, in response.[97] In mainland Europe as in Britain, then, both versions of the idea could be found during our period – but the balance between them was very different, and one detail of this difference is especially worth noting. European non-CIWL dining cars were 'unclassed', open to all comers travelling on that particular train, and willing to serve anything from formal meals to drinks and light refreshments – completely different from the British system of separate diners for separate classes.[98]

Tailpiece: parallels from America

In the USA, things were different again. Pullman's company maintained a large share of dining car building and operation. Further, no single centre or route served the function London and the lines to the North and Scotland had served in Britain; the closest equivalent was Chicago, and the services from it eastward to New York or Washington and westward to California. And despite Pullman's first US dining cars being earlier than those in UK, the starting date for the 'domino effect' in US was rather later, dating to the 1891 adoption of dining cars west of Kansas City.[99] Most important, however, were three specifically American differences – the development of a particularly wide-choice style of menu, the development of a high level of vertical integration of commissariat support services, and the development of both 'moderate comfort' dining and special luxury services by the same railroad lines.

Early US Pullman dining car menus had tended to be bills of fare rather than a formal menu for a table d'hôte meal. Initially, menus on lines such as the Santa Fé under Fred Harvey might seem to be moving closer to the British model. For instance, Bryant[100] remarks of the catering on the 'California Limited' of the 1890s:

'A typical "Limited" dinner might include the following:

Little Neck Clams Olives, Radishes
Consommé
Roast Squab au Cresson
New Potatoes in Cream
Stringless Beans
Lettuce Salad
Pistachio Ice Cream
Neufchatel Cheese, Fruit, Coffee'

This, however, represents not what was on offer but what an individual diner might have selected. The total offer was larger and more elaborate with a much richer range of options for the diner, as the menu for the 'Coronado' restaurant car ex-Chicago on 15 March 1889 makes clear.

This could not possibly be the menu for a single set meal: it is a highly sophisticated à la carte bill of fare. And this suited the American market perfectly: American diners classically want what they want, in whatever combination they want, and want it *now*. This is probably more than the result of mere whim: as early as 1886 the Baltimore & Ohio is advertising the range of choice on its limited trains in terms

---

The 'Coronado' leaving Chicago,
Friday 15 March 1889[100]

Dinner
Blue Points on Shell
Cream of Barley
Boiled Fresh Salmon, Shrimp Sauce
Sliced Cucumbers
Roast Beef, au Jus Loin of Veal,
Stuffed Young Turkey, Cranberry Sauce
Mashed Potatoes, Braised Sweet Potatoes,
New Leeks
Spinach, Asparagus on Toast
Sweetbreads Sauté, Petits Pois
Minced Ham with Eggs
Queen Fritters, Madeira Sauce
Roast Spring Lamb, Mint Sauce
Fresh Lobster, Chicken Salad,
au Mayonnaise Cold Ham
Sweet Potatoes, Dressed Lettuce
Apple Pie, Peach Pie
Rice Pudding, Vanilla Sauce
Assorted Fruit, Batger's Orange Jelly,
Assorted Cake
New York Ice Cream
Edam and Roquefort Cheese
Bent's Water Crackers, French Coffee

---

linking it to no less than the great Preamble to the Declaration of Independence:

'Nothing … has proved more satisfactory than the limited trains upon which … a man goes as he pleases, paying for what he may wish, and realising that he is in a country free as to railroad choice as to anything else.'[101]

This tendency of American train menus towards à la carte format increases as the period wears on. One good example is a Northern Pacific menu quoted by Mitchell, which can be dated to after February 1909, when the NP's dining car superintendent Hazen J. Titus introduced the 'Great Big Baked Potato'[102]. It was displayed in a folder shaped like a rounded casserole dish. Lifting the top revealed the food choices:

'Oysters As You Prefer 'Em 40c
Clam Chowder 25c; Chicken Broth in Cup 20c
Crab Meat au Gratin 40c
Hot Consommé 20c; Navy Bean Soup 25c
Sliced Tomatoes 25c; Head Lettuce with Egg 30c
Finnan Haddie 60c
Fresh Fish in Season 60c
Boiled Ham with Spinach 50c; Irish Stew 50c
NP Special Sausage with Mashed Potato 60c
Hamburger Steak, Creole Sauce 50c
Roast Beef Hash 30c
Chicken Minced in Cream with Pimentos 50c
GREAT BIG BAKED POTATO 10C
Mince Pie 15c; Apple Pie with
American Cheese 15c
Plum Pudding, Wine Sauce 25c; Fruit Cake 15c
Coffee, per Pot 10c; Tea, per Pot 15c
Chocolate with Whipped Cream 15c
Individual Bottled Milk 10c'[103]

The top cover showed a picture of a dining-car table setting, with underneath the legend 'NP Special Sausage – Our own Make'.[104]

This menu follows the approximate order of a table d'hôte meal, but any attempt to divide the text into courses is now missing; it is also much more down-to-earth than the 'Coronado' opus. This was not, however, true of all the NP offerings of this period: Hazen Titus at about this time had instituted a policy of featuring specialities of the regions through which the NP's train passed, which included:

'Potatoes and apples from Washington … fresh fish, dairy products and spring water from

Minnesota; breads made from North Dakota wheat; beers brewed with that state's barley and Washington hops; beef, buffalo and Rocky Mountain trout from Montana; Oregon prunes; Washington clams and salmon; and crab and reindeer from Alaska.'[105]

In fact, the Mitchell menu's ordinariness is deceptive: the clams and crabmeat are among Titus's regional specialities, and the 'fruit cake' concerned

This 1895 breakfast menu from the C&O's 'Fast Flying Virginian' service resembles a modern American hotel breakfast menu in size and layout, but is much more 'hearty' in its choice of main dishes than we would expect nowadays. *E. S. Hanger collection*

CHESAPEAKE & OHIO RAILWAY
DINING CARS
LIMITED

BREAKFAST

FRUIT	ORANGE 15c　　ORANGE, SLICED, 25c ONE BANANA 10c　　BANANAS WITH CREAM 20c
PRESERVES	PRESERVED PRUNES WITH CREAM 25c PRESERVED FIGS WITH CREAM 25c INDIVIDUAL ORANGE MARMALADE 25c
COFFEE, ETC.	COFFEE PER CUP 10c　　SMALL POT 20c LARGE POT 35c TEA, SMALL POT 15c COCOA, PER CUP 15c　　MILK, PER GLASS 10c CREAM, PER GLASS 20c
CEREALS	OATMEAL WITH CREAM 20c MAPLE FLAKE WITH CREAM 20c TOASTED CORN FLAKES WITH CREAM 20c
CLAMS	LITTLE NECK CLAMS ON HALF SHELL 25c CLAM STEW 25c
STEAKS CHOPS, ETC.	LAMB CHOPS (2) 40c (3) 60c MUTTON CHOPS (2) 50c SMALL SIRLOIN STEAK 80c TENDERLOIN STEAK 75c EX. SIRLOIN STEAK $1.50 WITH BACON 20c EXTRA WITH MUSHROOM SAUCE 25c EXTRA HAM 40c, WITH FRIED EGGS 50c BACON 40c, WITH FRIED EGGS 50c CALF LIVER AND BACON, 50c Bread and Butter with Meat and Fish orders.
EGGS AND OMELETS	BOILED, FRIED, SCRAMBLED OR SHIRRED (2) 20c OMELET PLAIN 25c WITH HAM OR JELLY 40c　　PARSLEY 30c
POTATOES	BAKED OR FRENCH FRIED 15c HASHED BROWN 15c
WHEAT CAKES	WHEAT CAKES WITH MAPLE SYRUP 25c
ROLLS, ETC	HOT ROLLS 10c　　PLAIN BREAD 10c DRY OR BUTTERED TOAST 10c MILK TOAST 20c　　CREAM TOAST 30c CORN MUFFINS 10c
	No order is served for less than 25c
Table Water from the Healing Springs of Virginia, Virginia Hot Springs.	As each order is especially prepared, some time is required to properly serve it. Passengers will please examine their checks before paying same

SPECIAL FOR BREAKFAST TODAY
CANTALOUPE, Half, 20c Whole, 35c
CLAM BROTH IN CUP, 15c
BROILED BLUE FISH, 50c
BROILED SEA BASS, 50c
BROILED SPRING CHICKEN, Half 50c, Whole $1.00
LAMB CHOPS, (2) 40c　(3) 60c
SPRING LAMB HASH WITH GREEN PEPPERS, 50c
SPANISH OMELET, 50c
SLICED TOMATOES, 20c

was baked to a prize-winning recipe that had taken the *grand prix* at the 1889 Paris World Fair.

Two further examples, one for breakfast and one for lunch, illustrate the development of the characteristic railroad à la carte menu at its most extensive. Both are from the 'Fast Flying Virginian' of the Chesapeake & Ohio Railroad; introduced in 1889, this was the C&O's first through passenger train, operating between Washington DC and Cincinnati, and was also the first C&O train to include diners.[106] The FFV breakfast menu from 1895 is reproduced here.

This menu closely resembles a breakfast menu in a good-class Southern hotel. It has the same comprehensive layout, the same careful organisation by sections, the same extremely wide range of choice, and the same individual item pricing. It is utterly different from the conventional British breakfast menu, and nothing could better illustrate the American belief that service implies variety and choice. One also notices the heartiness of the main dishes: this difference in food culture probably stems from the agricultural, pioneer nature of much early US society, where folk would put in several hours' work in the fields or on the range before returning with appetites well sharpened for breakfast. 'Who works hard, eats hearty', as the Amish proverb puts it.

The FFV 1918 lunch menu (not shown) continues and develops these cultural differences. Like the 1895 breakfast menu, it offers a wide-ranging à la carte choice, carefully classified into different food types for easy reading, to enable the customers to locate the dishes they want quickly. Like that menu, again, everything is individually priced. And also like the breakfast menu, it includes a range of specials of the day, some of which are really hearty. The surprise, however, is the proportion of dishes it offers that seem to have strayed either from a breakfast menu (boiled eggs, cereals, buckwheat cakes with maple syrup) or from a buffet bar-style snack menu (ham or tongue sandwiches, assorted cakes).

Again we are faced with evidence of a different eating culture: people who 'ate hearty' at breakfast were likely to want only a light lunch. But the notion of quality service as consisting of the instant satisfaction of any consumer demand means that due provision must be made for those who did *not* 'eat hearty' at breakfast, or who wanted to do so at both meals. Providing such a catering offer proves incompatible with a formal table d'hôte luncheon. The result is a fully 'opened-out' menu spanning both full meal and snack offers. The range of offers does not, however, imply any diminution in individual quality: oysters abound; both green and black olives are available on demand; Roquefort cheese is available either as a cheese course or as part of a salad; the pies are all home-made; and there is a range of speciality breads.

Providing such a diverse range of dishes involved considerable logistic complexity, given the 72-hour schedules of the 'California Limited' or the 'Coronado' between Chicago and Los Angeles, or the even longer five-plus days of the Northern Pacific's 'North Coast Limited' round trip run.[107] These journey lengths raised two distinct problems. The first was the question of how far any restaurant car could be stocked for such a journey, and where it was to be resupplied. On the Northern Pacific, for example, there were two main commissaries, one at St Paul, where the cars were shedded and serviced, and the other at Seattle.

But even so there were problems: cars were stocked at St Paul on the morning of Day 1, and left on the eastbound service after breakfast, reaching Chicago after lunch. They left Chicago westbound at noon on Day 2, serving lunch on departure: their return call at St Paul came between sittings of dinner, and the halt time was only 25 minutes, so there was only time to remove the garbage and take on new garbage cans. Restocking had to wait until the evening of Day 3, because only at Billings, Montana (reached around 10.30am on Day 3), was the next stop long enough to telegraph a restocking order ahead to a suitable company refreshment room. On Day 4 the train finally arrived in Seattle at 8.15am and left again at 1.30pm, having restocked a

second time at the commissary: the train then continued rolling eastward through Day 5, and served its final breakfast on the approach to St Paul on Day 6, where the restaurant car came off and its twin replaced it. Thus the train had to carry sufficient provisions for six meals before there was any possibility of restocking.

These operations now led to a second problem. Food is perishable, so how could one ensure that the right amounts, of the right freshness and quality, were available at the commissary and restocking locations when they were needed? On the Santa Fé, Fred Harvey used the same system of intensely policed local contracts he had already developed for his 'Harvey Houses'. On the Northern Pacific, however, Hazen Titus, with his dedication to fresh regional food, decided that the only way to guarantee timing and quality was for the railroad to own the units supplying its key perishable items. The result is described in the 1911 *North Coast Limited Handbook* as follows:

'The Northern Pacific has unusual facilities for supplying edibles to its dining cars. A 52-acre poultry farm at Kent, Washington … affords the supply of fresh eggs… The dairy farm, with 300 thoroughbred milch cows, provides the milk and cream supply, which is continuously inspected and tested.

This season an extensive truck garden is being laid out at Paradise, Montana, to supply vegetable products… Large bakeries in Seattle and St Paul, operated by the company, furnish

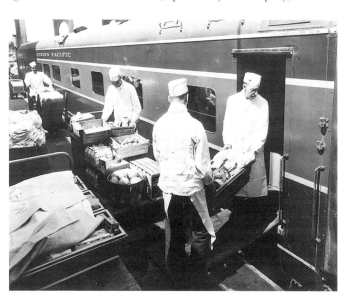

This 1940 photograph of a Northern Pacific dining car being stocked at St Paul shows the sheer volume involved in loading provisions needed for six meals (two days) before the next restocking point. The problem was just the same in 1883 or 1909 – if anything, even worse! *Courtesy of Minnesota Historical Society*

all the bread, cake, pies and French pastry. The butter used is unsalted... Wrappings of oiled paper protect it from contamination. The bread is also wrapped in tissue until cut for the table.'[105]

Indeed, to ensure freshness, from 1912 the unsalted butter was churned fresh on the train from the railway's own cream.

Thus far, late-19th/early-20th-century American dining car practice followed the same general principles of providing 'moderate comfort' as its British counterpart – down-to-earth rather than luxury menus, provided to patrons without restriction. Towards the end of our period, however, an innovation occurred that was much more like the 'trains de luxe' concept of Nagelmackers in mainland Europe.

By the turn of the century, the US economy had begun to evolve a plutocratic upper class of businessmen. This led to an increasing market for long-distance de luxe travel. To capture this market, a number of lines began to offer special de luxe trains, offering finer food and wine, greater comfort, extra services and, significantly, faster journey times than the normal run of services. A good example of this final American development is the 'Santa Fé De Luxe' of the AT&SF. Operated once weekly from 12 December 1911, the train cut 5½ hours off the westbound schedule and 7¼ hours off the eastbound, with a surcharge of $25 for the additional speed, luxury and services. Bryant describes it as follows:

'The services on the Deluxe more than compensated for the surcharge; travellers discovered a barber shop, ladies' maid, library, stenographer, daily market quotes, bathing facilities, and telephone connections at the terminals... The six-car trains included a club car, diner, and four Pullmans which contained compartments and drawing rooms with brass beds. The 70 passengers enjoyed First Class accommodations in the Pullmans ... while exquisite foods could be obtained in the "air conditioned" 30-seat diner, with its wicker chairs and vermillion [sic] mahogany panelling. The extensive wine list reinforced the "snob appeal" of the Deluxe, and the train was one of the few ever to have its own luggage sticker. For America's idle, and not so idle rich, the Deluxe became *the* way to reach Los Angeles.'[108]

Overall, the 'Santa Fé De Luxe' was of similar size to, and in many ways as luxurious as, the 'Orient Express', but very definitely business-oriented. The train only lasted six years (it was taken off when the USA entered the First World War), but it paved the way for the same company's 'Super Chiefs' and all the various Burlington 'Zephyrs' and the like that were to follow in the inter-war period.

5
DEPRESSION AND DEMOCRATISATION: COMPETITION AND LUXURY

1919-39

Prologue: the effects of the Great War

As summer 1914 dawned, dining car and ticket prices had been stable for over a decade, and for most people in employment real disposable income was steadily rising. But the Great War drew a line under that old way of life, for several reasons. First, war is inflationary, particularly for railways. Second, the war speeded up development of the internal combustion engine, creating new sources of competition. Third, the war distorted the economic and political life of Europe. The post-war world had new boundaries, régimes, balances of trade, and political ideologies. CIWL's *grands express Européens* agreements had all to be renegotiated, and the economic viability of the routes had changed.

There was also a sudden disjunction of social attitudes, rejecting the mores of the pre-war generation for an almost febrile modernism that on the surface embraced a frenetic pursuit of pleasure, while an underlying depression accompanied it. Like a post-traumatic stress disorder, it issued in a move towards frequent and compulsive snacking, destined to become a major agent for change in on-train catering:

'By the 1930s the fashionable ladies of London were consuming breakfast, lunch, afternoon tea, the "coloured wormcasts" of a cocktail buffet, dinner at 8.45 or 9, and supper in the small hours, in semi-darkness, and in snatches ... life between the wars was hectic, and it is hard not to conclude that people of almost every class were

The LNER's famous Art Deco poster advertising the 1928 'Flying Scotsman' restaurant service – a stylised close-up in black and grey of hands holding a cocktail shaker. *Courtesy National Railway Museum/Science & Society*

finding, in the multiplication of small meals, in the constant interruption of normal activities, a form of narcotic against the strain of existence.'[1]

Little wonder that the LNER advertised its new 'triplet' restaurant sets for the 'Flying Scotsman' with a poster featuring an Art Deco cocktail shaker!

Railways in wartime Britain came under the Railways Executive Committee, in terms that required the railways themselves to fund most of the costs of war-generated inflation. They also had to bear heavy extra passenger, goods and mineral traffic, and were called upon to manufacture everything from stretchers to gun carriages and shells, and to release 516 locomotives and 20,000 wagons for use overseas.[2] The effect of all this turmoil on normal passenger and restaurant car services has sometimes been underestimated. Rogers, for example, simply remarks

'…the railways had been initially hit by the large numbers of its [sic] staff who had left for military service, but … there seems to have been no difficulty in keeping quite a number of restaurant cars going.'[3]

Rogers is certainly right about the loss of staff: 49 per cent of the railway staff of military age joined up.[4] But it was the need to provide for military passenger and essential war freight workings that chiefly led to the curtailments. From February 1915 onwards, and again in 1917, the REC withdrew a range of 'competitive services': the sole morning Euston departure for Scotland was now the 9.30am to Perth, with St Pancras providing the sole Glasgow service and King's Cross the sole Edinburgh service.[5]

Restaurant car control formed part of this total package aimed at reducing railway fuel consumption by 10 per cent and freeing up 500 locomotives; as a result, there was no single pattern to the provision of dining services. Thus, on the LNWR and the East Coast route, all dining car services were suspended from 20 April 1916.[6,7] But the Midland's sole morning Glasgow service and most Great Central trains were allowed to keep their restaurant cars.[8,9] GWR dining cars were discontinued from 1 January 1917, but on the LSWR the morning West Country express retained its restaurant car throughout.[10] The SECR was very heavily affected by war traffic[11], but the Brighton line, after initially curtailing the 'Southern Belle' in 1915[12], allowed it to 'creep back into view' in late 1917[13], albeit on Sundays only. The general situation is well summed up by Reed:

'The consequence of this buoyant demand and restrictions on the railways' ability to serve it was a deterioration in travelling conditions: trains were fewer slower and overcrowded, fares were higher, and a wide range of facilities such as on-train dining had to be sacrificed to the overriding demands of the war.'[14]

The situation of the Wagons-Lits Company in mainland Europe was even more perilous, because half its fleet was under the Allies and half under the Central Powers. This forced the withdrawal of any services that crossed the warring powers' boundaries. Even the 'Simplon' express was truncated, since Trieste was part of Austria-Hungary.

Germany seized all CIWL and DSG restaurant and sleeping cars within its territory. Initially it used them to operate a new version of the 'Orient Express', known as 'Der Balkaner Zug', linking Berlin instead of Paris with Constantinople[15]: but on 24 November 1916 all the 116 DSG dining cars, together with 64 CIWL dining cars and 39 sleepers, were taken into the capital stock of a new company, Mitropa, to run international services between Germany, Austria and Hungary. Mitropa survived the war, and became a major competitor for Wagons-Lits. CIWL did eventually get 35 of its sleeping cars back, in very poor condition, but almost none of the dining vehicles were ever returned – and most were never paid for, either.[16]

Nevertheless, some CIWL operations kept going. The 'Rome Express' provided an essential top-level diplomatic and military link between London, Paris and the Italian capital.[17] The most elaborate of all the 'Orient Express' sets, Set PR, also continued in operation, for the French President Raymond Poincaré to conduct sensitive negotiations under the guise of courtesy visits.[18]

US railway passenger services were less directly affected. Some long-distance services were discontinued; there were a few re-routings, and sometimes the railways found themselves forced to use slightly odd motive power. But on the C&O the only effects on 'normal' dining car services were a few substitutions and a patriotic flag on the menu, and such trains as the SP's 'Shore Line Limited' continued to run full dining services.[19] Indirectly, however, US railways were almost as severely affected as those in Britain. They too came under Government control[20], and their financial compensation likewise failed to cover either war inflation or staff wage increases. Additionally, immigrant traffic from Europe dried up, and farm employees trooped to the colours in enormous numbers, resulting in farm abandonments and a decline in productivity that adversely affected freight income.[21]

New times, new tastes, new challenges

In all three areas then, 1918/19 found the railways in urgent need of rebuilding. But things could not simply be returned to the situation obtaining in July 1914: public attitudes and circumstances had changed. One part of this change was the result of inflation eating into customers' disposable income. People were less likely to put their hands in their pockets – and had less in their pockets to find if they did. Another part of the change was a carry-over from wartime of expensive, slow, inconvenient, crowded and uncomfortable travel; as late as 1920 London to Inverness still took 2 hours longer than in 1914.[22]

Meanwhile, the growth of modernism led to a whole range of new phenomena, including the growth of road and air travel. In Britain and Europe this competition was primarily via public transport, with bus and tram services replacing local trains, and motor-coaches for longer-distance journeys. The newly grouped railways recognised the competition, buying into the Eastern, Western and Southern National bus companies[23], but this did not solve the problem of declining rail passenger revenue. In America, by contrast, the competitor was the private car and farm lorry, but the effect was the same in both nations:

'During the decade of the 1920s passenger revenues declined sharply. The average distance each passenger travelled increased, but total revenues declined as local travel transitioned from … local trains to the automobile.'[24]

The challenge to the passenger railway industry was thus to persuade the travelling public to patronise its services, rather than the cheaper bus and coach companies – or, for the wealthy, the glamorous and speedy competitor of air travel. The provision of economical travel was one key element, but it was far from the entire solution. Doughty puts the problem particularly well:

'Railroads became acutely aware that if their services were to be attractive to the public, they had to appear in touch with the times by appealing to the public's aesthetic tastes. Simply put, they had to make travelling by train

popular, and it was imperative that they make their patrons feel as though they were travelling "in style".'[25]

This chapter will look at how the railways attempted to achieve these two seemingly incompatible objectives of style and economy.

Encouragement and economy

One immediate way in which the railways could seek to generate more traffic was by adding cheaper options to their services. From 1927 most major European international services conveyed Second Class passengers, and CIWL's 'trains de luxe' followed suit from 1931. In 1932 Austria, Holland, Romania and Yugoslavia added Third Class to their international consists, with France following suit between Paris, Marseilles and the Cote d'Azur in 1933.[26] In the late 1930s Second Class was even admitted on the 'Orient Express'.[27] American railroads did likewise. Before the war many major US long-distance trains conveyed parlor and club cars only; however, from around late 1916 records such as that of the consist changes for the Southern Pacific's 'Shore Line Limited' show such comments as 'two coaches added'. Later, marked 'effective 4/30', 'discontinued all Pullman Parlor Cars, now carries smoker, coaches and diner', and the authorial text on the same page comments, 'it was difficult to sell parlor space … so the three cars were converted…'[19]

In Britain, railway companies altered the proportion of Third to First Class seating, including dining car seats, as Charman's figures for 'Cornish Riviera' restaurant car seating make clear:

'It is interesting to note that in 1904 the dining capacity for First Class was 18 and for Third Class 32, while in 1929 it was 24 First Class and 95 Third Class.'[28]

The LNER's 'Sheffield Pullman Limited' of 1924 similarly had

'…a five-car rake of Pullmans, of which only one was First Class; this meant six times as many Third Class as First Class passengers could be carried.'[29]

The railways also encouraged passenger revenue by offering reduced-rate fares with emphasis on leisure travel, tailoring their offers as closely as possible to match road competition. The developing bus and coach operators could undercut standard Third Class fares by about one-third and were catering more and more for precisely tailored pick-ups.[30] But the coach companies could not compete on speed, not could they provide on-board refreshment. The railways therefore needed to match the coach companies as closely as possible on price and popular destination, while still trading on their two trump cards of speed and on-train services.

To cater for this new market, in 1933 the LNER introduced its famous Tourist Stock – open stock, with large windows with tables at each, modern bucket-seats, gloss finish and Rexine decoration, bare light bulbs in close-fitting sockets, and Art Deco-style chrome fittings.[31] The external finish was green and cream. Many were built as articulated twin sets, made up into rakes of 12, each containing two of Gresley's other economising innovation, buffet cars.[32] The Great Western built similar open stock, though not articulated and with bench seats, which it called 'Excursion' stock. This stock had kitchen cars serving meals at all tables and overcame the dining service problem by adopting another economising innovation in dining operation – 'plated meal' rather than 'silver service'.

In addition to being available on excursion trains, cheap returns were usable on many regular British services, often at heavily discounted rates: the 1926 weekend return from Waterloo to Ilfracombe was only 33s 9d, against an ordinary return of 50s 6d.[33] US railroads also offered reduced fares. Their offers were more aggressively advertised than in Britain, and much of their advertising focused on the classic 'tourist strengths' of the train, scenic experience, relaxation and comfort (including dining).

Cutting the costs of comfort

The railways succeeded eventually in holding passenger numbers steady, but at the cost of lower total passenger revenue receipts. To balance the books they needed also to control operating costs, especially the cost of restaurant car staff, which could be as great as all other on-train staff combined. Also, on-train dining services generated opportunity costs – seats used for 'fluid' dining added to hauled weight but generated no ticket revenue. Yet it was clear that dining provision was crucial to the 'travelling in style' that passengers required to woo them away from road competition.

In principle, the problem could be solved in several possible ways:

- Selling some dining-car seats as ticketed space
- Inducing maximum take-up of 'fluid' dining seats
- Increasing the maximum number of meals able to be served from the kitchen
- Devising new and more economical alternatives to the traditional dining car

Let us now look in more detail at each of these strategies.

'All the way in the dining car'

This solution allowed fare revenue to be collected from dining car seats. It was particularly favoured by the LMS – especially on services such as the 'Mancunian', with a 17-coach loading possible at peak periods.[34] Not all dining car seats could be thus reserved, as space had to be left for diners from other parts of the train, and the economics of the system meant that this facility was more often available to First Class passengers than to Third.

The LMS also operated a further version of this idea, where a Kitchen Third diner was paired with a *semi-open* First; the open saloon section functioned as a fluid diner, while the compartments conveyed fare-paying passengers.[35] (On the 'Royal Scot', the generous design of these compartments made it possible for extra tables to be inserted on which meals could be served if wanted.[34]) The Southern under Bulleid went even further, and teamed a semi-open First with a Kitchen Third diner *and* an open Third, to give a total of 120 fluid dining seats.[36]

'Go ye into the highways and byways, and compel them to come in'

A further way of controlling operating costs was to make maximum use of staff. Partly this could be implemented by careful rostering, but the real problem was to get the public to use the dining car services fully. In Britain, both the LMS and the LNER made substantial efforts to advertise their dining cars to this end. The LNER's use of advertising to attract dining car custom perhaps went furthest, particularly in its series of 1935 adverts alerting the passenger to the fact that there were '200 Restaurant Cars' on the LNER system. A degree of mystery surrounds this figure – Hughes claims that 'over 200' cars were handed over to the LNER by its constituents, but Harris lists only 165 as being in service in 1926.[37] The accuracy of the claim, however,

This 1935 restaurant car poster uses a whole raft of pictorial and typographical effects to make its points – including a suggestion of modern women's independence.
Courtesy National Railway Museum/Science & Society

fades into insignificance beside the ambiance of A. R. Thompson's poster illustrated here.

This remarkable design vividly contrasts the chaos and discomfort of an early railway journey with the comfort, order and cosy elegance of a contemporary restaurant car. The modern diner is gently lit from a table-lamp against a dark background and the figures are carefully grouped in a rock-steady tableau that contrasts strongly with the contorted lines of the 1835 train and the discomfort of the figures huddled in driving rain over their picnic hampers, reminding us how much better the 'modern' is than the 'ancient'. The typefaces reinforce the same message: 'Then' is printed in a fussy, hard-to-read Victorian type, while 'and NOW' is in the world-famous sans serif face designed for the LNER in 1929 by Eric Gill.[38]

And finally, the modern figures themselves repay study. The elegant man and the stylishly coiffured woman are clearly enjoying a late dinner (it is completely dark outside); all three figures are fashionably smart, including the attendant waiting to take the order. But here yet another aspect of 1930s modernism becomes apparent – the growing move towards feminine independence. He and she are clearly a couple: he appears, if only slightly, to be older than she – but *it is she, not he, who is clearly deciding the order*. In 1935 you couldn't get much more up-to-date than that!

Other UK railway companies, though, did not advertise restaurant cars in general in the same way as the LMS and LNER. In mainland Europe, too, posters involving portrayals of on-train dining almost always advertise specific 'trains de luxe'. Likewise, dining services are mentioned in US inter-war advertising such as this 1937 example, simply as one inducement among many to ride a specific train service, often alongside cheap offers:

'Here is the train you asked for between San Francisco and Portland – the friendly Beaver for Tourist Pullman and chair car passengers exclusively... Challenger-style dining car service for all passengers...' [Alongside is a picture of a family happily ordering in the dining car, then, inset:] 'Breakfast 25c Luncheon 30c Dinner 35c.'[39]

'Doing more with less'

A third way of reducing dining car costs was by cutting the per-capita costs of producing a meal. UK staff wages were cut across the board by 2½ per cent in 1928-29, and several more times during 1932-37.[40] But the direct costs of meal production also needed to be addressed. Cooking costs were not a source of economy, except by increasing the number of cold dishes; actual meal provisioning and ingredients costs therefore needed to be tackled.

The development of the LMS lunch menu demonstrates how this was done. Early inter-war menus still quite closely resembled the 1906 menu quoted in the previous chapter, but by June 1929 the menus are beginning to show distinct signs of a move towards cost-efficiency. There are no hors d'oeuvres – we start directly with the soup. The fish course is cold and there is only one roast, with 'assorted cold meats' as an alternative rather than a separate course. The menu cards are still relatively expensively produced, with the company's crest at the head, but the menus themselves have been designed for general use across the entire LMS system; the ingredients are being bought in bulk, with attendant economies of scale.

The process was complete by the lunch menus for August 1939. Again for the whole system, implying bulk purchase economies, they were produced more cheaply, without the complicated company crest. Printing the wine list on the reverse instead of on a separate sheet also saved money. Most important, though, was the reduced format of the meal; with these menus, we arrive at the 'typical British' standard meal of just three courses, with either a sweet or cheese on offer, but not both – which appears to give the lie to Palmer's assertion[41] that the habit of ordering 'three courses, never more and never less' was a product of Second World War rationing. The price also rose, by 10 per cent, from 2s 6d to 2s 9d, despite the falling cost of living.

American railroads also offered shorter, simpler and cheaper meals, for example the 'Challenger' menus of the Southern Pacific mentioned in the advert quoted above. The 'Challenger' trains were low-fare, low-cost expresses designed to attract custom during the Depression. In keeping with this, they provided a cost-cutting meal service, but achieved it by reducing choice rather than by shortening the menu. Thus, where the 'Daylight' menu offered nine main courses, the 'Challenger' menu[42] offered only two – roast turkey or scrambled eggs with mushrooms – and included only hot dinner rolls and ice-cream dessert with them, rather than the range of multiple choices on the 'Daylight'. The à la carte section on the 'Challenger' menu was likewise much shorter.

The effects of these economies were also different. In Britain, the more economical meals continued to be served at the same price as before: in the USA, however, almost all of the saving was passed on to the customer – the price of a 'Daylight' 'Selection' was generally around $1, but that of the 'Challenger' dinner was an astonishing 35 cents. These savings were intended not to control costs but to generate custom – cost benefits came from extra turnover or from staff economies. Indeed, most lines, in both countries, also maximised staff productivity by extending the number of meals served. There were several ways of doing this, all exploiting the fact that, as Jenkinson puts it, 'the kitchen was well able to produce far more meals than the typical seat capacity of the car could consume'.

Coupling a First kitchen-diner with an open Third substantially increased the number of seats available for any one sitting; thus the limiting factor on the number of meals per sitting was now the number of main course portions the chef could deal with. But all kitchen-diners had a pantry as well as the kitchen – many had two. Many open saloons intended for meals service also had a pantry at one end. These pantries included storage cupboards, a hot plate and a sink; as Harris puts it[43], 'their main purpose was to relieve the work carried out in the kitchen of the adjoining restaurant car'.

This ability to 'split' the work increased the total number of customers served. Each main course order would take the kitchen a specific time to prepare, and delivery to the diners would take a specific number of waiting staff a specific time. The total times and numbers involved formed an upper limit to the number of seats that could be served. But if the staff, instead of serving all the diners at the same time, were to start serving one part of the catering rake ahead of the other, this would then enable the two pantries to work on different stages of the meal at any one time. The forward pantry could serve starters to First Class, then the aft pantry could serve starters to Third Class while the forward pantry served main courses, then the forward pantry could serve sweets while the aft pantry served main courses in its turn, and so on.

This time-sharing division of the work, known as 'swing service', almost doubled the amount of time available to the chef to finish main course dishes. And because it normally took three waiting staff to silver-serve the main course, but only one or two to serve starters, sweets and cheese, it meant a maximum of five waiting staff would be needed at any one time, leaving two available to work in the kitchen itself throughout. On the 'Mancunian' or the 'Merseyside Express', where two rakes of catering vehicles served up to four sittings each[34], 'swing service' could extend the possible meals total by up to 50 meals per rake at each sitting – a further 400 in all.

The Great Western took this second element even further by substituting for main course silver service the cheaper alternative of serving excursion customers direct with plates of food ready made up. This rapidly spread to holiday trains in general, and Charman relates that in the immediate post-war period this 'plate service' still applied on Saturdays on the 'Cornish Riviera':

'I can remember going direct from Truro to Paddington… There was a special lunch menu of cold ham salad, roll and butter, and the sweet was tinned mixed fruit… We did literally hundreds of these meals, but did not mind as they were "plate service" where the usual meals were "silver service".'[44]

The notion of operating a 'swing service' from a central kitchen also developed in the USA, often, as on the Southern Pacific, marrying both strategies by combining a dining car and a 'coffee shop' car serving plated meals. The New Haven Rail Road's 'grill cars' of 1937 took plated service even further, presenting the entire meal on a single cafeteria-style tray – though the tray was still brought to the customer by an attendant. Tray service of this kind may sound airline-style, but the food was cooked fresh on the train, and Doughty comments that the results 'look[ed] better than any airline food'[45].

'There is an alternative'

A fourth way of controlling costs was by finding cheaper alternatives to the conventional meal. The American 'coffee shop' cars and 'grill cars' both implied such a concept, as did the Great Western's 'plate service', with its reduction to just salad and sweet, but the biggest meal cost savings were to come from the realisation that many people actually wanted not full meals but smaller snacks at more frequent intervals. The great protagonist of this change in Britain was the LNER.

The LNER faced road competition on the King's Cross-Cambridge service.[46] Gresley suggested using steam railcars, but Wedgwood preferred the 'short, frequent, fast service with a refreshment counter' concept of the old Great Central. Since the GCR buffet cars had met with resistance, Gresley was cautious; in 1932 he converted a few GNR open Thirds, and used them from King's Cross to Cambridge on weekdays and on excursions at weekends.[47] They proved a huge success – the undergraduates called them 'the beer trains', and flocked to them in droves[48] – and the Sunday excursionists liked them too. Accordingly, in 1933 Gresley ordered the design for his 'Tourist' sets[49], plus further cars in 1934, in conventional teak livery, operated on a wide range of services previously without catering. By 1937 the total build had reached 25.

All versions of the design had a kitchen containing a grill with a boiling ring over, which led directly from the staff side into a bar area with bottle-rack, showcase, tea and coffee boiler and, at the far end, a cashier station, and had modernist tubular metal seating for 22-24 persons. The Gresley buffet cars were seen as offering particularly good value for money. For 2s 6d you got a three-course lunch plus coffee, with a choice of grapefruit or soup, a selection from six cold main courses with salad, and a choice of cold sweet or cheese.

The other 'Big Four' companies also invested in buffet cars, though not to the same extent. The initial

| 2/6 | BUFFET CAR MENU | 2/6 |

Grape Fruit
Tomato Soup

Cold :

Veal and Ham Pie

Cold Ham   Pressed Beef   Ox Tongue

Galantine of Chicken
Roast Beef

Various Salads   Potato Salad

Fruit Salad
or
Cheese and Biscuits

Rolls and Butter

Tea or Coffee

The LNER's buffet car lunch menu, available all day, provided three courses and coffee for 17 per cent less than the equivalent menu in a formal dining car – 2s 6d as against 3 shillings. The food was cold (apart from a soup option), but there was a substantial choice of main courses. *Courtesy British Railways Board (Residuary)*

LMS design involved a very different design concept from Gresley's. Its self-service Cafeteria Car had 20 seats, on one side of the coach only, with a long rail separating them from a gangway, in which the customer queued up to approach the curved counter, then took a tray, placed it on the 'specially prepared runway for trays'[50] and ran it past the 'snack stand' to the far end. Here there was a 'girl serving drinks and cutlery and taking cash'. The customer then walked back along the opposite side of the rail to the seating area. The tables were fixed, but the chromium-plated chairs were 'placed to allow passengers maximum amount of freedom'. The public, however, did not take to the design, and Stanier rebuilt it with a Gresley-style buffet counter plus small kitchen, to which form he built four more cars in 1936.[51]

On the Southern, the area immediately south and south-east of London involved journey times too short for a full meal service to be feasible. The Southern already had a Pullman buffet service on its Brighton trains, but for the 1938 Mid-Sussex electrification Bulleid (who had been Gresley's chief assistant at Doncaster) designed new non-Pullman buffet stock featuring a kitchen with electric stove, refrigerator and serving hatch for meals to be delivered to seats, a bar with a scalloped outer edge and ten bar stools, and an open area with 16 seats, grouped round two scalloped tables each side, with a window over each table.[52] The scalloped edges to the tables resembled the styling of the 1937 'Coronation', and bar stools at a curved counter recalled the 1932 'Flying Scotsman' cocktail bar.[53] The food on offer was common to all the Southern buffet services, Pullman or not – a grilled 'Club Breakfast' up till 10am, followed for the rest of the day by à la carte service and various snacks.[54]

The principal refreshment needs of the Great Western were for heavily loaded holiday trains, on which they used plate service to cope economically with periodic heavy demand. However, the GWR too invested in a small number of buffet cars, to three different designs, all of which again suggested transatlantic influence, and one of which was specially designed to win back custom to an eroded service.

The first (1934) design was for two 'Quick Lunch Cars' with a small pantry with grill, boiling plate and wine cupboard, plus a single 40-foot bar counter with 12 bar stools in front of it.[55] The design, intended to feed people rapidly in small batches, closely resembled the 'lunch counter' to be found in American refreshment rooms. The second design was a cross between this and a conventional buffet car; there was a small kitchen with a proper range as well as the pantry, and the bar counter was now only 17ft 3in long, with eight stools on the passenger side. Twenty-one low-backed seats arranged in conventional 2+1 format around tables occupied the rest of the space, rather as in the 1928 NP 'Café Cars'. A phone passed orders from the bar/pantry to

the kitchen. Jenkinson comments that 'as all-purpose catering vehicles they were hard to better'.

The third design married the buffet car with a lightweight diesel-powered railcar, which the GWR used in 1934 to revive its badly eroded Birmingham-Cardiff service. The car had 44 roomy seats in 2+2 configuration around tables, lavatories, and what Jenkinson[56] describes as 'a small but extremely well-equipped buffet section at one end'. No menus have survived, but the GWR *Magazine* of 1934 pictures a steward serving coffee at seat to passengers.[57] As a result of the cars' success, two-car sets entered service in 1940-41[58], comprising two gangwayed single-ended diesel railcars coupled back to back. One car housed the buffet, and the other the toilet facilities.

American railroads also provided lower-cost alternatives to conventional dining car meals, often combined with more traditional offers. Where buffet-type service was provided, the name under which it went varied: a 1930s 'coffee shop' car, for example, could have tables positioned like those in a conventional dining car, but served with 'plate meals' rather than silver service, or it could have a lunch counter very similar to the Great Western 'quick lunch cars' of 1934, still serving plated meals but with the cooking 'in full view of the passengers'[59]. To confuse matters still further, the Northern Pacific, which had been running a version of the 'coffee shop' car with a half-length lunch counter *plus* some conventional coach seats since 1928, called their stock 'café cars'.

This 1959 photograph shows Southern Pacific 'tavern snack' car 10315. The vehicle was built in 1938, and is of typical 1937 Pullman-Standard 'moderne' design. Note the blank central section, the two balanced sets of windows, and the lack of any exterior doors. *Courtesy of California State Railroad Museum*

The interior of car 10315 illustrated opposite, looking towards the bar from the leading saloon. The seat design and configuration are clearly visible, as is a coffee percolator and hot-dog steamer, and the speaker grilles for the SP's radio/PA system. *Courtesy of California State Railroad Museum*

Two further noteworthy developments of the US 'coffee shop'/'café car' occurred in 1937. The Southern Pacific introduced what it called 'coffee shop-tavern' cars, making use of a new Pullman-Standard Co design also used by the New Haven RR for its 'grill cars'. This body design had a central 'short-order' kitchen and bar area within a blank-walled section of the coach, with seating areas either side; it also had no exterior doors, access being solely through internal gangways. Each passenger space could be fitted out with a 24-seat lunch counter or with 18 soft seats, positioned in groups of three round semicircular tables, back to the window.[60] The interior of one of the 1938 SP full tavern cars is illustrated here.

The 1937 New Haven 'grill cars' likewise had both a short-order kitchen and a bar in the centre, but in their case each passenger section contained inward-facing tables and bench seats. They advertised themselves as serving 'Dinner … at Cafeteria Prices'. A specimen menu of 'TYPICAL MEALS – TYPICAL PRICES' reads

BREAKFAST	LUNCHEON	DINNER
35c	60c	60c
Orange Juice	Broiled Lamb	Fried
Bacon & Egg	Chop	Chicken
Roll & Butter	Mashed Potatoes	French Fried
Coffee	String Beans	Potatoes
	Roll & Butter	Roll & Butter
	Lemon Meringue	Ice Cream
	Pie	Coffee
	Coffee	

with a picture of the tray meal concerned displayed to the left of each meal menu.[43]

In mainland Europe dining car policy had always been to provide an 'all-comers' service, with a single diner permanently open to serve a range of orders, from a simple beer or coffee through snacks such as chocolate torte to cooked meals. Away from CIWL, all service was 'plate service', with rarely more than two waiters needed. As a result there was little need for European railways to introduce a separate buffet car régime. But some buffet cars were introduced in 1932-33, together with Second and Third Class sleeper services, and 'in France, and certain Central European countries, a restaurant-cum-bar car offered a more informal service'[61].

Our final examples of buffet car operation saved not money but weight. Even during the Depression, a niche market still existed for more expensive and luxurious travel. Two of these 'Supertrains' in Germany, and around a dozen in the USA and France, were high-speed self-propelled ultra-lightweight diesel-powered multiple-unit sets. To operate these at the advertised speeds every last ounce of weight had to be saved. Dining cars were out: at-seat buffet service was essential.

The earliest of these trains were the German 'Fliegender Hamburger' and 'Fliegender Kölner' of 1933. Each only two coaches long, they had their origins in the Nazi Government's needs for a technological propaganda coup.[62] Thus in addition to their high speed they had to offer a recognisable luxury service at the same cost as the ordinary Second Class fare. A contemporary account describes the result:

'As soon as the passenger is seated, a waiter of the "Mitropa" appears with a list of ... drinks and cold refreshments, and small portable folding tables are placed in front of the passenger. There is a bar in the middle of the train. It is just large enough for the bar-keeper. It is ... a wonder of room economy, for the attendant can conjure up all the liqueurs, mineral waters, beer, wine, the sandwiches, coffee, tea and bouillon ... *à la carte.*'[63]

The origin of the 1934 US lightweight high-speed diesels – the Union Pacific's 'Cities' and the Burlington 'Zephyrs' – was much more directly economic; to counter airline impact on the rail passenger market, railroads were seeking to offer trains that would go from New York to California in less than 60 hours. In the original UP layout, the front coach contained the power unit, a post office and a baggage compartment, the middle coach held 60 passengers in a 2+2 configuration in reclining seats, and the rear car held washrooms, a further 56 seats, and a small 'buffet kitchen' at the extreme rear. The layout diagram contains almost no detail of how the buffet-kitchen was fitted out, but again a contemporary description gives an indication of this and how it was used:

'... the buffet kitchen is replete with space-saving devices for the preparation of light meals. On one side is a refrigerator box for carrying ice-creams, cooling drinks and the like, and on the other side are two coffee urns, a grill and other cooking apparatus. An electric icebox is built directly into the entrance end of the coach. The traveller can obtain occasional refreshments at the counter. Light meals are also prepared in the train kitchen, and passengers are served on little trays which can be attached to the seats... Meals are served from a special dinner wagon, the top comprising a steam-heated table, with lower shelves for dishes, silverware and linen of a special weave. The dishes ... are made of a special composition, very light in weight, and gaily coloured.'[64]

(The American liking for one-off nomenclature, though, meant that when a buffet kitchen was added to the rival Burlington 'Zephyr', it was named a 'Dinette'.[65])

The French 1934 sets, also intended to compete with airline traffic[66], included a central buffet kitchen 'complete with a refrigerator and gas-cooking apparatus'. The meals were served at seats, with 'removable tables and large, upholstered armchairs'.

Trains and Supertrains

The need to protect the premium market against car travel and the new airlines also led to the development of the 1930s 'Supertrains' – fast, of sophisticated Art Deco design, often streamlined, and offering a high degree of comfort and added services. Some, like the 'Orient Express', the 'Flying Scotsman' or the 'Twentieth Century Limited', were existing trains reborn or upgraded. Others, like the 'Rheingold', the 'Silver Jubilee' or the 'George Washington', were new, designed as 'star turn' attention-getters. These trains formed only a small proportion of the passenger services but they had a tremendous publicity value – they made rail travel feel glamorous.

CIWL: the 'Orient Express' enlarged?

Mainland Europe's 'Supertrains' built on the pre-war Wagons-Lits 'train de luxe' format. By 1930 the CIWL map showed not one 'Orient Express' but six[67] – the route through Strasbourg; the 'Simplon-Orient' via Venice; its *Branches correspondantes* for Bucharest and Athens; the 'Arlberg-Orient' via Basle, Zurich and Vienna; the 'Ostend-Istanbul Express'; and feeder services from Berlin via Budapest. The new trains, and CIWL's other 'trains de luxe', such as the 'Train Bleu' of 1922 with two sittings of lunch leaving Calais[68], now sported all-steel rolling-stock and admitted Second Class passengers. The restaurant cars (built in France, with Art Deco marquetry panels from Britain) could seat 56 people, in a 2+2 configuration, and had rather severe bench seats – more space-intensive and less luxurious than their pre-war predecessors[69]. CIWL also introduced 'buffet cars for short journeys, with light refreshment bars'[70].

Yet another set of changes occurred at the Eastern end of the route. In 1923 Kemal Ataturk moved the Turkish capital from Constantinople (renamed Istanbul) to Ankara. Thus political travellers now needed to be conveyed onwards to the new capital. For them CIWL instituted in 1927 a connecting service, the 'Anatolia Express', which prided itself on its menu every bit as much as its brethren on the western shore.

Indeed, the CIWL went even further. To cater for up-market trips to the Middle East and Egypt, the

'Taurus Express' was instituted in 1930, with two parts, one for Baghdad and the other for Cairo and, via the 'Cairo-Luxor Express', the tombs themselves. The venture was highly successful; at its height 20 dining cars were needed for the complete 'Taurus' service.[71] A contemporary account of the train shows dining cars very similar to the 1928 French-built stock, even down to the marquetry panelling and bench seats[72], but with louvred shutters to keep out heat and dust.

Back in Europe, however, CIWL had a competitor: Mitropa, the company set up in Germany at the outbreak of the First World War, now operated five Supertrains in competition with CIWL's 'trains de luxe'. Two – the 'Fliegende Hamburger' and 'Fliegende Kölner' of 1933 – have already been discussed. The other three were slightly older. The earliest was the 'Berlin-London Express' (via the Harwich-Hoek ferry and the LNER) of 1923, using the refurbished ex-Kaiser's Imperial Train, a direct competitor with CIWL's restarted 'Nord Express', then came the 1924 Warnemunde-Basle 'Scandinavian-Swiss Express', using new sleepers.

Finally, there was the 1928 'Rheingold' (London-Hoek-Lucerne-Milan, competing directly with the 'Golden Arrow' and the 'Simplon-Orient'), with its violet and white Pullman-style saloon coaches and its superb dining cars and wine list (Mitropa had invested in a major commissary and wine store in Berlin and in the Franz Klein winery at Traben Trarbach). This train was an instant success, especially with British passengers, who got the overnight part of the journey over in cabins on the boat and started fresh with breakfast leaving Hoek. Behrend describes the on-board facilities:

'…immediately beside the gangway … stood the train… Rheingold passengers now had only to take a few … steps … and enter the train's heated saloons. At once the passenger was in Germany… Customs inspection took place on the train, which comprised luggage van, First Class dining saloon with kitchen and Second Class dining saloon without kitchen…

Prussian-blue chairs were thick-cushioned and the tables laid with cruets and pots of English marmalade. Unlike the Wagons-Lits staff, whose international language was French and whose English was slight, halting and poorly pronounced, the Germans asked in perfect English what the passenger wished for breakfast (a full one if desired) as the train moved off beside the canal.'[73]

A contemporary account indicates the general level of competition offered to CIWL on Mitropa services:

'The Mitropa cars are similar to those of the International Sleeping Car company: in the Third Class the berth is harder than that of a British Third Class sleeper … but spotlessly clean bedclothes are inevitably provided. The Second and First Class sleepers are exceedingly comfortable. Of the restaurant cars, little need be said, save that they provide the passengers with good and plentiful food. But the finest train of the Mitropa Company is the "Rheingold Express", which consists entirely of First and Second Class Pullman-type coaches, running between the Hook of Holland, Basle and Zurich. The "Rheingold" is among the handsomest and most comfortable trains on the Continent.'[74]

However, with the exception of the two German diesel fliers and the Paris-Brussels 'Blue Bird', these trains lacked one major characteristic of a Supertrain: they were not particularly speedy, none averaging more than 60mph overall. Nevertheless, by 1935 the 'Orient Express' had cut its journey time to Vienna by 7¼ hours, and to Bucharest by 21¼ hours. The 'Simplon-Orient' had cut 36 hours off its time to Istanbul, while the 'Nord Express' had reduced its journey time to Berlin by 3½ hours and to Warsaw by 5, and further journey time had been saved in 1932 by attaching the 'Rome Express' and 'Train Bleu' sleeping cars leaving Calais to the 'Flèche D'Or'.

The British 'Dalziel' Pullmans

The 'Flèche D'Or' (or 'Golden Arrow') was the earlier (1929[75]) of two 'trains de luxe' to operate both in the UK and on the European mainland. (The other was the 'Night Ferry', which started in 1936.[76]) British responses to the Supertrain niche market fell into three well-defined groups:

- Extensions under Dalziel of the Pullman services
- Upgrades to existing 'named trains' (and sometimes to other existing services, then given names, such as the 'Atlantic Coast Express')
- Supertrains proper – a small group of fast, luxurious, streamlined and extra-fare trains, from 1935 onwards

At the beginning of the inter-war period there were five regular Pullman services – the 'Southern Belle', the Sundays-only Pullman services to Eastbourne and Ramsgate, the 'Clacton Sunday Pullman' with its weekday individual Pullman car workings on regular East Anglian expresses, and the evening 'Hook Continental' boat train.[77] This was an alarmingly insecure commercial base: only two services were aimed at any regular business market, and of those the weekday East Anglian services proved economically questionable, except for the Harwich boat trains.[78]

Dalziel therefore set about developing his services in three main directions – finding more profitable routes for his LNER Pullmans, initiating a further luxury 'Belle' express to Bournemouth, and linking the Pullman operations on the Southern with his Wagons-Lits operations in France, through the 'Golden Arrow' and the 'Night Ferry'. In these operations he was assisted by two of the most forward-looking railway entrepreneurs of the inter-war years – Sir Ralph Wedgwood on the LNER and Sir Herbert Walker on the Southern. Both men were aware that for the upper end of the market 'trains de luxe' were still an important prestige element; the issue was to make sure that the routes selected were economically viable. The East Coast and 'Golden Arrow' services especially needed careful monitoring.

The origins of the first of the East Coast Pullmans – the 'Harrogate Pullman', later extended to Edinburgh and renamed the 'Queen of Scots' – are something of a mystery. Both the LNER and Dalziel were looking for a more cost-efficient use of the cars, but it is uncertain who made the first move. Wedgwood claimed, in his speech at the 'Harrogate Pullman' inaugural dinner, that

'...the Harrogate Corporation came forward with their proposal for a Pullman train service which should combine the last thing in luxury with the best thing in speed, [and] they ... found the Railway in responsive mood.'[79]

But according to Hughes, the LNER management first initiated discussions over varying the use of the cars, and the Pullman organisation suggested Harrogate, Leeds and Bradford as destinations. Hughes also indicates that the LNER's Passenger Managers initially resisted the proposal, but Wedgwood overruled them.[80]

In the actual schedule, a stop was made at Leeds, but from Harrogate the train then ran on to Ripon,

Darlington and Newcastle, giving them a London Pullman, and providing a fast Harrogate-Newcastle service. The timings maximised the opportunity for meal service: the down Pullman left King's Cross at 11.15am, while the up service left Newcastle at 9.20am and Leeds at 11.45am. This enabled down Leeds and Harrogate passengers to take morning coffee and lunch, and Harrogate-Newcastle passengers to take afternoon tea, while up passengers from Newcastle or Harrogate could take morning coffee followed by lunch, which those joining at Leeds could also enjoy.[81]

A 'Sheffield Pullman' was added in 1924, aimed at the business market, but it proved uneconomic, and was withdrawn in 1925. The analysis, however, had shown that Leeds traffic paid, so from 1925 the Harrogate and Newcastle service cut out Leeds but was extended to Berwick and Edinburgh, while a new 'West Riding Pullman' service to Leeds, Bradford and Halifax replaced the 'Sheffield Pullman'. These changes proved successful too, and in 1928 the Edinburgh train was renamed the 'Queen of Scots' and extended to Glasgow, while the 'West Riding Pullman' (later 'Yorkshire Pullman') was retimed clear of it in both directions, and also called at Harrogate. With a section to Hull added in 1935, the service continued until the Second World War.[82]

The problems faced by the 'Golden Arrow' were, however, more severe. Declining passenger numbers from 1929 onwards led, first to only one boat being used for both the 'Golden Arrow' and for the ordinary boat train, then in May 1932 – with cross-Channel passenger journeys dropping by one-third in three years – to the two trains being combined, and from 1935 to the London-bound service being re-timed to allow one rake of coaches to be used on the French side also.[83]

Other factors were at work too. 'Going abroad' was seen as an expensive and exclusive pursuit, and there was also a difference in convenience. While the traveller on the East Coast Pullmans could settle down and relax with morning coffee, sherry, lunch and afternoon tea, the break of journey and time differences of the 'Golden Arrow' service meant that the best one could hope for was the standard Southern Pullman buffet service, plus something on board the steamer *Canterbury*. Fryer sums up the overall problem like this:

'The ... "Golden Arrow" was ... dependent on favourable economic circumstances for its success, and the times were not propitious. Not only the slump of the early 1930s, but also the increasing use of aircraft to convey passengers from London to Paris in a third of the time that the train-and-boat service required, limited its period of exclusive "de luxe" splendour to a mere two years.'[83]

A 1936 account adds an intriguing further insight, suggesting that it was Britain's departure from the gold standard, as much as the recession in general, that was behind the problem.

'When the "Golden Arrow" was first introduced, an all-Pullman train was provided on either side of the Channel, ten large cars, First Class only, being run… But a phase of depression of cross-Channel traffic followed the devaluation of the pound… Since then, although the number of passengers crossing the Channel has again increased, the conditions … compelled the "Golden Arrow" to abandon its exclusiveness. The First Class barrier was banished and Second Class coaches were included.'[84]

The naming game

The second response was the upgrading of existing 'named train' services and the creation of new ones. The 'Big Four' indulged in a spate of train-naming or upgrading around 1925-28, the peak coming in 1927, when the LMS named no fewer than 16 of its services, including the 'Royal Scot' and the 'Irish Mail'[85], and immediately included them in a special new page in its timetable headed 'FAMOUS LMS TRAINS', leading one writer to comment 'note the publicity man's use of "famous" for something he has just thought up'[86].

These named trains usually involved a stock upgrade, with on-board dining services playing a major part in any improvements. The market leaders in this upgrading process were the 'Cornish Riviera' and the 'Flying Scotsman', with the latter the more spectacular. When on 11 July 1927 the LMS named its competing 10am departure the 'Royal Scot', and introduced a glamorous new engine type to match, the LNER responded by making its train non-stop from May 1928; the LMS made one non-stop-run attempt, but could not match the LNER in regular service.[87]

For the 1928 non-stop 'Flying Scotsman' service, the LNER built a special restaurant triplet set, with the First Class saloon sporting individual armchairs and 'Louis XIV' decoration. They also included a ladies' retiring room and a hairdressing salon, and

introduced an on-train newsvendor selling newspapers, magazines and books.[88] The LMS countered in late 1928 with new 2+1 open Thirds, a semi-open dining First design in which the compartments had only four seats each, and 'a First Class lounge brake, with armchairs and settees, picture windows and occasional tables'.[89]

In 1930 the 'Flying Scotsman' in return received new passenger stock, including two 'super Firsts' with winged armchairs with adjustable seats and backs, footstools, and pressure ventilation.[90] The LMS riposted by building further new 'Royal Scot' sets, with lower waistlines and larger picture windows.[91] The LNER replied by altering the hairdressing carriages in 1932 to include a cocktail bar at one end; a further suite of 'French-style' First Class coaches was added in 1935, and in 1938 a further complete set of new stock included a buffet-lounge car with a separate side corridor to ensure privacy to the loungers.[92] The LMS initiated further upgrades during 1933-37, including new kitchen-diners together with open stock.[93]

These responses were quite deliberate: instruction notes on the building programme for the 1930 'Flying Scotsman' stock, for example, include the comments 'as per the stock on the West Coast' and 'in view of the improved stock which the LMS is using'. And upgrades of on-train dining and associated services played a central role in each offer; contemporary accounts of both services[94] go out of their way to draw attention to the dining arrangements, with illustrations of the chef of the 'Flying Scotsman' at work in the 'wonderful all-electric kitchen' or 'Mealtime on the 'Royal Scot':

'The serving of meals in comfort while the train is travelling at high speed is now a commonplace in railway travel. The extent to which this service is appreciated by the public can be gauged by the fact that nearly eight million meals are provided annually on British railways.'

A similar competitive pattern occurred on the Great Western and Southern's West of England services, and again on-train dining featured heavily in the competition. The Great Western had already introduced new articulated stock on the 'Cornish Riviera' service in 1925.[95] The Southern's 1926 'Atlantic Coast Express' was initially introduced with no stock upgrade, but from 1927 to 1934 Maunsell introduced new improved stock on the 'ACE' and other West of England services, including paired kitchen First and 2+2 open Third diners with

This shot of a single dining car bay shows just how much attention to detail went into conveying the atmosphere of 'dining at speed'. Note the table napery, the vase of flowers, the menu card, the wines, the rolls and the bread basket laid out in advance. *Courtesy National Railway Museum/Science & Society*

a transverse open space between the kitchen and the forward pantry to enable courses to be served from both without the staff getting in each other's way.[96]

The GWR responded with new 'Cornish Riviera' stock in 1930, also with a transverse gap between pantry and kitchen, and with chromium door handles, Art Deco seat design and ribbed glass styling to the dining saloon partitions, and further updating of the stock in 1935 with end-kitchen Firsts, and separate armchairs in the First Class dining saloon.[97] Maunsell's reply was to increase the number of restaurant sets allocated to the 'ACE' services during the summer till on summer Saturdays almost every section of the 'ACE' had a through restaurant working.[98]

Food and menu quality were central too. Cost considerations were not to be allowed to affect

dining on the 'Titled Trains' and some of them gained a reputation for serving very fine food indeed.[99] One such, the 'Irish Mail', left Euston at 8.30am, serving breakfast and lunch; the First Class menu for 29 June 1937 is reproduced here.

The menu is distinctly more elaborate than its ordinary counterparts. Luncheon has five courses: cheese is additional to a sweet and the fish course is additional to the roast, retaining the Edwardian format that more general restaurant car menus had lost; there is a choice of sweets, and a choice between soup and grapefruit as a starter. And the breakfast menu is actually even *more* elaborate than pre-First World War examples.

The diner is expected to be willing to pay for this more lavish provender, though. luncheon costs 3s 6d

The menu for the 'Irish Mail' for 29 June 1937 demonstrates inter-war 'Titled Train' catering at its best. Notice the elaborate formality of the luncheon; notice too the stylised menu cover, redolent of the romance of a sea passage (the Irish Sea was rarely this calm!). *Courtesy British Railways Board (Residuary)*

as against the 2s 9d of the ordinary luncheon menu, and the extra charge for coffee is 4d rather than the usual 3d. A similar price and quality differential existed on other lines too: the Great Western's restaurant car tariff shows luncheon as 2s 6d and 3 shillings, but notes that 'The charge for the Table d'Hôte Luncheon served on the "Cornish Riviera Limited" and "Torbay Limited" Expresses is 4/- per head'[34], and Boston indicates what travellers on the 'Torbay Express' got for their extra money when he quotes the following six-course menu layout (plus coffee, 4d extra):

> Soup, Grapefruit or Tomato Juice
> Fish – Halibut, Turbot, Brill or Sole
> Entrée Coffee and Liqueurs
> Meat or Poultry with vegetables in season
> Sweet
> Savoury[100]

Four streamlined Supertrains

There were only four British streamliners, all but one on the LNER, and their entire career only spanned 1935 to 1939, yet for most people they *were* the romance of rail travel in between the wars. Their appeal rested on several things. They were fast and they were glamorous. They were ultra-modern in design and décor. But most of all, they embodied a sense that things were at last getting better.

The Supertrains resulted from responses to several factors. One was potential competition from air travel, another was renewed inter-company competition. By around 1934 people were again beginning to want to travel, but mainly at low prices, still only providing a reduced income. Thus the premium market – the one part of the service that could still be guaranteed to pay – was pursued with increasing urgency.

Two more factors were special to the LNER, Sir Ralph Wedgwood's policy of combining continuous economy with continuous quality improvement, and Gresley's dislike of the restricted comfort of the German high-speed diesels. It seems to have come as a shock when he discovered that the best the German designers could come up with for a proposed London-Newcastle 4-hour service was 'a three-coach articulated train, seating 140 passengers in accommodation much more cramped than that provided for *Third* Class passengers in Great Britain'[101]. Wedgwood suggested that even a standard 'Pacific' locomotive with ordinary coaches could make better time. Gresley tested this idea with 'A3'

loco *Papyrus* and a six-coach train, and *Silver Link* and the 'Silver Jubilee' train were born.

At least, that is the usually accepted version, but one contemporary account suggests that other factors influenced the decision to offer a steam-hauled streamliner. The review of the 'Silver Jubilee' service in *Railway Wonders of the World* ends with the following patriotic flourish:

> 'Diesel propulsion has been avoided with the express intention that British native fuel – coal – shall be used rather than imported fuel oil. And in any event, as compared with the "Flying Hamburger" or the "Flying Cologner", although the speed of the "Silver Jubilee" is not quite so high, it has double the seating accommodation of either of these German units, in more spacious conditions, and with full restaurant car accommodation as compared with merely a cold buffet.'[102]

'Native coal' was an obvious choice, given Wedgwood's watchword of 'continuous economy', but it would also have been a major public relations gaffe to have offered a train for the North East that ran on anything else! The question is, who told Winchester and Allen's author?

The 'Silver Jubilee' went into service on 27 September 1935 on a 4-hour timing between Newcastle and King's Cross, with a stop at Darlington. The train, articulated throughout to save weight, consisted of seven coaches – a restaurant car triplet in the centre flanked by two First Class coaches (one semi-open to allow for 'swing' overflow) forward and two Third Class compartment coaches aft, providing seating for 198 passengers with 10 per cent weight saving over traditional stock. All seats were reservable, at a supplement of 5 shillings First Class and 3 shillings Third. There was no 'fluid' dining – if you wished to dine you booked a seat in the dining section.[103]

The train's 4-hour schedule at last put Newcastle in the position where a businessman could leave at 10am, lunch on the train, arrive in London for half a day's business meetings, dine on the 5.30pm return journey and arrive home late that same evening. But the 'Jubilee' did not only cater for business traffic, and the lunch menu in particular allowed for that, as the 1938 specimen illustrated here shows.

Instead of separate First and Third Class menus, a single table d'hôte menu was offered, with two variations – a five-course luncheon for 3s 6d, or a two-course 'joint luncheon' for 2s 6d. Coffee was

The amazing 'Silver Jubilee' lunch menu card – probably the closest a British railway ever came to the US style of a dining car bill of fare. Note the provision of children's meals, and also the warning to make sure that the bill is written out in front of you. *Courtesy British Railways Board (Residuary)*

extra, again at 4d a cup rather than 3d. But the 'Silver Jubilee' luncheon had many more choices than were available on the LMS 'namers' – three fish courses, entrées and sweets. Even the 'joint luncheon' allowed you to choose a main course from any fish or entrée option, and a dessert from any of the sweets or cheese. And the à la carte offers included most table d'hôte items as well as anything from a complete mixed grill through a cold buffet to snacks, pastries and sandwiches.

Loading at 86 per cent, the 'Silver Jubilee' grossed six times its operating costs[104], while its publicity value stimulated overall traffic by up to 12 per cent. Wedgwood recommended to the Board in 1936 that

two more streamliners should be run the following year, to Edinburgh and to Leeds/Bradford.[105] These two trains, the 'Coronation' and 'West Riding Limited', were even more luxurious. Each train comprised eight coaches in four articulated pairs. There were no separate dining cars: catering was at-seat throughout the train, from two kitchen-diners. Jenkinson describes the coaches as follows:

'The open Thirds were as nearly like orthodox First Class dining cars as anything else. Subtle shades of fawn and green combined with excellent attention to detail and … marvellous riding quality gave the next best thing to

This dinner menu from the 'Coronation' is perhaps somewhat less innovative than the 'Silver Jubilee' lunch menu, though it still represents a level of fine cuisine well above the ordinary for the period. Note particularly the much more limited à la carte section – but also the wide range of drinks available, including one or two really fine wines, and Harrogate spa water. *Courtesy British Railways Board (Residuary)*

Pullman travel that I can remember. What was particularly thoughtful was the way in which, when not laid up for meals, the table tops would fold along their long axis to make it much easier to reach the window seats…

As for the … Firsts, here the "French" influence crept back… Single swivelling armchairs were arranged down both sides, and each four-seat bay was divided from its next-door neighbour by a full height partition which … also had lateral "wings" forming a sort of alcove into which each armchair was snugly ensconced… Even the table shape, with its scalloped edges, was designed to make eating simpler, and one could even arrange the chair at an angle so as to part face the window while enjoying the meal.[106]

The 'Coronation' left London at 4pm and Edinburgh at 4.30.[107] The First Class dinner menu illustrated compares interestingly with the 'Silver Jubilee' offer. Separate First and Third Class menus and prices have returned: dinner in First Class is 5 shillings, with a choice of sweet and an inclusive dessert course (at 4s 6d, Third Class had only one sweet and dessert was extra). The menu has less choice than the 'Silver Jubilee' – no choice of fish course, and only two entrées. But this is the result of an even more radical innovation – at-seat silver service to everyone on the train. Close examination of the train consist schematic shows that the forward kitchen served to 45 seats, and its trailing pantry to 48, while the rear kitchen served to 57 seats and its trailing pantry to 66. Such a task was only feasible if menu choice was strictly controlled.

The LMS responded by also producing a streamlined Supertrain, the 'Coronation Scot', hauling nine coaches with a tare weight of just under 300 tons between Euston and Glasgow in 6½ hours. Exact details of how the LMS heard about and decided to 'trump' the LNER's proposal are impossible to discover; we only know that Wedgwood reported the success of the 'Silver Jubilee' in October 1936, that Stanier organised high-speed Euston-Glasgow trials with 'Princess Royal' 4-6-2 *Princess Elizabeth* and a 'fair-sized though by no means heavy train'[108] at around the same time, and that both Supertrains began work on the same day, 5 July 1937.

The 'Coronation Scot' was longer and heavier than its LNER counterpart, its nine coaches being refurbished from existing stock rather than specially designed. The on-board services were slightly different, too: passengers in the open sections were offered an at-seat service of meals, 40 Firsts and 34 Thirds were in side corridor coaches with no catering available, like the 'Silver Jubilee'. It did, however, have two double-pantry kitchen cars, rather than the kitchen-diners of the 'Coronation', which made meal service a lot easier; each pantry served to 42 seats, leaving kitchen staff free to concentrate on food preparation. The supplement was 2s 6d, in either class.

The 'Coronation Scot' menu also differed in emphasis from its LNER counterpart, though at the same price (5 shillings). It was a completely set table d'hôte meal, but much more elaborate – seven courses, with asparagus added as a vegetable savoury before the sweet, and the cheese course replaced by a

The 'Coronation Scot' menu and wine list for June 1939 shows by contrast how the LMS concentrated on its traditional 'table d'hôte' set meal approach, together with light refreshments available 'out of hours', pioneered by the Midland as early as 1893. *Courtesy British Railways Board (Residuary) and Harpenden Railway Museum*

cooked savoury. Yet it also has a traditional English feel to it, as does the offer of 'light refreshments available when table d'hôte meals are not being served', reminiscent of early Midland menus.

Thus, despite the economies forced upon ordinary train menus by the Depression years, British 'Supertrain' food fully justified Tim Petchey's judgment of it in the opening of his chapter on Railway Catering in *A Collector's Guide to Railwayana*:

'On-train catering reached its peak in the first dozen or so years of the 20th century, the First Class diners at least enjoying sumptuous surroundings and services to match any hotel… The crack expresses of the 1930s carried on the tradition of the previous days, with … standards … second to none.' [109]

Three American case-studies

US railroads responded to airline competition and the beginning of up-market resurgence in a range of ways. The Southern Pacific combined the prestige of named trains with cost-cutting strategies (though it offered both a streamlined version of the 'Daylight' and a non-stop Houston-Dallas streamliner, the 'Sunbeam', in 1939).[110] The Union Pacific and the Burlington concentrated on ultra-high-speed lightweight self-propelled diesel streamliners. The New York, New Haven & Hartford RR put its money into upgraded and new streamlined passenger stock and innovative diners across as much of the system as

possible[111], rather than into specific high-profile services (apart from the 'Yankee Clipper' between New Haven and Boston).

The New York Central upgraded the stock on its existing 'Twentieth Century Limited' service, which often ran in several sections, to Art Deco designs by Henry Dreyfuss[112], with single-room sleeping cars, barber shop, valet, ladies' maid and manicurist, fresh-and salt-water bathrooms, day Pullman cars with single and double roomettes and drawing-rooms, a business service including stock market reports and an on-train stenographer, dining cars serving dinner and breakfast, and club and observation lounges[113] serving cocktails. The main train left Grand Central Station at 2.45pm, any second section left at 1.45, and its dining car also served lunch.

Some roads, however, did introduce or upgrade titled trains in a manner similar to those in Britain – among them the Northern Pacific, the Chesapeake & Ohio, credited with the first completely air-conditioned train, and the Santa Fé, operating the world's first full-length diesel-hauled streamliner, the 'Super Chief'. These three roads all had in common a mixture of provision for tourism and for premium services.

The Northern Pacific's 'North Coast Limited' had been running between Chicago and Seattle since 1900[114], and hence NP policy resembled that of the New York Central. Where it was different, however, was in combining upgrades of the 'Limited' with operating a train aimed at the transcontinental tourist market, the 'Yellowstone Comet'.

The development of the 'North Coast Limited'

This picture shows the interior of one of the Northern Pacific's 1910 Barney & Smith dining cars as remodelled by Pullman in 1921 for the 'North Coast Limited'. Note the panelling and the dining chairs, and the jugs of iced water and fresh roses on every table. *Courtesy of Minnesota Historical Society*

and the 'Yellowstone Comet' began in 1921 with an upgrade by Pullman of 1910 dining cars by Barney and Smith[115]; the result was a very substantial wood-panelled clerestory vehicle, with elegant concealed lighting, pull-down shades to the windows, and individual dining chairs. In cuisine, the railway was one of the few western roads to resist sacrificing meal quality to cost reduction, but it did have to make some compromises. McKenzie comments:

'As ... patronage fell off, however, reductions had to come. Some of the more elaborate meals disappeared ... and less expensive ingredients were substituted in many recipes to cut costs and make them seem more like "home-style" cooking. On the other hand, crew size remained intact...'[116]

But the railway believed service quality would eventually produce an upturn. In 1930 it ordered further new dining cars and added a hairdressing salon-cum-soda fountain to the facilities of the 'North Coast Limited'. In 1933 it started an air-conditioning upgrade of the whole fleet, beginning with the observation and dining cars of the 'Limited', and by 1935 it was offering at-seat tray service along the train. By then, though, the worst was over: from 1934 passenger revenues began to pick up again, putting the line back into profit by 1937, though, as McKenzie says, 'through it all, the dining cars lost money, as expected'[117].

What then can we learn from the 'Limited' and 'Comet' menus of the period? An early example (not illustrated), 'Some Northern Pacific Club Meals', demonstrates that company's first attempts to 'hold the line' over quality while meeting demand for cheaper prices, by reducing portion sizes; choice is still available from a full à la carte menu, but the 'Club Meals' all specify reduced portions. A slightly later menu from the 'Yellowstone Comet' (illustrated here) demonstrates a second and perhaps more common method the NP used. Here, the formal heading 'Dinner' is replaced by 'Evening Club Service', and there are five levels of Club Meal to choose from – four at 75 cents and a fifth at $1. Three of the five alternatives involve a choice of soup, main course or vegetable, but instead of the portion size it is the range of alternatives that is reduced. The list from which patrons can choose their Club main courses is very much shorter than the old à la carte menu.

If the Northern Pacific reflects a policy of soldiering on, the Chesapeake & Ohio demonstrates

The 'Yellowstone Comet' menu offered a choice of 'club meals'. Note how the saving is effected not by reducing portion size but by shortening the range of choices. Note, too, how 'Evening Club Service', with its homely, relaxed overtones – so appropriate for a tourist train – has replaced the formality of 'Dinner'. *Courtesy of Minnesota Historical Society*

innovative flexibility. Its initial response was to continue running the 'Fast Flying Virginian' while it sized up the most productive reaction to the economic maelstrom. One thing its officers saw clearly was that tourism, in a depression, attracts more custom than business trains – but business trains, *if they are special enough*, pay better. Their response was to launch two of America's most famous trains, the 'Sportsman' in 1930 and the 'George Washington' in 1932.

'The Sportsman' embodied a simple but audacious principle: if you have major up-market tourist areas at both ends of your route, each peaking at a different season, and more along it, then a service connecting them, which also passes through major business centres, can scarcely fail to make money. The train's route ran from Newport News to Detroit, via Russell KY, Columbus and Toledo OH. As E. S. Hanger has put it, it 'connected the Virginia seashore and the summer resorts along the Great Lakes ... with the

Dining Service
The George Washington
CHESAPEAKE AND OHIO LINES

☆

Mount Vernon Dinner $1.25

Spring Onions   Garden Radishes
                    Tomato Juice Cocktail
                         CHOICE
Spring Vegetable Soup   Consomme
                         CHOICE
            Broiled or Fried Fish, Lemon Butter
Baked Young Chicken with Dressing   Breaded Veal Cutlet, Tomato Sauce
      Lamb Chops   Dinner Steak
                     CHOICE OF TWO
    Potatoes, as desired   Fresh Asparagus, Drawn Butter
Fresh Green Beans   Creamed Cauliflower   Fresh Spinach

              Lettuce and Tomato Salad
                  French Dressing

                  Assorted Bread
                       CHOICE
Ice Cream with Cake   Apple Pie
            Fruit Jello, Whipped Cream
   Roquefort or Martha Washington Cream Cheese with Wafers
      Tea   Coffee   Milk   Cocoa

                         ☆

Tavern Dinner 75c
              Broiled or Fried Fish or
Breaded Veal Cutlet, Tomato Sauce, Fresh Green Beans
   Mashed Potatoes, Lettuce Salad, Assorted Bread
                    Apple Pie
               Tea, Coffee, Milk

                         ☆

  ❧   *Suggestions*   ❧

Broiled or Fried Bass, with one Vegetable 85
Dinner Steak, with one Vegetable 85
Baked Young Chicken, with Dressing 75
Breaded Veal Cutlet, Tomato Sauce 65
Omelet with Mushrooms 65
Imported Frankfurters, Potato Salad 60
Chicken Salad (Mayonnaise) with Saltines 50
Chicken Sandwich (Toasted) 50
Oven Baked Beans with Brown Bread 35
Fruit Jello, Whipped Cream 25

You are welcome to take this Menu Card. The Steward will provide an envelope.

Service a la Carte

☆

RELISHES

Spring Onions 15   Garden Radishes 15
Green Olives 15   Tomato Juice 15   Mixed Pickles 15   Celery 25

SOUP
             Spring Vegetable 25; Cup 15
        Consomme, Cup, Hot or Jellied 15

FISH
Broiled or Fried 75   French Sardines 50

EGGS
Boiled, Fried, Scrambled or Shirred (2) 30   Plain Omelet 35
   Ham or Jelly Omelet 50   Spanish Omelet 50

FROM THE GRILL
Single Sirloin Steak $1.25   Lamb Chop (1) 35, (2) 60
Bacon and Eggs 50   Ham and Eggs 50   Virginia Ham, Broiled 75
   Ham 30   Virginia Ham, with Eggs 90   Bacon 30

VEGETABLES
Potatoes Hashed Brown 15 Home Fried 15 French Fried 15 Lyonnaise 25
   au Gratin 25   Stewed Tomatoes 15   Stewed Sugar Corn 15
Peas 15   Lima Beans 15   Spinach 15   String Beans 15

SALADS
   Lettuce with French, Thousand Island or Mayonnaise Dressing 35
Potato Salad 25   Lettuce and Tomato 35   Sliced Tomatoes 25
   Asparagus, Vinaigrette or French Dressing 35
        Roquefort Cheese Dressing, extra 25

CHEESE
      Martha Washington with Wafers 20
Roquefort with Wafers 35   Philadelphia Cream with Wafers 25

BREAD, ETC.
Bread or Rolls 10   Corn Muffins 10   Dry or Buttered Toast 15
      Milk Toast 25   Cream Toast 30
      Boston Brown Bread 10   Saltine Crackers 10

DESSERTS
Apple Pie 15   Grapefruit 15   Ice Cream with Cake 25
Fruit Jello, Whipped Cream 25   Sliced Hawaiian Pineapple 25

BEVERAGES
Coffee, Single Pot 15   Tea, Small Pot (for one) 20   Cocoa, Pot 20
   Milk, Half Pint Bottle 10   Instant Postum, Pot 20
Buttermilk, Half Pint Bottle 10   Chocolate Malted Milk (large glass) 25
                    Kaffee Hag 20

INDIVIDUAL PRESERVES
Marmalade 25   Strained Honey 25   Prunes 25; with Cream 30
Strawberry Jam 25   Texas Figs 30; with Cream 35   Raspberry Jam 25
               Bar le Duc Jelly 25

Ask the Steward to show you The George Washington double-deck bridge set
            Specially priced at 50 cents.
Alvon Spring Water from White Sulphur Springs is used exclusively on this car.
   H. S. CALCUTT, Superintendent, Dining Car Service, Cincinnati, Ohio.

                         C. W. REUSCH, Steward

---

springs of the Virginias being along the route between.'[118]

The train did not merely operate on a lucrative choice of route, it also featured highly luxurious and innovative stock. Hanger describes it thus:

'The Sportsman's great innovation in railroad passenger service was its "Imperial Salon" cars – cars with seating arrangement of 15 single swivel seats along one side with 15 paired swivel seats along the other, all at no extra fare. The train offered no standard "coach" seating.'

But in 1932, George Washington's 200th anniversary, the C&O launched an even more impressive and up-market train, the 'George Washington', inaugurated on commemoration day itself, 22 April. Connecting Newport News and Washington DC with Louisville and Cincinnati, it was the first completely air-conditioned express in America.[119] It too sported 'Imperial Salon' cars, together with sleepers, diners, and an observation car. Hanger describes it thus:

'The car interiors were decorated in Colonial motif and each was named for a person or place

This menu from the inaugural year of the 'George Washington' (1932) fully justifies E. S. Hanger's claim that the train served 'the finest food available'. Note the range of choices, including 'potatoes as desired' (any one of five different ways) on the set dinner menu, sliced Hawaiian pineapple and Texas figs with cream on the à la carte section, and Oven Baked Beans with Brown Bread (a Boston speciality recipe) under the chef's suggestions. *E. S. Hanger collection*

of significance in Washington's life. The dining cars featured the finest food available ... served on china modelled after dinnerware of the colonial era, and decorated with gold leaf striping and ... Stuart's famous portrait of Washington.'

Menus from the two trains justify Hanger's appraisal of the food aboard the 'George Washington'. Both menus follow the long-standing US tradition of a large à la carte section, together with one or more set meal offers, certainly not designed or priced for economy. The 1930 'Sportsman' dinner menu (not illustrated) offers a five-course table d'hôte meal, the 'Sportsman Dinner', with five choices of main course for $1.25, or a simpler two-course meal, the 'Sportsman Special', for 75c. The initial 'George

Washington' menu (illustrated here) is even better: it too features a $1.25 dinner and a simpler 75c alternative, named like the railroad cars after places connected with George Washington – 'Mount Vernon' (his family home) and 'Tavern' (Michie's Tavern, 'gathering place of the patriots as the Revolutionary storm began to blow'). But the 'Mount Vernon' dinner offers six courses as against the five of the 'Sportsman' – cheese has become a separate course additional to dessert.

These two trains' catering made little concession to the drive for economy, though from about 1935 a 'club diner' was added to the formal dining car service. But the set meals were still at $1.25 and 75c, now with a cold buffet option, also at $1. And the à la carte menu offered a brand new luxury, the individual salad bowl. The strategy was successful – both trains lasted to the very end of individual US company passenger railroading.

If the Northern Pacific sought to 'hold the line', and the Chesapeake & Ohio to create new trains, the Santa Fé responded by throwing itself with ever-increasing vigour into competition with the airlines and its neighbours' high-speed diesel streamliners. The Santa Fé's response was to operate full-length, fast, luxurious extra-fare Supertrains, and to link them with the glamour of Hollywood.

The first of these Supertrains was the Santa Fé 'Chief', inaugurated in 1926 with the stars of MGM's *War Paint* as VIP passengers. The seven-car train carried a $10 supplement on top of the First Class Pullman fare. Initially the Chicago-Los Angeles run took 63 hours, cut to 54 hours by 1934[120]: the stock was upgraded several times. This is how Winchester and Allen described the dining arrangements of the 'Chief':

'The first air-cooled diner … in the West was installed on the "Chief" – a desirable innovation for summer-time travellers. Fine table linen, gleaming silver, harmonious decoration and immaculate daintiness everywhere serve to whet the appetite for the feast prepared under the skilled auspices of Fred Harvey… Midway in the train and next to the diner is the special ten-section lounge car, with its luxurious settees and chairs and its tables with reading lamps. It is a recreation rendezvous, and … it forms a pleasant meeting-place for friendships so often formed on long-distance trains of this nature.'[121]

By the time this was written, however, the 'Chief'

was already being superseded as the Santa Fé's premier train. In 1934 the UP and the Burlington introduced their high-speed self-propelled diesel flyers. The Santa Fé's President was convinced that a full-size luxury train could match the UP's 'City' series for speed, given lightweight stainless steel stock, upgraded track and a power source that did not have to make intermediate stops. The result was the 'Super Chief', whose inaugural run took place on 12 May 1936, taking just over 39 hours from Chicago to Los Angeles. The original 'Chief' remained the Santa Fé's fastest daily train, while the 'Super Chief' ran once a week in each direction (increased to twice weekly in 1938). The nine-car sets, air-conditioned and fitted with large picture windows, catered for 104 passengers each

'in incredibly beautiful surroundings, with southwestern colours, and an array of wood veneers … the cars generally received ivory ceilings and grey-green frieze upholstery. The sleepers … contained panelling of avodire … satinwood … rosewood, sycamore, holly, ebony, cypress and oak. The lounge … with its barbershop … contained a bar of zingana wood, a Navajo rug, and was painted in beige, blue, brown and orange. The observation sleeper "Navajo" carried out the Indian motif with turquoise ceiling, goatskin lampshades, sand paintings encased in glass, and upholstery in Navajo designs.'

The arrangements for on-train dining were equally resplendent. The dining car

'received a color scheme of warm brown, orange and brick red. Mary Elizabeth Coulter, a 35-year veteran of the Harvey system, designed the china and silver, basing her concepts on the fish characters of the Mimbreno Indians of southern New Mexico. Steward Peter Tausch produced a "yard long" menu, which included beluga caviar, larded tenderloin ($0.95), mountain trout, raisin pie and Cheshire cheese. A sirloin for two cost $2.75. The diner contained 78 seats.'[122]

With this effort, US luxury on-train dining may well indeed have reached its peak. The success of the 'Super Chief' led to 12 new streamlined trains being released throughout the Santa Fé system in late 1938. But in the following year America was already re-arming, and in 1941 the Second World War became a reality for the US railways too.

6
AUSTERITY, BUREAUCRACY AND PASSENGER ATTRITION
The idea in decline, 1939-77

From September 1939 the railways became convulsed in a second World War, with effects on passenger traffic much more severe than those of its predecessor. And though everywhere the ultimate effects were that, as Martha Thorne puts it,

'With the end of the Second World War, train service began to suffer a steady decline... The automobile was most definitely the main competitor in the USA and Germany as well as to some degree in other European countries... For long distances, air travel was providing stiff competition',[1]

the roads that Britain, Europe and the USA took to this impasse were different.

The detailed effects of the war differed between the three regions. US railroads suffered direct impact on matériel and troop movements rather than on passenger services, but these troop movements led to very heavy dining car usage, which, combined with a degree of rationing, resulted in a reduction in menu quality and service standards. At the other extreme, services in mainland Europe fell prey both to the Nazi war machine and to being fought over by the advancing Allies, though the post-war Marshall Plan helped European railways to recover after the war relatively easily The passenger services of Britain, though, had to endure both the war and the upheavals of 'austerity' and nationalisation following it without Marshall Plan help.

'Is your dining car really necessary?'

UK railways came under the control of the National Railway Executive immediately Britain declared war, and all restaurant cars were withdrawn from 11 September 1939, to allow crews to be drafted into the Armed Forces, additional coaches to be run for the same train weight, and some cars to be refitted as ambulance coaches. Subsequently, however, some diners were re-introduced, reaching 426 runs per day in late 1941, but dwindling to 65 by May 1942[2]; the LNER ran 90 of its buffet cars on long-distance runs, which had previously featured full dining services.[3]

The Railway Executive was caught in something of a cleft stick over these restaurant car services. It wanted to keep people off the railway to free up trains and train paths for essential war movements, but it also needed to keep up civilian morale. As Whitehouse and St John Thomas put it:

'...posters began to appear to enquire "Is Your Journey Really Necessary?", but the discomfort of weekend travel was probably the greater deterrent. Troops went on weekend leave, parents visited their evacuated offspring, and there was busy ordinary weekend traffic ... despite the questioning posters.'[4]

The Executive maintained a balancing act for as long as it could. It issued the 'questioning posters' but also restored cheap weekend tickets and permitted on-train refreshment services as long as possible. But juggling troops and civilian passengers eventually got too much, and from April 1944 all restaurant services were withdrawn.

The food on offer was limited. The restaurant car meat ration was two-thirds of a penn'orth per portion, based on the number of portions served the month before[5], but the individual ration was 1 shilling's worth per week (plus 2d worth of corned beef), which averaged out at 1d per meal[6] – half as much again as the catering allowance. Fish was not rationed, though it wasn't always as fresh as it might have been[7]; sausages, kidneys and liver were off-ration too, but they were often in short supply[8]. A. E. Rogers's monograph summarises the general level of provision like this:

'A standard charge of 2s 6d for Breakfast, Luncheon or Dinner was made … and no more than three courses could be served. There was … a monotonous diet of soup, with a main course too often a choice of meat pie, sausages or fish (generally cod) followed by a simple sweet (which wasn't very sweet) and a cup of tea or coffee was 4d. To these prices was added 3d for gratuity.'[9]

When dining cars were restored in October 1945, rationing actually got worse. Meat remained on ration until 1954, and a world wheat shortage led to bread becoming rationed too – diners could have potatoes or bread, but not both. Three courses maximum were permitted, and few took less – you took what you could get, especially if it gave you a meal 'outside' your personal ration card allowance! Staff on the cars made heroic attempts to

supplement the meagre ration allowances. Fish, sausages, offal and game were pressed into service to provide additional menu offers. The fish was now often either whalemeat or snoek, while the 'game' included pigeon, rabbit and Lord knew what else; the major railway hotels supported the hard-pressed dining cars by baking large game pies of indeterminate contents, which were re-heated on board on demand. 'Rabbit, sir?', one of Rowland Emett's funniest railway cartoons, vividly conveys the train staff's harried determination to please the passenger on a nearly nil budget.

This understanding, sardonic, and very British humour seems to have been the commonest way people coped with the situation; the railways themselves even harnessed it in a celebrated poster by Fougasse. The harassed chef in '…and twenty more for dinner just coming in…', intended to urge passengers to be patient over catering limits, shows this 'Blitz'-style humour at its best.

It is difficult now to realise just how bad British cuisine became during those years of wartime and post-war austerity. Palmer puts down to the war the habit of 'ordering three courses, never more and never less, from a bill of fare'; he is not entirely correct, but there is no doubt that the regulations helped. More insidious, though, were two other influences he noticed – the tendency towards 'snacking', and the tendency to confuse mere filling-up with culinary satisfaction:

'… since the restaurants, too, were rationed, clients soon learned that an early arrival, before the best dishes were exhausted, had

'Rabbit, sir?': this famous Emett cartoon – perhaps of all his work the most appropriate to the 1947 rationing situation – had no caption other than its title. The picture says it all! *Courtesy Rowland Emett,* The Early Morning Milk Train, *and John Murray (Publishers) Ltd*

" ..... and twenty more for dinner just coming in ...."

British Railways have little or no surplus margin of food for unexpected guests. They are rationed just as you are! For the same reason, Refreshment Baskets have had to be abolished.

Fougasse's famous drawing of the 'harassed chef' was intended, like his wartime posters, to exhort the reader to be careful and patient – but it was also superbly drawn, and very funny! *Courtesy National Railway Museum/Science and Society*

advantages… By the end of the war the majority of Londoners were eating as much as they could get at noon, having a light meal early in the evening, and indulging more and more their old fondness for odd morsels at odd times.'[10]

It took an awfully long time for both cuisine and public taste to recover from this austerity. Even in the early 1960s a dinner menu from the post-war 'Queen of Scots Pullman'[11] provided an interesting 'give-away' on just how bad things had become. The menu overall is quite reasonable, but the soup is listed as 'Real Tomato Soup with Golden Croutons'. That an organisation with the quality standards of Pullman should have had to tell the diner that it was serving *Real* Tomato Soup, rather than 'Colouriser Soup' (a basic bland white stock, flavoured and coloured as required – in this case with tomato ketchup[12]) suggests just how far standards had fallen.

Matters were not helped by the nationalisation of the railways in 1947, which affected dining services adversely, in several ways. One was, quite simply, that it politicised them: nationalisation was at the core of the Labour Party's ideological manifesto, and thus inevitably relations between the newly nationalised railways and the travelling public became contentious. As Wooler remarked:

'Under Nationalisation, the railway ticket barrier and buffet counter began to look suspiciously like extensions of that popular enemy, the Whitehall desk.'[13]

Nationalisation also abolished the competitive stimulus behind previous drives to upgrade on-train services; the railways were now 'a public service' with 'notions of quasi-monopoly … and the maximisation of traffic volume irrespective of cost'[14]. It replaced competition with

'overblown bureaucracy, with its numerous committees and its mass of paperwork, much of which was produced by administrators … insensitive to the changing needs of customers.'[15]

And finally, the restructuring under nationalisation not only removed on-train catering from the former operating companies but also centralised it in a separate Hotels Executive, which

'devoted most of its resources to where the profits could most quickly be found… The restaurant cars, needed by the railways as a passenger service but financially embarrassing to the Executive controlling them, now became a major bone of contention.'[16]

On the ground, dinner prices rose by 1951 from the immediate post-war 4 shillings (at which they were making a loss) to 6 shillings[17], and what you got was very much a matter of chance, as early Hotels Executive menu cards demonstrated. The menus were carefully laid out to give as much impression of variety as possible, but the truth emerged in the bottom line: 'The choice in each instance will be served as available'.

'There is a tavern on the train'

On-train dining in Britain thus faced a series of interconnected problems. First came the problem of

'…Until they release the new dining cars, we'll just have to do our best': this equally famous Emett cartoon again gently invokes the spirit of British improvisation in adversity, this time with a sideways nod at the NP's renowned 'Great Big Baked Potato'. The moustached gentlemen and their Memsahibs sitting on their luggage in the snow, wearing party hats like Governor-Generals' plumes and waiting for their potatoes baked in Nellie's firebox on the fireman's shovel, radiate the same mixture of the ludicrous and the entirely admirable that has made *Dad's Army* one of TV's most successful series. *Courtesy Rowland Emett, The Early Morning Milk Train, and John Murray (Publishers) Ltd*

coping with shortages and engineering a return to normal service. Second came the problem of dealing with a major shift in public taste caused in part by those very shortages. Third came the problem that, by 1949, conventional on-train meals were publicly admitted to be making a steady loss, under a Hotels Executive formally charged with returning a profit.[18] And finally, all this needed to be dealt with within a badly flawed management and operational framework.

The solutions were interconnected also. For example, the shortages were not simply of food: there was also a shortage of equipment, as Rowland Emett again noted with gentle glee. Many of the refreshment vehicles were at the ends of their lives. But if public demand really *had* changed during the wartime hiatus, of what sort should the replacements be? And profitability entered into these decisions

too: buffet and cafeteria cars required fewer staff than diners.

The Hotels Executive, however, had made one really excellent choice of senior manager – the LNER's E. K. Portman-Dixon ('P-D' for short), who became Superintendent of Refreshment Rooms (including on-train catering) from 1948. P-D was an active and innovative manager with a real flair for attempting solutions to difficult problems; he had handled the LNER's wartime buffet operation to general acclaim, and was to bring similar ingenuity to BR on-train dining services.

Initially, little could be done about rationing, but while food was going to be gloomy for some time, the Southern and the LMS attempted to bring some jollity into their catering through those other elements of on-train dining, drinks and snacks. The Southern was first off the mark, with an entirely new design – the now notorious Tavern Cars designed by Oliver Bulleid in 1946-47 and put in service under the new BR régime from May 1949. These extraordinary vehicles have often been presented as an error of taste by Bulleid, unpopular with the travelling public and poorly patronised – 'a gimmick that the public did not like'[19]. The public certainly disliked the lack of windows, but much of the rest of the commonly accepted version is far from accurate. The reality is both different and more complicated.

Bulleid was attempting both to cater for post-war customer demand for a wider range of refreshment offers, and to solve the problem that food lost money, but drink – particularly beer – made a profit. He had already begun to address these problems with the Bognor buffet cars' long bar counter layout and the introduction of draught beer instead of bottled ale. The logical next steps would be to extend the idea to trains offering full meals as well as other services, and to run an actual pub as part of the catering consist. It was this that the Tavern Car sets were designed to do. Apart from the windowless diners (which he in fact fitted with full-size windows the next year) as used on the 'Atlantic Coast Express' service for which they were designed, the Tavern sets did extremely well. Far from being unpopular, they were well patronised; Austin records that they had 'the best takings of any catering vehicles on the railways'[17]. And it was this that led to the furore that followed.

The Hotels Executive allocated six sets to the Eastern Region, where they ran foul of the Methodist Church and the National United Temperance League, which had been campaigning to ban alcohol on restaurant cars. Cars that not only served alcohol without a meal but bore pub names and even looked like pubs thus attracted their special venom. Questions were asked in Parliament, and though Ministers defended the design, no more were built. The Taverns themselves, however, continued to operate until 1959, when they were rebuilt as standard BR Mark I buffet cars.[17,20]

In the meantime, a number of further designs were created from old LMS coaches. BR used these rebuilds to trial two major types of food service car under consideration for P-D's Mark I Restaurant Car programme – the RKB kitchen/buffet car and the RB buffet car. Seven trial RKBs were converted from pre-war kitchen-diners by removing most of the dining seats and replacing them with a buffet counter opening out of the forward pantry.[21]

The trial RBs came in two main types, 'party cars' and 'Cafeteria cars'. Both had a kitchen occupying the centre third of the car; the other sections contained either a central counter with bar stools around it or an 18-seat dining saloon. Party cars had bar counters at each side and serving counters at each end of the kitchen unit. Cafeteria cars had a bar stool set on one side and a dining saloon on the other, and were arranged for patrons to help themselves.

British Railways' own initial 1951 designs replicated the stock that was being phased out – five two-car sets of kitchen-restaurant First plus open Third for the Western Region, and ten three-car sets of full kitchen car plus open First and Third either side for all the regions. This initial build was only a holding operation, however: the main prototypes came out in 1956, and the production series during 1957-63, by which time it had become clear that, as Parkin puts it,

'social patterns in Britain had changed, due in large measure to the traumas of WWII. This was felt … as a demand for cheaper, less substantial, food and more "unaccompanied" drinks, both alcoholic and temperate.'

This perception affected P-D's post-1956 fleet ordering policy. Of 500 catering vehicles built, only a few were conventional kitchen-restaurant cars, and they were mainly unclassed; they had propane gas cookers, and seated 29-33 in the dining saloon.[22] A much larger group had their pantry opened out into a buffet bar counter, with a circulating space, wall shelving and seating areas for either 12 or 23. Their kitchens had normal stove equipment, so they could also serve full meals into an adjoining open car.[23]

Thus by the end of 1962, almost all catering vehicles offered buffet-bar service, whether the train also featured a full dining service or not.

P-D's quest for an economic response to the changes in customer demand continued. The design built in the largest numbers was the Miniature Buffet, created by taking two seating bays out of a standard Mark I open Second coach, and fitting a serving bar on one side, and a passenger circulating space with drink shelves on the other. The rest of the coach had 44-48 standard 2+2 seats for normal revenue-earning passengers. The bar itself was a little miracle of design: Parkin describes it as containing

'an incredible amount of equipment in its 50 square foot floor area. A refrigerator, dresser and shelves were tucked behind the sliding entrance door. A sink, propane gas-fired boiler, egg boiler and pie warmer occupied a stainless-steel-lined recess at the other end. The rear wall, with concealed lighting, held and displayed bottled liquid refreshment while the serving surface supported a display cabinet for comestibles.'[24]

These cars were frequently used as the sole catering vehicle on lightly loaded cross-country services.[25] They were eventually followed by an even smaller design, the Micro-Buffet, created by removing a single seating bay at the forward end of an open Brake Second, into which a drinks and sandwich trolley could be slotted, which was also then pushed through the body of the train for at-seat sales.[26]

P-D's last design to go into series production harked back to Bulleid's Tavern Cars by seeking to 'offer the amenities of a good pub', as Parkin again puts it. This was the now famous 'Griddle Car' design, with a central kitchen with a propane gas 'griddle', a hot plate surrounded by glass splash screens, on full view to the passengers at one end of the counter. On the 'griddle' side of this kitchen was a buffet counter, and beyond it a buffet saloon with conventional table seating. On the other side was a curved bar counter, and a saloon with soft seats arranged in two inward-facing gentle curves, with drinks tables.

The Griddle Cars were used primarily on runs expected to pick up casual dining trade. They required two staff against one for the Miniature Buffets[27], but as the menu reproduced here shows, they offered a wider and more interesting range of casual meals than the RMBs could. The Western ran them on the 7.15am Paddington-Bristol, and the 1.30pm return; the LMR ran them on the 10.28am

The Griddle

is on your train

APPETISERS	"ANGUS" 1/9	SUNDRIES
Tomato Juice ... 1/3	Hot, fresh, griddle - cooked Aberdeen - Angus beef in toasted Bread Roll, with savoury butter	Cereals, with hot milk 1/–
Orange Juice ... 1/3		Biscuits, per packet 6d.
Grapefruit (half) 1/3		Wrapped Cake 8d.
(in season)		Fruit and Ice Cream 1/6
		Roll and Butter 5d.
	"ABERDEEN" 3/–	EGG
SOUP 1/3	An " Angus," with fried egg	Boiled egg, with brown or white bread and butter 1/9
Oxtail Tomato		
(with roll, or Ryvita)		Poached egg on Toast 1/9
	"TARTAN PLATE" 6/6	
FILLED ROLLS	Entrecôte steak, with a fried egg, grilled tomato, roll and butter	BACON & EGGS
All rolls generously applied with pure butter and double filling		Bacon (two rashers), egg, roll and butter 4/–
Ham ... 1/6		
Egg ... 1/6	COLD HAM 6/6	
Cheese ... 1/3	Cold Ham and Salad roll and butter	CHEESE BOARD
		A selection of cheeses with biscuits, butter and salad *(in season)* or mixed pickle 2/–
COFFEE per cup, 10d.	TEA per pot, per person, 1/3	

This Griddle Car menu is from the Scottish Region service, as witness the range of Aberdeen Angus specialities offered in the middle column. This menu also demonstrates Portman-Dixon's commercial flair: headed 'The Griddle is on your train', it formed a flyer distributed on open-stock tables throughout the train, not just restricted to the buffet itself. Note also the level to which prices had risen by this point (1962): the 'Tartan Plate' cost more than an entire three-course meal in 1950. *Courtesy British Railways Board (Residuary)*

Derby-Bristol and 5.00pm return. The Scottish Region, which found them particularly suitable, ran them on the Inverness-Edinburgh route – up on the 8.20am cooking breakfast and back on the 4.03pm serving high tea.

Competition, inflation, attrition – and the death of Pullmans

So far it might seem as if Portman-Dixon had made a pretty good job of dealing with the changes in UK consumer demand, and that the erosion of dining car services towards the end of the period by inflation and the desertion by passengers for competing road and air travel was simply an unfair blow of fate. At a deeper level, though, it involved a complex and

long-standing competition between conflicting ideas, at three levels – between ideologies, between the train and the refreshment room, and between ideas about quality. Nowhere is this deeper competition seen better than in the demise of the Pullman services.

The post-war period presented the competing ideas about the social paradigms behind 'dining at speed' in a peculiarly acute form. The same spirit that had led to nationalisation raised the question of what the railways were 'for', and in particular, how far 'competition' was permissible within a publicly owned railway enterprise. Initially, of course, the questions scarcely arose: as Rogers put it, 'there was no question ... of looking for business on the cars.'[9] But later, when there *was* a need to 'look for business', the railways were much hampered by not having any clear answers to these questions.

Competition also arose from the lumping together of responsibility for on-train dining and station refreshment rooms. P-D and his successors seem consistently to have put the latter first, even as late as the Travellers-Fare policy releases of 1984-85.[28] Commercially, they were probably right – the refreshment room business had a larger customer base and greater profit potential than on-train catering – but both were necessary railway services. A similar conflict affected the actual operation of the cars. Here again, P-D seems to have approached the problem of what sort of services to provide more from the 'refreshment room' view of satisfying the maximum volume of casual demand than from creating a high-quality on-train experience. Again he was probably commercially correct: re-educating public taste would have been a chancy experiment. But it can be argued that the railways missed an opportunity to influence a captive audience to their advantage.

There were now also competing definitions of quality service in on-train catering. From the inception of dining cars, notions of on-train dining quality had depended on key individuals' conceptions of ways the experience 'could be so much better'. These personal visions had developed in a consistent direction for more than 70 years. Now, however, that legacy had been broken by the hiatus of wartime restrictions and austerity. In the resulting vacuum another definition of quality experience had arisen, the extent to which it satisfied immediate customer demands.

All these factors came together in the demise of the Pullman Company. Pullman's private status sat awkwardly with a nationalised railway service;

accordingly, the BTC in 1954 bought out all the ordinary shares in Pullman, though it continued to operate as a separate company. This still, however, remained a bureaucratic anomaly, and the NUR objected strongly to any profits from railway operation ending up in private hands.[29] In 1962, therefore, the BTC bought out all the preference shares also, and from March 1963 Pullman became a sub-division of British Transport Hotels reporting to P-D, and in March 1967 it ceased to exist as a separate business.

Pullman train operations reflected these changes, falling roughly into three periods. Post-war re-establishment of 'traditional' Pullmans, together with a number of new trains, was followed by a period post-1954 when the stock got older, the passengers and services gradually became fewer, and the catering became more expensive. Finally, in the 1960s there was an attempt to re-start a very different type of Pullman service.

The first restored Pullman services were the 'Golden Arrow' on 15 April 1946 and the 'Bournemouth Belle' and 'Brighton Belle' in October. The 'Devon Belle' was added for summer 1947, when the 'Night Ferry' also resumed, and the 'Thanet Belle' (later 'Kentish Belle') came out in May 1948. I described in the Introduction the feelings of pleasure and excitement that the coming of the 'Devon Belle' aroused in passengers, and Fryer confirms this for the 'Bournemouth Belle' too:

'Its re-appearance was welcomed … after wartime neglect much of the SR's ordinary coaching stock was in a poor state, and to travel in a train that was not only luxurious but clean, with bookable seats and refreshments to hand, was an experience which made the modest supplement seem negligible.'[30]

For Fryer, this train offered 'a passenger experience … more rewarding than on any other … journeys in southern England'; he described that experience in terms of the scenery – but also, significantly, in that

'Meanwhile, one could sip one's morning coffee appreciatively during the outward journey … and regale oneself with dinner on the return'[31]

– proof that the idea of the 'dining at speed' experience was at this point still alive and well. Indeed, BR Southern Region management attempted during the late 1950s and early 1960s to cash in on this very effect through a series of posters

In the poster featured here, a (still somewhat Art Deco) young couple enthuse in silhouette over glasses of wine. No meal is portrayed as such – possibly because despite the claim in the text you couldn't actually dine on the 'Brighton Belle', in the strictest sense of that term, though you could of course on the 'Bournemouth Belle'.
Courtesy National Railway Museum/Science and Society

featuring the slogan 'You can wine and dine on these all-Pullman trains / every day of the year'.

The slogan, however, was not strictly accurate. You could 'dine' in the proper sense on the 'Bournemouth Belle', but not on the Brighton and Thanet/Kentish 'Belles' because journey times were too short – even on the 11.00pm late-night down journey of the 'Brighton Belle', the advertising said only 'Supper served from 10pm'.[32]

Details on the immediate post-war menus are not easy to come by. The 'Devon Belle' (see Introduction) experimented with Lyons' 'Frood', but though of high quality it was expensive and neither attendants nor passengers liked it.[33] On the 'Brighton Belle' and other South East services the Pullman Company by 1957 had introduced a fast-food snack service, shown below as listed in Morel[34]:

CLUB SNACK SERVICE

Fruit Juices: Grapefruit, Tomato Cocktail, Fruit Cup	1/-
Hot Green Pea Soup with Croutons	1/-
Omelette and Grilled Bacon	3/9
Grilled Frankfurter and Spaghetti Milanaise	3/-
Cold Collation with Seasonal Salads	5/6
Hamburger, Tomato, Bacon, Chipolata, Fried Egg and Sauté Potatoes	5/6
New England Gateau	1/-
Cheese Tray	1/6
Oven Crisp Roll and Curled Butter	6d
Coffee	Cup 7d, Pot 1/2

Like other BR innovations of this period, this menu shows a transatlantic influence, with the inclusion of frankfurters and hamburgers in the grill. But the Spaghetti Milanaise that accompanied the Frankfurters points to a rather different change in public taste; by 1957 we were well into coffee-bar culture, of which Espresso, Spaghetti Milanaise (properly 'Milanese') and Bolognese were staple ingredients. Morel claims that this menu was popular with passengers, and I don't doubt he is right – even though a single dish cost more than an entire meal on the early 1950s menus.

The East Coast Pullman services took slightly longer to restore. The 'Yorkshire Pullman' returned in 1947, followed by the 'Queen of Scots' in 1948 and the 'Harrogate Sunday Pullman' in 1951.[35] There were also two further additions. The first of these, the 'Tees-Tyne Pullman', introduced in 1948, replaced the old 'Silver Jubilee' between Newcastle and London. Running on a similar schedule to the 'Jubilee' (but taking an hour longer), it proved very popular – Fryer describes it as 'the prestige train on the East Coast main line'[36] – and helped inspire British Railways' fightback against road and air competition. And from 1958 to 1971, the 'Master Cutler' over the old Great Central route was replaced by a Pullman service into King's Cross.[37]

Not much information seems available about the actual catering on the post-war East Coast Pullmans either. All the trains were timed to serve at least one main meal on each journey. The 'Queen of Scots' served both lunch and dinner in both directions, plus afternoon tea leaving Darlington; the offer was similar to the 'Golden Arrow' afternoon tea menu discussed below. Morel also singles out the 'Master Cutler' (which ran two up and two down trips each weekday, departing Sheffield at 7.30am and only finally returning at 10.05pm) for special mention as having timings that

'ran through all the meals of the day – breakfast, luncheon, afternoon tea and dinner... A single Pullman crew worked all trips, but rosters were so arranged that each man only worked four days out of the five.'[38]

BR provided new stock for these services (and for the 'Golden Arrow' for Festival of Britain year). Built by Metro-Cammell, they were essentially luxury versions of the standard BR Mark I restaurant stock, with very similar cooking facilities in the kitchens, including propane gas. The stock for the 'Tees-Tyne Pullman' also included the famous 'Hadrian Bar' – though this was taken off in 1969, and re-appeared as the 'Nightcap Bar' on the Euston-Glasgow sleeper service.[39]

The subsequent fate of the traditional post-war Pullmans was a sad mixture of passenger attrition and lack of imagination. The first to succumb was the 'Devon Belle', which was peculiarly susceptible to road competition. In 1950 it was still largely fully booked, but by 1954 car ownership had begun its inexorable rise and, despite an attempt to increase revenue by using the set for luxury excursions to cathedral cities, it did not re-appear in 1955. The Pullman Company made use of the coaches, without the observation cars but with a bar, from June 1955 on a new service from Paddington to Cardiff and Swansea, the 'South Wales Pullman', attempting to repeat the business success of the 'Tees-Tyne Pullman' and its companion 'Yorkshire Pullman' with London businessmen wishing to visit the Principality. The service proved successful, and lasted till the opening 'fightback' services replaced it during 1960-61.[40]

The next to go was the 'Queen of Scots', a victim of the growth of the much faster air competition between London and Edinburgh or Glasgow. By 1963 it was no longer running profitably north of Harrogate, and in June 1964 it was cut back to the Leeds-Harrogate area and renamed the 'White Rose'. It was finally taken off in 1967[41], as was the 'Bournemouth Belle'; the 'Thanet Belle' (renamed 'Kentish Belle' in 1951) had already gone, in 1958. These 'Belle' withdrawals, however, were not due to lack of patronage – the 'Bournemouth Belle' continued popular to the end, and the 'Thanet/Kentish Belle' seems also to have paid its way – but to a curiously shortsighted stock replacement policy by BR, which in turn impacted on the 'Brighton Belle', which was likewise withdrawn in 1972.

When the Second World War had broken out the

Southern Railway had been part way through a third-rail electrification programme, using multiple-unit self-propelled stock. At the onset of war, two major areas had remained to complete the scheme, the Kent Coast lines and Waterloo-Southampton-Bournemouth. These were completed after the war, to Margate and Dover in 1959 and the remaining Kent Coast in 1961, and the Bournemouth route in 1967.[42] When 'the juice' reached Margate and Ramsgate it was thus clear that EMUs would take over all the workings from 1959, and the same would happen on the Bournemouth line within eight years. This could have created an opportunity for a new standard class of Pullman EMUs capable of running on any of the three 'Belles', but the mind-set at the top of British Rail equated multiple-unit electrification with commuter services. The Kent Coast electrification was seen as catering for outer-suburban commuter traffic, with 'a regular interval service … vestibuled and [with] refreshment facilities, but no Pullman cars'[26] and the 'Kentish Belle' and later 'Bournemouth Belle' were taken off. This meant that when the 'Brighton Belle' stock reached the end of its working life there was no Pullman EMU to take over its duties. BR would either have to replace the units with a small, non-standard class, or scrap the train altogether. Pleading 'the interest of maximum utilisation of stock' it did the latter, and the 'Belle', which had 'become something of a national institution', and at 2,600 revenue-earning miles a week was both popular and profitable, finally ceased to run at the end of April 1972.[43]

Because the 'Brighton Belle' lasted so long, its menus show how far price inflation and BR menu standardisation had changed the food offer. Morel quotes an 'all-day bill of fare' for 1966[44]; most of it is now taken up with thoroughly British dishes – fish and chips, steak and chips or sausage and mash, or 'teashop' items-on-toast, and prices have escalated since 1957 by between 50 and 100 per cent. One of the most direct comparisons – the Cold Collation and Salad – which was 5s 6d in 1957, is now 8s 6d, and the grill has gone up from 5s 6d to 12s 6d – though it does now include sirloin steak.

The sole remaining old-style Pullman services were now the 'Golden Arrow' and the 'Night Ferry'. Of these, the 'Golden Arrow' only lasted a further five months; the British and French operators both tried a series of increasingly desperate 'trimming' measures, including replacing the Second Class Pullmans by ordinary coaches with a buffet car, to keep it alive, but as Fryer says,

'The end was now in sight… Paris was now only two hours from London by air and more and more people chose to go that way. The train's final journey was made in September 1972.'[45]

The 'Golden Arrow' timings had always presented problems over what to serve, but the Pullman organisation grappled well with this intractable problem – as indeed did the French on their side, with a respectable if slightly early lunch leaving Paris.[46] Morel lists a 1963 menu containing, in addition to the usual coffee, sandwiches and other sundries, the following highlighted sections:[47]

AFTERNOON TEA 4/-
Toasted Tea Cake, Hot Buttered Toast
Fruit Loaf, White and Hovis Bread and Butter
Teatime Biscuits, Individual Preserves, Quality Cake
Pot of Tea (Indian of China)

A LA CARTE DISHES Featured on the Inward Service

Smoked Salmon with Lemon Wedges	9/6
Omelette to Choice	7/6
Pan Fried Egg and Grilled Bacon (single)	3/3
(double)	6/6
Grilled Dover Sole with French Fried Potatoes	10/6

The 'Inward Service' à la carte menu was for its time decidedly up-market. It also sheds an interesting light on the rate of inflation during this period; it is three years earlier than the 'Belle' menu and the eggs and bacon retails at 6s 6d as against 8 shillings on the 'Belle' – 25% inflation across three years. The Afternoon Tea offer was likewise opulent, and is very similar to the offer I remember from the 'Queen of Scots' ten years earlier.

This now left just the 'Night Ferry', and here too reductions in patronage were rapidly felt. Indeed, after 1976, when it sometimes mustered just one sleeper each for Paris and Brussels, it seems to have been regarded as a nuisance on both sides of the Channel. The train left both London and Paris at 20.30 and arrived at 09.10 (London) or 09.30 (Paris) next morning. Outward, a two-car restaurant and buffet-bar set operated by Pullman staff was attached to the sleeping cars, serving à la carte suppers. It stayed at Dover overnight and joined the morning inward service serving breakfasts on the way back to London. A similar rake of French vehicles did the same thing across the Channel.[48]

Initially Pullman and Wagons-Lits treated the train as one of their most prestigious services, with dining arrangements organised accordingly. As late as 1962 Morel recorded a supper menu a good deal more extensive than the 'inward service' menu of the 'Golden Arrow' – soup, eggs and bacon, ham salad (9s 6d, slightly more expensive than on the 'Brighton Belle') or a 2s 6d ham sandwich if preferred, grilled minute steak with potatoes and seasonal vegetables (also 9s 6d), fruit salad and cream, or a cheese tray.[49] And Behrend describes the breakfast scene on the French leg of the journey:

'Swaying to the motion of the train with accustomed skill, a waiter comes round brandishing enormous silverine pots of coffee and hot milk from which he pours simultaneously and with expert accuracy. But he just gives you time to stop him, if you prefer tea. For her English guests … the Company long ago devised what is always known as "le meat breakfast" … bacon and eggs, served still frying in the almost red-hot metal dish, brought in on a plate, and placed on top of the one already on the table.'[50]

Once patronage began to decline, however, it was a very different story. In September 1977 Travellers-Fare replaced the dining car by a micro-buffet offering sandwiches going out and a £1.30 Breakfast Tray coming back; anyone wanting full breakfast was asked to wait till Victoria.[51] In May 1978 SNCF replaced its breakfast car with a snack vendor trolley service, though the remaining British business travellers created such uproar at the loss of their 'meat breakfast' that the breakfast car was restored for the remaining two winters.[52] The train ceased to run in 1980.

Price inflation and passenger attrition were not restricted to Pullmans. The railways' market share declined from 27.6% in 1947 to 7.8% in 1973.[53] The annual number of dining car meals was reduced to 3½ million by 1973 and 2 million by 1980, and the resultant loss was *not* made up by the increase in buffet car sales[54] that resulted from trains getting quicker and eating habits becoming lighter. And the BR Mark I cars were now in turn reaching the end of their lives.

At the same time, on-train dining became more standardised and less of a 'special experience', so that people felt they were being asked to pay more for declining quality. In 1961 individual menus were still offered at least on some named trains, and there

was some attempt to return to pre-war catering standards with a fish course re-instated and separate cheese or savoury courses available at an extra charge. But by 1968 menus were back to the 'one size fits all' single standard menu. The dishes could all be served 'from stock' – bacon and egg, steak and chips, fish and chips, cold meat and salad. The range was small, and the prices were large: lunch and/or dinner were around 15 shillings, an increase of 20% over 1961. The dreaded 1950s words 'Tariff as available' re-appeared too. Only the famous Newcastle-London 'Steak and Kidney Pie Trains' redeemed the situation.

Post-decimalisation, menu prices continued their inexorable rise; quality and choice, however, did somewhat improve, though there was still an awful sameness about the lunch and dinner menus. But the price of lunch went up by more than 40% and dinner by almost 60%, and coffee service charge doubled. Afternoon Tea rose still more, by 75%, though it did now include *both* assorted sandwiches *and* toasted teacake, and High Tea cost around 45% more than previously, as did Breakfast.

The fightback begins

Though all UK Pullman trains except the 'Manchester Pullman' had ceased by 1975, it was one successful group of them that led to the revival of passenger services and dining by Inter-City to be described in the next chapter. The story began with the popularity of the 'Tees-Tyne Pullman' with business passengers, who could use it to attend meetings in London without having to be away overnight.[55] The 'Yorkshire Pullman', the 'South Wales Pullman' and the 'Master Cutler' were popular with business travellers too.[56] Similar patronage was also experienced on fast non-Pullman services, such as the London-Wolverhampton 'Inter City'.[57] Some businessmen, it seemed, actually *preferred* to travel by train because on the train they could both relax *and* work. This was not new: in 1947 Emett had noted the British manager's fondness for starting work before actually getting there. But it was new for it to be observed so consistently

To cater for this niche market, BR brought into service from 1961-62 a series of fast Pullman diesel sets, running from Manchester to St Pancras (the 'Midland Pullman') and from Wolverhampton and Birmingham to Paddington; a similar service ran from Bristol, and the new sets were also used on the 'South Wales Pullman'. The 'Midland Pullman' was all First Class, while the others conveyed both First

'I wish they'd have their Board Meetings when they GET to Town!': this classic Emett cartoon of c1947, of businessmen holding a board meeting in the parcels van on the 9.35 to the City, catches beautifully the first moments of the post-war tendency to work every hour God sends, including train journeys. Incidentally, the nameboard on the crowded station platform at which the '9.35' has pulled up is just visible and appears to read 'Haywards Heath' – on the route of the 'Brighton Belle' rather than on one of the lines on which the 'Blue Pullmans' were later to run! *Courtesy Rowland Emett, The Early Morning Milk Train, and John Murray (Publishers) Ltd*

and Standard. The Manchester service was replaced in 1967, when West Coast electrification was complete, with a locomotive-hauled 'Manchester Pullman', and the Birmingham service with a fast

A specimen à la carte menu

Scotch Smoked Salmon with Lemon Wedges 7/6

Chilled Fruit Juices: Pineapple 1/6; Tomato 1/6; Orange 1/6

Crème Argenteuil with Golden Croûtons 1/6

From the Grill

*English Lamb Cutlets 8/6   *Scotch Salmon 8/6

*Fillet Steak 12/6   *Barbecued Chicken à l'Américaine 8/6

*Price of main dishes includes:

Parsley, New and Olivette Potatoes, Sweet Corn, Baby Carrots

and Broccoli Mornay

Cold Buffet: Salmon Mayonnaise or

Half a Chicken with dressed Salads 8/6

Fresh Fruit Salad with Dairy Cream Ice or

Crème Chantilly 2/–

Continental and English Cheese Tray 2/–

Coffee 8d.

Bread Basket of White and Hovis Rolls

Ryvita and Curled Butter 6d.

non-Pullman train, both running into Euston. The Bristol and South Wales services continued until the advent of HSTs in 1972-73.[58]

Going after this market involved two major changes to the idea of 'dining at speed'. One was to restrict the range of patrons for whom the service was provided to a special group; the other was to change from providing a space in which to eat and relax to one in which to eat *and work*. These made themselves felt in almost every aspect of the offer. The advertising emphasised high speed and getting things done, rather than relaxing and 'train magic'. In First Class 2+1 seating replaced 1+1, to enable businessmen to hold meetings over their meals; the internal furnishings were

'comfortable and convenient rather than "artistic"; a contemporary business executive wished to study what was in his briefcase rather than regard marquetry or fancy brasswork.'[59]

And in keeping with an attitude that saw dining as an adjunct to working rather than as a pleasure in itself, the main menu became entirely à la carte.

The 1960 BR/Pullman joint commemorative booklet for the opening of the new WR 'Blue Pullman' services included this 'specimen menu', entirely à la carte, though with food of the quality of the best offers of the 'Golden Arrow' 'inward service' or the 'Night Ferry'. That this style of menu carried through into the regular runs is clear from an almost identical example quoted by Morel as in use on the 'Midland Pullman'. *Courtesy British Railways Board (Residuary) and Harpenden Railway Museum*

As the official 'specimen menu' alongside shows, however, the food was selected with some attention to attracting the clients through *haute cuisine*. Menus from the non-Pullman business trains likewise demonstrate attempts to attract the new market, featuring invitations to consume an aperitif, wine suggestions for particular dishes, offers of liqueurs, cigars and cigarettes, and willingness to accept Luncheon Vouchers.

Mainland Europe after the Second World War: 'facing both ways at once'

Mainland Europe's long-distance rail infrastructure had been even more damaged than Britain's by the Second World War, since much of it had been fought over (and Mitropa had again 'requisitioned' more than 100 CIWL sleeping and dining cars).[60] But the Wagons-Lits company's services seemed to have a curious resilience. Morel comments:

'Through wise commissariat, supplies were never short, special trains were put at the disposal of the Vichy government in unoccupied France, for the German rulers in occupied France, and then for the Allied commanders during the liberation of France. Trains ran whenever and wherever they could; when they did, the CIWL restaurant cars, in particular, were well patronised... Even in wartime it was business as usual to an extent.'[61]

But though CIWL ended the war fit and raring to go, a totally new force entered in competition from 1957: the 'TEE' network, international expresses operated by the *national* railways, aimed at winning business passengers away from the airlines and roads.[62] Thus the story of the 'period of decline' in mainland Europe faces in both directions, with decline going on in one area but fightback in another.

The demise of the 'trains de luxe'

The earliest train to be restored post-war was again the 'Orient Express', the preferred route being the Simplon-Orient through Venice, Trieste and Belgrade. Several other trains were also added, the best-known being the 'Tauern Orient'[63], running to Athens from Ostend (again see Introduction). The

trains, however, were increasingly subject to airline competition: from 1956 direct flights between European capitals catered for political and business travellers more efficiently than the 'train de luxe', and with that came once again a change of attitude to what travel was about. As Burton remarks,

'The journey was no longer something that was there to be enjoyed for its own sake, it was simply the quickest route between two points.'[64]

CIWL tried various devices to stem passenger attrition on the 'Orient', but no solution was more than temporary. In May 1962 the 'Arlberg Orient' was cut back to Vienna and became simply the 'Arlberg Express', and the 'Simplon Orient' was cut back to Venice and similarly lost the 'Orient' part of its title. The 'Direct Orient' struggled on, but all pretence at 'train de luxe' status rapidly vanished. Here is Burton again:

'It set out from Calais with a single YU-class sleeper, a survivor from more spacious days... It was joined by two composite coaches, with First and Second Class compartments... Coaches came and went, it seemed, at every stop... There was no longer even any pretence of attracting the old style of wealthy passenger. In time, even the dining car was sacrificed, and the best that anyone could expect was a hurriedly grabbed snack at a buffet, or a plastic tray of apparently plastic food... The wise took their own provisions.'[65]

The end finally came on 19/20 May 1977, and from then on the train that ran on the same service did so only as far as Trieste, conveyed ordinary SNCF sleepers, and was known simply as 'Train 225'. In that same year, French rail authorities officially declared 'the age of the Trains de Luxe is over.'[66]

The history of the other restored 'trains de luxe', and of dining on them, mirrors that of the 'Orient Express'. In *Grand European Expresses*, published in 1962, Behrend offers a series of vignettes (with occasionally a formal menu) of dining on these trains around 1960, when road and airline competition was beginning to take its toll.[67] They make fascinating reading: both their tone and their content suggest a service poised between success and decline and showing indications of the onset of the latter – which is just what we would expect from considering the story of the 'Orient Express'. The two menus quoted formally are still firmly in the *haute cuisine* tradition (five courses for the 'Blue Train' dinner, four for the

'Italia Express' lunch) and some individual dishes earn high praise – the Florentine strawberries on the 'Italia', for example.

But there is a curious unease about the description of the food, especially on the 'Nord Express'. The smaller and cheaper version of the dinner available on leaving Paris, the spaghetti cut up to suit non-Italians, the very ordinary vegetables, the sweet prepared off-train in the Gare du Nord kitchens, the fact that the train out of Paris was using a buffet car, and its kitchen was 'stretched' by a full meal service – all suggested a service struggling to remain true to what it had been pre-war. Breakfast is passed over with little comment, but lunch, though it begins well with a Scandinavian smorgasbord, goes down hill fast, through a second dose of creamed spinach in 24 hours and a rather lack-lustre macedoine of potatoes to a ghastly sweet made from prunes.

Descriptions of the dining vehicles give the same sense of living in the shadow of former greatness. The 'Blue Train' saloon bar car was converted from a former Pullman. The 'Nord Express' made do with a buffet car whose kitchen was barely able to cope with dinner, and the windows wouldn't open; the 30-year-old restaurant car that took over the following morning was 'more comfortable to eat in than modern innovations', and on the 'Italia Express' the new bodies on the old Pullman frames 'wrecked in the war' are described as starkly modern in décor – 'the ceiling lights are of neon strip'. In both vehicles and food Behrend is chronicling the close of an epoch.

'The Empire Strikes Back': the Trans-Europ Expresses

By 1977, then, the 'train de luxe' was dead, but since 1957 an alternative had been under development. It was called 'TEE', and its smart, fast red-and-white trains were operated jointly by national railway companies. Though initially First-Class-only multiple-unit diesels, from 1970 most TEEs featured electric locomotive-hauled stock and from 1978 many conveyed Second Class also. Advance reservation was essential, and they were among the first trains to make use of computerised booking systems. Most TEE trains offered at-seat meals service at every seat, though some – for example the new 'Rheingold', which was partly saloon and partly compartment stock – conveyed a formal dining car.[68] An at-seat trolley coffee and snack service was available outside meal times. Like the UK's 'Blue Pullmans', the TEEs were overtly aimed at

businessmen. Once again, this introduced a new variation into the idea of 'dining at speed': emphasis on speed rather than dining. The dining now was no longer a key experience of the journey, simply an added-value service.

Two vignettes from my own journeys illustrate these opposing aspects of on-train dining in post-war Europe. TEE services were not really aimed at the British traveller, so those journeys that involved them mostly fell outside mealtimes; I can, however, confirm that the at-seat trolley service was excellent, the coffee in particular being properly percolated rather than the instant variety one got back in UK. The one TEE meal service I *did* sample was on the 'Rheingold' leaving Hoek in 1975: the diner opened promptly at 7.30, and coffee was available by the kännchen, 'extra stark' if you wanted it. Mitropa's old eggs-and-bacon breakfast had gone, though; what you got were rolls (crisp and hot) with a selection of cheeses or cold meats, including ham and German salami, unsalted butter, and little pots of preserves.

My other vignette dates from 1981. I had decided to travel right through to Berlin by train – the famous '07.17' from Hoek, successor to the 1920s Berlin-London express. Mitropa – which since being taken over by the DDR had confined its activities to Eastern Europe – had just begun once again to run dining cars right through to Hoek, and I wanted to see what the experience would be like.

Entering the Mitropa dining car was like stepping into a time warp. Although painted externally in Mitropa red, I strongly suspect that the vehicle was one of the former blue CIWL cars 'purloined' during the Second World War. The frame was long, large and spacious, allowing for easy 2+2 dining, with a wide passageway in between. The tables had white napery, and the seating was entirely composed of movable chairs. Every table had a small vase of flowers placed on it (though I discovered on close inspection that the flowers were plastic). The waiters – never more than two visible at any one time – wore uniforms of high-buttoned white jackets over black trousers; as on the pre-war Mitropa trains, they all spoke excellent English. The one concession to people's democracy was that there was no silver service – everything was plated in the kitchen.

The food throughout was once again of excellent quality. Breakfast again started promptly at 7.30 and the car quickly filled up. Cheese or cold meats were available, and so were soft-boiled eggs. Kännchens of coffee came round once again; tea was also on offer, but I eschewed it in favour of the coffee, and watched deer grazing in the woodlands beside the dykes through the morning mist outside the window. After breakfast I adjourned to my compartment, returning for coffee service around 10.30; an all-day à la carte menu was now available, including a splendid sticky chocolate torte, which accompanied yet another 'kännchen kaffee extra stark' extremely well.

The menu promised that there would also be a lunchtime special, and around Hannover it came on stream – *Wiener schnitzel mit sauerkraut, salat und rostkartoffeln*, those splendid German sauté potato pieces that have alas so often now been cast out in favour of the ubiquitous 'frites' – delicious! Each schnitzel was cooked to order and served separately plated. As an added bonus, there was also Raderberger Pilsner 'luxus klasse' available – next to Pilsner Urquell (the original from Pilsen itself) and 'real' Budweiser (from Budvar in Czechoslovakia), the finest railway beer in Europe. Since Raderberg was in the DDR it came in true Communist spirit in bottles of all colours and shapes: the factory used whatever containers they could lay hands on. But the beer tasted divine whatever colour of bottle it came out of. I was only sorry I couldn't sample dinner, but that wasn't served until the train left Berlin for Warsaw.

'Pride goeth before a fall': wartime and post-war on-train dining in the USA

US railroads did not go through physical devastation during their war, though they did go through a period of shortages and heavy overloading. So, when British and European railways were rebuilding, US railroads were enjoying a belated 'streamliners' finest hour'.[69] But once passenger attrition started, it proceeded very much faster in the USA than in Europe, with little or no attempt at fightback until the formation of Amtrak in 1971.

The main wartime effect on the railroads was a vast increase in train movements and loadings, plus restrictions on 'critical war materials'[70] preventing more than minimal purchase of new vehicles.[71] In addition to enormous troop movements,

'the rationing of tyres and gasoline caused civilians to turn to trains, adding to the crush, and job seekers going to … defense plants swelled the throngs.'[72]

Bryant, in fact, estimates that Santa Fé passenger numbers increased sixfold.

Almost all these people wanted feeding. Food on official troop trains was not the railroads' problem, but large numbers of service personnel travelled on civilian trains, both on postings and on leave; on postings 'all came armed with tickets redeemable for a dollar a meal per person', and even going on leave 'Few of them ignored "mess call", even though they had to pay for it themselves', and this attitude of 'enjoy it while it's around' spread to civilian travellers too:

'Most rail travellers … had money to spend for the first time in half a lifetime, and even if none took it seriously, they seemed to adopt the fatalist's philosophy of "Eat, drink, and be merry". What better place to apply it than on a train, travelling as they had fantasized – and what better time than when in full flight from a … depression, especially when there was a war on?'[73]

The railroads responded to the flood of demand in various ways. On the Northern Pacific, dining cars opened at 6am, and GIs were called to the car first and served with standard plated meals. Staff on the cars and in the commissaries worked extended hours. To cope with possible meat shortages, menus were redesigned so that items could be 'tipped' on and off by changing a small insert. Even the NP's trademark 'Great Big Baked Potato' became a wartime casualty: it took up oven space for much too long.[74]

The Santa Fé doubled the diner fleet, and also re-opened former Harvey Houses and re-introduced meal stops for some of the trains running in multiple sections. The SF also used on-train 'news agents' to sell drinks and snacks.

'Harvey news agents on the trains were soon selling 150,000 bottles of milk and 500,000 sandwiches a month; on one trip, the passengers on the "Scout" consumed 4,400 sandwiches… Standard 36-seat diners fed 350 people in 10 sittings of 30 minutes each, and frying 50 to 60 dozen eggs for breakfast became a routine… Harvey … ended the "bottomless cup of coffee", but kept the standard of quality as high as possible.'[75]

Possibly the most extreme conditions of all were faced by the Southern Pacific, which claimed to have served 23 million meals during 1943. It too served GIs first and used plated meals, and also attempted to limit lunch service entirely to military passengers;

civilians would be offered two meals a day – breakfast, extended till noon, and dinner, starting from 4pm.[72] The SP explained this somewhat draconian rule to its customers in a series of advertisements that played a similar role to the British 'Is Your Journey Really Necessary?' campaign.[76]

To further speed up meals service, a number of the triplet diner/kitchen/coffee shop sets had their diners altered to run as second coffee shops, for example on the 'San Joaquin Daylight' – which, thanks to that heightened capacity, *could* continue serving lunch.[77] Much food was prepared in shore-based commissaries for finishing on-train. Finally, the SP too made extensive use of 'news agents', selling 15,000 sandwiches and 6,500 box lunches a day in 1944.[78]

The effect of all this on menus was predictable. 'Meals Select' were phased out almost immediately; they took too long to prepare and called for too great a range of food to be carried. May 1945 'Daylight' coffee shop menus printed breakfast and 'combination plate' menus on opposite sides of the same card.[79] Breakfast offered three set choices, the only variable being the main course: cereal, French toast with preserves, or two eggs, boiled, fried or scrambled. The short à la carte section allowed four strips of bacon or two doughnuts. The 'plate combinations' similarly offered three alternatives, all of two courses. Again the only variable was the main course – baked fish, spaghetti with meat patty, or braised beef – though the two more expensive menus did offer ice-cream as an alternative to fruit cobbler

for sweet. The à la carte section offered liverwurst on rye, tomato and lettuce or chopped egg sandwiches.

Overcrowding plagued eastern railroads too. The diners on the 'George Washington' became 'almost the equivalent of a mess hall on wheels'[90]. The massive à la carte sections went, but the menus were not totally reduced to coffee shop status. With its sense of style tattered but not defunct, the 'George Washington' breakfast involved three alternatives, as on the 'Daylight', but there were more choices within each, some, like scrambled egg with chicken giblets or corn meal griddle cakes with syrup, retaining a feel of 'the old south' while avoiding the ration card. Various other little touches survived, too – cream with the cereal, hot biscuits as an alternative to corn muffins, and coffee by the pot. In the same spirit, the November 1943 dinner menu (reproduced here) retains the 'Mount Vernon' and 'Tavern' Dinners and the Sandwich Combination Plate. There is no à la carte selection, but the dishes on offer are stylish and again often characteristically Southern (the crabmeat cakes, the browned chicken fricassée) and manage beautifully to avoid the 'red meat on ration' problem; and a separate salad course is retained.

Hubris and Nemesis: the triumph of road and air

The US railroads were justifiably proud of their wartime performance. At the war's end they were

Mt. Vernon Dinner 1.25

Orange Juice or Grapefruit Juice
Bisque of Oyster Soup
——— CHOICE ———
Chicken a la King
Fried Fresh Crabmeat Cakes
Broiled or Fried Fresh Fish, Lemon Ring
Browned New Potatoes   Fresh Vegetable

Lettuce with Sliced Radishes, Diced Celery
(French Dressing)

Assorted Bread

——— CHOICE ———
Fresh Apple Pie   Chilled Grapefruit (Half)
Rice Pudding, Sweet Cream   Ice Cream, Sweet Wafers

Tea   Coffee (Pot)   Milk   Cocoa

Sandwich Combination Plate .75

Assorted Finger Sandwiches
Chicken Salad
Tea   Coffee (Pot)   Milk

Tavern Dinner .85

Bisque of Oyster Soup

——— CHOICE ———
Browned Chicken Fricassee
Omelet with Jelly
Broiled or Fried Fresh Fish, Lemon Ring
New Potatoes, Persillade   Fresh Vegetable

Lettuce Salad
(French Dressing)

Assorted Bread

——— CHOICE ———
Rice Pudding, Sweet Cream   Ice Cream

Tea   Coffee (Pot)   Milk

Patrons Will Appreciate, Under Existing Conditions, Our Inability To Serve Meals Outside Dining Car.

"All prices listed are our ceiling prices, or below. By Office of Price Administration regulation, our ceilings are our highest prices from February 1, 1943, to April 10, 1943. Records of these prices are available for your inspection at Room 212—Yard Service Building, Terminal Yards, Cincinnati, Ohio."

This wartime dinner menu from the 'George Washington' is shorter and simpler than the pre-war equivalent, but still unmistakeably in the special style of that famous train. Note the statutory declaration about wartime controlled prices. *E. S. Hanger collection* exhausted but confident, placing 3,000 new car orders for 1945 and 1946[80], including orders for a completely refurbished 'Super Chief'[81] and the C&O's brand new 'Chessie', named after the company's legendary mascot kitten that was supposed to ride the sleepers curled up in comfort, and incorporating 'hostesses, music piped to each individual seat, theatre car, children's playroom [and] the first dome cars in the east.'[82]

But on 17 April 1944 the *Los Angeles Herald Express* carried an account of the first Lockheed Constellation flight, from Burbank, CA, to Washington, in 7hr 3min, with Howard Hughes at the controls of the 65-seater.[83] The Southern Pacific saw the potential threat, and by 1946 was running advertisements headed 'A short course in Railroading … for Airline executives', emphasising that the SP 'Daylight' streamliners provided the cheapest fares between California's major cities.[84]

The problems stemmed from the very victory itself. America's factories were intact, her returning troops were looking for jobs, and her governments desperately wanted to ensure no return to the Depression years: the Marshall Plan and similar policies boosted employment. As Gerald Parshall put it, 'American factories … were soon producing half the goods and services in the entire world'[85]. And this upbeat economic scenario rubbed off on individual psychology; the romance of air travel had begun to overtake 'the romance of the rails'.

The railroads were also hampered by the nature of US geography. Major commercial and industrial centres were separated by distances that required at least a 20-hour train journey; even San Francisco-Los Angeles by rail took 7 hours – the time the Lockheed Constellation's 1944 maiden flight took to cross the entire continent. The philosophy of speed thus meant that the business traveller was bound inevitably to fly. The effect on passenger rail traffic was swift and devastating. Total US ridership was 90 million in 1943, 45 million by 1951, and just 30 million by 1959[86] – figures crucial to on-train dining, because irrespective of journey length passengers tended to make the same demands per head on dining services. Fewer passengers meant less patronage.

Initially, once wartime restrictions eased, full dining car services were re-instated, and menus returned to almost their pre-war length and variety. I particularly like this pair of items from the Southern Pacific's 'Noon Daylight' Dinner Select menu for March 1949 – steward D. L. Ernst, subsequently of Broadway acting fame[87]:

6 – THE SILVER PLATTER   2.00
Slices of Chicken or Turkey on Toast, Topped with Green Asparagus, Fresh Mushrooms, Covered with American Cheese Sauce Flavored with White Wine and a Sprinkle of Parmesan, au Gratin, Garnished with Broiled Tomatoes and Shoestring Potatoes

WINE adds to your dining enjoyment
California RED or WHITE TABLE WINE
Especially bottled for Southern Pacific
Half bottle (serves two)   75c with meal

The grandeur was short-lived, however; by late 1949 the 'Daylight' triple-unit diners were rebuilt again in a coffee shop/kitchen/hamburger-grill format, and many of the 'heavyweight' diners converted to coffee shop or snack-bar use, at a saving of several hundred jobs[88], and most of the remaining new building was in coffee shop/lounge format.[89] The hamburgers were 'Served in Basket with Ripe Olives, Slices of Pickle and Potato Chips' (some light meals – for example Salisbury steak with spaghetti[90] – were also available) and instead of a wine invitation the menu showed 'Beer and Ale available at prevailing prices'. Clearly the SP now expected to serve 'a steadily increasing percentage of chair car passengers'[91].

As the decline went on, the SP looked for still more ways to reduce meal service costs. In 1961 its workshops rebuilt surplus tavern cars as automats, marketed as 'Quick lunch for families', with the bar or some booths replaced by vending machines, rather unpleasant-looking vinyl seats and mean little tables. Seventeen conversions were carried out in all, and they were assigned to everything from the 'City of San Francisco' streamliner to the overnight 'Lark' and the 'San Joaquin Daylight'.[92] They saved money all right, but they were not liked: Richard Spence, the first President of Conrail, commented of them:

'Because dining car losses were so horrendous, we built those damned vending cars… Unless cold sandwiches and hot casseroles in cans are your thing, you would not have cared for the cuisine. Someone in the Dining Car Department suggested an automat menu with the heading "Hobo's Lunch".'[93]

When Amtrak took over in 1971, one of its first actions was to get rid of them.

The Santa Fé by contrast chose to retain as many of its premier services for as long as possible to the high quality standards inherited from Fred Harvey.

New higher-capacity equipment, including the first double-deck dining cars (80-seat saloon above, kitchen underneath, connected by dumb waiter), was purchased for 'El Capitan' in 1956, and for the 'Super Chief' in 1962-64. Bryant comments:

'Standards were not lowered … fresh fruit, freshly baked pies, live mountain trout and hot rolls still flowed into the diners from the commissaries… Food quality remained high, the same waiters and dining car stewards served the cars, and fresh yellow roses still graced the tables.'[94]

However, in September 1967 the US Post Office moved almost all its railroad mail carriage contracts to the airlines. For the AT&SF alone, this created a loss of $35 million per year, and was the single major factor that led the Class I railroads to support the creation of Amtrak in 1971.[95]

The Northern Pacific's ridership problems were different. A substantial portion of its ridership came from patrons who had sampled its 'Famously Good Food', and *preferred* to travel NP rather than fly. Accordingly, it attacked the problem on two fronts: an 'economy buffet car' staffed by just a short-order cook and a cashier[96] on its 'second-string' train the 'Mainstreeter' and on connecting services, but retaining on the 'Limited' the ambience and cuisine that had made it famous.

The result of this policy can be seen in the 'Limited' Dinner menu for June 1961 reproduced here. Although this is late in the period of railroad decline, it still has a substantial à la carte section, and caters for a variety of eating styles. The set dinner menu, however, demonstrates a new departure: each meal now offers choices between a formal six-course table d'hôte offer, a plated meal or a 'salad suggestion'.

There was also a lighter offer available on the 'Limited' from 1955, but it was aimed at retaining custom rather than cutting costs. In that year a buffet-lounge car, the 'Lewis and Clark Traveller's Rest', was added, running just ahead of the dining car proper. The lunch counter buffet served a limited range of meals from 7am onwards, while the lounge section offered all-day beverage service; magazines, cards and radio were also available. The buffet *did* offer a hamburger, but served on a plate not in a basket.

Finally let us look yet again at the Chesapeake & Ohio. The C&O celebrated the end of the war by ordering stock for an entire new streamlined Supertrain, to be called the 'Chessie', including Vistadome high-level cars, the 'Chessie Club'

Dinner

Table d'Hote

Chilled Washington Apple Juice
or
Chicken Broth with Rice Soup
Hearts of Celery   Rosebud Radishes
Broiled Fresh Fish (In Season) $3.35
Fried Spring Chicken (Disjointed) A La Maryland $3.65
Broiled Ham Steak, Florida $3.75
N.P. Big Baked Potato
Washington Green Asparagus
Waldorf Salad
Dinner Rolls
French Apple Pie   Vanilla Ice Cream
Imported Roquefort Cheese, Toasted Crackers
Coffee   Tea (Hot or Iced)   Milk

**Broiled Choice Sirloin Steak, Fresh Mushrooms
With Above Dinner, $5.50**

**Plate Dinner
$2.50**

Broiled Fresh Fish (In Season)
or
Baked Meat Loaf, Creole
Choice { Whipped Potatoes
of   { Whole Kernel Corn
Two   { Red Cabbage Slaw
Dinner Roll   Hol-Ry
Berry Tart, Whipped Cream
Coffee   Tea (Hot or Iced)   Milk

**Salad Suggestion
$1.90**

Tossed Green Salad, Strips of Chicken and Ham
Whole Wheat Toast   Ry-Krisp
French Vanilla Ice Cream
Coffee   Tea (Hot or Iced)   Milk

Form 8294-D—6-61

This June 1961 'North Coast Limited' Dinner menu demonstrates the tenacity with which the Northern Pacific was still clinging to its culinary tradition of 'Famously Good Food'. Choice is still extensive, and food is still in general of high quality: Room Service to Club travellers in Pullman private rooms is once again possible, though the surcharge has doubled. Meal prices are showing signs of inflation too, just as in Britain; the set meals are two to three times as expensive as their pre-war or wartime equivalents, and the famous 'Great Big Baked Potato' has doubled in price since before the war. *Courtesy of Minnesota Historical Society*

club/lounge car, and new dining cars that were displayed at the 1948-49 Chicago Railroad Fair under the 'Chessie Club' title.[97] The management even opened a training school for dining car staff and standardised recipes under the gourmet chef Michael DeZutter of New York to ensure quality and consistency of food service on all the trains.[82]

But the 'Chessie' never ran. By the time the complete consists were delivered, the passenger traffic decline had set in. Most of the new stock was sold, and the 'Chessie Club' mark became used as a public-relations menu title.

The 'Vistadome' car, with its all-round upper-level view lounges (once described as 'like riding in a travelling greenhouse') was a must for the sophisticated flagship US streamliners of the late 1940s. This preserved example is from the Burlington Northern. *Ray Ruffell Collection, Silver Link Publishing Ltd*

Typical main meal menus for 1948 and 1953 illustrate the effects of these events. The 1948 menus show a similar range to their pre-war counterparts, plus one striking new offer – dishes from the charcoal broiler now available on the new cars. By 1953, though, the traditional range and layout have gone in favour of attempts to win over the passenger by a 'bright and breezy' style. 'Chessie' and her (non-existent) 'Club' have now made their appearance, but only one charcoal-broiled dish (sirloin steak) is now available, and the à la carte section has been replaced by items from the old 'Sandwich Special' quoted individually. Prices have continued to rise, too, and in response to this a 'Chessie's Budget Special' of frankfurters and beans has been introduced (costing as much as the entire pre-war 'Mount Vernon Dinner').

The final example in this survey makes even more depressing reading. It is 1967: under pressure of falling revenues the C&O has merged with the Baltimore & Ohio. They now take credit cards, and they still use the 'Chessie' logo – but really all you can get are sandwiches (though the two 'Specials' are pretty substantial). This isn't, in any real sense, a diner any more – it's a buffet car.

By the 1970s, then, the traditional concept of 'dining at speed', with the emphasis on comfort and the quality of the experience itself, was under attack on several fronts – airline and road competition, cost and price inflation, and changing attitudes to eating. Just as the respectability of lunch had generated on-train dining almost a century earlier, so now a move to lighter meals and more snacking and an increasing demand for speed were combining to kill it. In Europe a fightback was under way, becoming well established on the continental mainland, though only really just starting in Britain. But this implied a different, and less inclusive, concept of on-train dining – as a part of a business-class package rather than as a major element of travel in its own right. And this crucially depended on somehow matching overall rail journey times with those by car or plane, which US geography rendered singularly difficult.

Dating from 1967, after the C&O/B&O merger and just a year before the demise of most of the C&O 'named trains', this menu shows what things had come down to as rail market share dropped remorselessly toward 7 per cent. Gone is any pretence at 'dining' – all this really is now is a buffet car menu – but 'Chessie' still sleeps eponymously through it all. *E. S. Hanger collection*

Appetizers . . .

CHILLED FRUIT OR TOMATO JUICE   .35

LETTUCE AND TOMATO SALAD   .50
(French Dressing)

Chessie Sandwich Specials . . .

HOT ROAST BEEF, GRAVY, WHIPPED POTATOES,
Choice of Beverage and Dessert 2.25
HOT ROAST TURKEY, CRANBERRIES, WHIPPED POTATOES,
Choice of Beverage and Dessert 2.25

Sandwiches . . .

CHICKEN, WITH LETTUCE AND MAYONNAISE 1.00
HAM OR BACON AND EGG 1.25
BACON, LETTUCE AND TOMATO 90
HAM 75
CHEESE 65

Desserts . . .

BAKED APPLE WITH CREAM   .40   STEWED PRUNES   .35
INDIVIDUAL PIE   .25

Beverages . . .

COFFEE, Pot   .35   TEA, Pot   .35   MILK (Ind.) .25

Please write on meal check each item desired.

Car in charge of

American Express, Diners Club and Rail Travel Credit Cards Honored

C&O/B&O PASSENGER FOOD SERVICE
K. S. Cox, Superintendent

Chessie

7
'CENATOR REDIVIVIUS'
The revival of the idea, 1977-97

As the not-quite-Latin of the chapter title suggests, the notion of on-train dining, by the early 1970s apparently terminally ill, mysteriously revived, in some areas at any rate, during the following quarter century. If the made-up word 'cenator' was real classical Latin, it would mean something like a 'diner' (the person, not the carriage) in the individual and private rather than the public and formal sense – somebody eating a meal, rather than someone attending a banquet: thus it perfectly suits the state of affairs in post-1970s on-train dining, where the lavish banquet-like repasts of the 'Orient Express' and the other 'Grand European Expresses' were for the most part a thing forgotten. And just as the title looks like classical Latin but isn't, so the form of 'dining at speed' in this period outwardly resembled the classical concept, but was in fact something different – less luxurious and dreamlike, more part of an overall package of added value, more angled to the business travel market rather than leisure travel, more subservient to the prime competitive notion of speed as part of the attempt to counter passenger attrition and the resultant loss of revenue.

In Britain, by the 1960s a 'fast business niche market' was being served by trains such as the 'Blue Pullmans' and their Manchester successor. In mainland Europe, a similar movement had started with the development of the TEE network as early as 1957/58. Only in the USA was there no real fightback before the formation of Amtrak in 1971; the Pennsylvania Railroad's Washington-New York 'Metroliner' high-speed trains were put into service in 1969, but their design was technically flawed – they only reached two-thirds of their rated top speed and 'rode like a cork on a windy pond'[1] – and the Penn Central went bust.

In all three areas, then, the stage was set by the mid-1970s to develop specialised business-oriented high-speed train services able to compete successfully with air and motorway travel, and the new version of the 'dining at speed' idea that formed part of them.

From British Rail to Inter-City: the belated rediscovery of 'train magic'

By the late 1960s British Rail was beginning to make extended use of its discovery of a demand for fast business rail services between major cities. The 'Mancunian' and the 'Blue Pullmans' were recording regular capacity loadings. But the real eye-opener was the sustained surge of traffic that followed the 1966/67 Euston electrification's speedy fixed-interval services; after just three months of hourly 100mph trains, Liverpool-Manchester-London passenger traffic had grown by 66%, and the same thing happened on the Birmingham line. Furthermore, the customers stayed.[2] This fast and frequent new service between London, Manchester and Liverpool was given the title 'The Inter-City Service'; the InterCity brand name was shortly thereafter extended even further, to cover all fast main-line operations.[3]

Two further stimuli hastened the re-emergence of a commercially oriented InterCity business. The first was the requirement in the 1968 Transport Act, repeated in 1980 by the Thatcher Government[4], for BR routes to pay their way. The second was the development of the HST 125 sets, introduced on the Western Region in October 1976 and on the East Coast route in May 1978; on the WR ridership rose by 15% in six months, and by 33% over the following two years.[5] InterCity's publicity people started to talk of the 'nose cone effect', and coined the slogan 'the changing shape of rail'.

But BR didn't entirely realise what it had uncovered. That business approved of the new fast services was clear, but the media pundits feared ordinary travellers would perceive a high-speed service as 'not for them', and went to considerable trouble to promote it as 'the people's train'. When this involved such images as a family speeding away for the day to meet London relations, or Jimmy Savile declaring 'This is the Age ... of the Train', it was harmless enough, and it was probably still relatively harmless to play down 'speed for speed's sake [or] images of luxury travel'[4]. But this attitude also got inside the heads of BR management, and led to some unfortunate decisions over HST design.

This was particularly true of the dining cars. The prototype HST, the first 20 WR sets, and some East Coast sets, had an unclassified kitchen-restaurant car with 24 seats (TRUK) *and* a buffet car with 36 seats marshalled together in the centre of the train between First and Standard Class. Subsequent WR sets, however, were built with buffet cars only, while the final 12 East Coast and further WR sets were built with a single combined vehicle (TRUB) that featured a 17-seat dining saloon forward, plus a kitchen amidships capable of serving 41 main meals (or 65 breakfasts) and a buffet bar (but no seats) aft. Brian Perren, in his contribution to *The InterCity Story*, claims that this was simply a response to customer demand:

'In the light of experience, it became apparent that two separate catering cars in a eight-car train were more than was needed on most services.'[6]

Nicholas, however, writing in 1979, is less charitable:

'The speed with which catering policy on HST sets has changed reflects the alternate economic optimism and pessimism which has been such a feature of the HST decade... The intention was to build the 27 sets for the Western Region with two catering vehicles in each. A mood of pessimism then set in, and the TRUK was omitted from the later portion of the fleet.'[7]

And although both saloons were 'unclassified', they were at the First Class end of the car, with a small swing half-panel marked 'First Class Only Beyond This Point' separating them from the buffet; the entire coach was marked '1' externally, marking the first retreat from the provision of dining services to all classes since 1881.

Indeed, only in 1987, with InterCity about to become a commercial company, did a re-branding exercise re-discover the core concept of 'train magic', the idea that had fired 'dining at speed' from its outset. Michael Beswick's chapter for *The InterCity Story*, 'Building a Winning Brand', describes it like this:

'...increasingly there was an emotional content with much more subjective associations... InterCity identified this missing link in the idea of "train magic". On an InterCity train people were cocooned in an environment away from the cares of the world and could relax.'[8]

But even this insight was seen as carrying a danger of being 'viewed as highly elitist' and 'for expense account travellers'. Thus this rediscovery of 'train magic' resulted in advertising slogans, such as 'Relax! – Let the Train Take the Strain', cheap leisure fares, and customer welcoming teams wearing nice new claret-and-blue uniforms[9], rather than in any return to on-train dining comfort provision for all. The general terms of InterCity's commercial strategy were correct, though – 1991 was its third year in profit, and it operated the most trains at 100mph-plus overall in Europe.[10]

From Travellers-Fare to On-Board Services

The development of on-train catering had been hindered by being a subordinate part of British Transport Hotels. Now, however, it was to change rapidly. In 1973 British Rail Catering was renamed 'Travellers-Fare', and in 1978 gained a separate Board of Directors, famously including the cookery writer Prue Leith. In 1982 it finally became a separate division of the British Railways Board with the formal status of in-house catering provider to BR, but although it had been freed from the incubus of the hotels, it still combined on-train catering and refreshment rooms – two areas of catering that were becoming steadily more and more different.[11] Only in 1986 was on-train catering separated out, placed directly under InterCity[12], and renamed 'On-Board Services'[13] – the direct ancestor of today's Rail Gourmet organisation, the catering supply service to most privatised train operating companies.

How well did the Travellers Fare?

The new Travellers-Fare continued the drive towards standardised menus, but with a difference. It was plain there were different levels of customer demand on different services, from something approaching *haute cuisine* at one end to simple buffet takeaway griddle dishes at the other. Travellers-Fare therefore standardised menus across the network at four different levels. Nicholas describes the top three of those levels like this:

'The cheapest is the "Grill" menu, which is served all day and encompasses an à la carte range with one main dish changed a week. It is served on train services which do not have a high volume of demand at conventional meal times... The next type of menu is the "Main Line", which is served on a large number of trains were demand justifies silver service... A rotation of menus is served to provide the regular traveller with adequate variety... The "Gold Star" series of menus cover breakfast and dinner on trains where demand is considered to justify a more elaborate meal at a higher price...'[7]

Nicholas's example of the 'Gold Star' dinner menu from November 1979 offers four courses plus coffee, with price based on the choice of main dish – a starter (choice of asparagus soup with fresh cream, various fruit juices, or Ardennes paté), a main course, with parsley and sauté potatoes and a choice of green beans and broccoli or a fresh salad made to order, a sweet (pears in orange cream or fresh fruit) and a cheese course, with Scotch woodcock as an alternative. The main dish choices were Baked Gammon with Cumberland Sauce at £5.75, Fillet of Sole Bonne Femme, also at £5.75, and Selection of Cold Roast Beef, Ham and Tongue with Mixed Salad, £5.15.

The fresh-cream asparagus soup and the Ardennes paté both offered a touch of *haute cuisine* (the paté was particularly adventurous for the period), and the provision of a cheese course additional to the sweet, with a savoury offered as an alternative, 'carries on a traditional part of dining car dinner menus', as Nicholas puts it.

On the 'Main Line' menus the starters were less adventurous, and cheese was an alternative to the sweet, not an addition; overall, they had more of a feel of the previous period about them. The price was a little cheaper, too. The Inter-City Grill menus (which included Breakfast and a range of Afternoon and High Tea menus) were still simpler and more standardised. They were readily capable of being served from a TRUB kitchen, or even from a Griddle Car. The basic main meal was two courses, with the starter available as an extra; this, and the regular

Salad Special offer, gave these menus an American flavour. With these menus, Travellers-Fare began actively to seek custom; they could be found not simply in the dining or buffet car itself, but on tables in ordinary stock right the way through the train.

In the ten years since the latest menus listed in Chapter 6, one would have expected prices to roughly double, but the dinner menus actually increased four- or five-fold, and even a humble plate of sausage, bacon and tomato from the buffet now cost as much as an entire dinner in 1971. Some at least of that price increase was deliberate commercial policy. Nicholas comments:

'The statistics of meals served clearly demonstrate that on a wide range of trains putting up both price and quality of meal increases custom. Indeed, scale of unsatisfied demand is a growing problem where journey time and/or fixed train formations prevent more than one sitting.'

In other words, if the meal is a good one, the punters will pay top whack for it.

Several sources indicate that the general quality of cuisine and menu choice was high during this period.[14] Nicholas again comments:

'Travellers-Fare splendidly upholds some of the traditions of British catering. Any chief steward knows that a big crusty pastry steak and kidney pie (often with mushrooms) is likely to be more popular than any other main course. Roasts still feature in many menus ... the results of real effort to increase the quality and value of meals are clearly detectable more often than not.'

And Kitchenside, also writing in 1979, remarks:

'Travellers-Fare policy ... is to use as much fresh food as possible, particularly meat, although a certain amount of frozen vegetables are used and some convenience foods in buffet cars ... steak, kidney and mushroom pie ... is freshly made in the kitchen of the restaurant car, although chefs have a choice of using proprietary pastry mix or making their own. The frozen complete main meals of the 1950s cafeteria cars have no place in today's BR menus.'[15]

But in just over five years this emphasis on food freshly prepared on-train was to change radically, under the influence of four stimuli: the need for faster turn-round and greater reliability, changes in kitchen design, the development of 'cook-chill' technology, and an unexpected side-effect of the introduction of the at-seat trolley.

The 'cook-chill' revolution

Business travellers demanded higher standards of quality, reliability and availability. But at the same time journey times decreased, and with them serving and preparation availability times. The impact of all of this on the work environment in the cars was substantial. Breakfast was a rush, and joints for dinner on down trains often had to be started during the morning up run, adding to the complexity of work scheduling and oven use – and, since one team now no longer necessarily stayed with the train all day, might well involve a second crew taking over the finishing.[15] At the same time, staff on the TRUB cars had to run both a buffet and a dining saloon. Clearly, a way had to be found to streamline the catering crew's job.

The answer came from a number of innovations that came together during the 1970s and 1980s. The earliest was the development of microwave ovens, fitted as standard on the new Mark III catering vehicles. Initially these were used to shorten cooking times, but they could equally well be used in conjunction with the technique of 'cook-chill' meal preparation, initially developed for use on airlines. This involves preparing a dish to a given state, then chilling it very rapidly to about 3°C, at which it will keep for several days. The dish can then be quickly 'regenerated' as needed, and because it warms from the middle outwards a microwave oven is ideal. Two variants of this technology were available. One – favoured by airlines and mainland European rail companies – was to bring the food as close as possible to the finished state before chilling, and do little more on-train than warm it through. The other – the one selected by InterCity – was to bring the food to an advanced intermediate stage of readiness before chilling, but still leave some additional finishing to be done on-train.

The reason for this choice was a rather interesting one. The 'finishing' option did not necessarily produce any higher quality dishes than the 'warm-through' option; the sole determining quality factor was the amount of money one wished to spend on the dish.[16] The major factor that led InterCity to select the 'finishing' option was the British travelling public's fondness for a silver-served cooked breakfast. The 'Great British Breakfast', as they came to call it, accounted for half of meals sales, and

'while it was perfectly possible to produce good-quality cook-chill lunch and dinner items … it was conversely very difficult to re-heat a fried egg or toast.'[17]

'Cook-chill' technology, of course, meant that the earlier stages of food preparation could be conducted off-train, greatly simplifying and shortening the on-train kitchen process. It also allowed economies of scale through mass-production of dishes at central points, a wider range of dishes, and standardised portion control, as well as more consistent product quality. But how was the chilled food to be got into the kitchen, or stored once it was there? The answer was via the on-train trolley, originally introduced on MicroBuffet cars to carry pre-prepared snacks and drinks; after use it would be unfastened and wheeled off the train at its destination, the empties removed, and the stock replenished ready for the next journey.

The trolleys were not initially designed to facilitate the 'cook-chill' revolution, but it became clear that they could also be used for handling the loading and storage of 'cook-chill' provisions, and on busy services the 'regenerated' meals could even be served direct from them, just as they were on aircraft – though BR catering management felt that the ambience created by 'silver service' gave InterCity a major advantage over airline competitors, and used that form of presentation, at least for main courses, whenever it could.[14]

The first new 'cook-chill'-based catering service began operation in August 1985, between Euston and Manchester, under the name 'Cuisine 2000'.

The Anglia restaurant car steward presents the breakfast grill tray to a mid-morning business traveller on the 10.30 Liverpool Street-Norwich service on 16 November 2000. *Author*

EXPRESS DINER

MENU 1

Appetizers

Duck Liver Terrine	£3.75

A smooth duck terrine served with a salad garnish and hot toast

Prawn Cocktail	£2.95

Succulent prawns with lettuce, cucumber and lemon. Served with brown bread and butter

Soup of the Day	£2.15
Garlic Bread	£1.05

Entrees

Grilled Rib Steak	£13.95

A prime Scotch rib steak, grilled to your liking and topped with Sauce au Poivre or melted stilton. Served with grilled tomato, peas and chips or jacket potato or a crisp side salad

Traditional Fillet of Cod with Chips	£6.95

Served with peas, lemon and tartare sauce

Kashmiri Chicken with Pilau Rice	£6.95

Pieces of chicken gently cooked in a mildly spiced creamy curry sauce, served on a bed of pilau rice with a crisp side salad

Chilli con Carne or Vegetable Chilli	£7.95

Served with white and wild rice, tortilla chips and a crisp side salad

Vegetarian

Fresh Tagliatelle Verde with Tomato and Mushroom Sauce	£6.95

Served with Parmesan cheese, roll and butter and a crisp side salad

Desserts

Warm Toffee and Banana Pancakes or Apple and Cinnamon Pancakes	£2.95

Topped with whipped cream

Selection of British Cheeses	£3.75

Served with celery and biscuits

Drinks

Coffee Service or Freshly Brewed Tea	£1.50

Decaffeinated coffee available on request. Served with InterCity Chocolates

A wide range of soft drinks, beers, wine and spirits are available. Please ask your steward for details

Food supply contracts were let to Trust House Forte's airline kitchens at Luton and Manchester airports, but actual service was by Travellers-Fare staff. Official photographs of the initial operation show that it was a slightly odd hybrid of dining car and at-seat trolley service; the 'Great British Breakfast', for example, was served Pullman-style at-seat throughout First Class, and arrived in several stages – place settings on one trolley, starter choices on the next, and finally the main course silver-served.[14] The arrival of 'Cuisine 2000' coincided with the re-launch of the Pullman marque, now indicating a level of comfort and service analogous to that formerly associated with Pullman cars themselves, on specific trains and nominated on-station lounges.[18]

Thus by 1986 On-Board Services (OBS for short) covered on-board service proper, food supply via 'cook-chill' trolleys from 28 shore bases, menu planning and food procurement.[19] The Pullman marque became OBS's 'flagship' provision on specific business trains on major routes, featuring an at-seat service throughout First Class; other levels of service, each with its own clearly defined quality standards, included First Class specified meals on major trains, Express Diner menus – a limited range of lighter options for more lightly loaded routes, served all day – and Silver Standard, an at-seat service of light refreshments aimed at business travellers travelling full fare but in Standard Class.[17] The name 'Cuisine 2000' was retained as late as 1988, but by 1992 it had effectively vanished and documents simply list the various menu levels by individual name.

It was InterCity's boast that it provided catering services on every IC train (though some trains were entirely buffet-car served).[20] The overall range of dishes – increasingly wide, thanks to 'cook-chill' modularisation – was standardised across the entire system, but different selections were made from the range for different menu levels and routes. Many selections were also grouped in four-week revolving cycles, changed weekly; new selection cycles were introduced every six months.[21]

The design of such menus – complex, despite the greater freedom given by 'cook-chill' cuisine – was constructed on a matrix system. Each menu needed to have a red meat dish, a white meat dish, a fish dish

The general lunch/dinner Express Diner menus used on more lightly loaded services changed on a four-week cycle, of which the first menu of the set is shown here. The steak offer and one starter changed week by week; however, the other items did not change. *Courtesy British Railways Board (Residuary)* and a vegetarian option, while all the main cooking equipment – grill, stove top and microwave oven – needed to be used as near equally as possible in the finishing process; if one item was called upon for too many servings, the kitchen would be unable to cope with demand. Finally, all cooked dishes had if possible to be capable of being finished on two alternative items of kitchen equipment, in case the power failed on one.[22] The economic and quality range advantages of the new cuisine had thus been purchased at the expense of greater advance planning and fail-safe provision.

The quality of these menus was high, even when the offers themselves were relatively simple, as in the Express Diner menu reproduced here. Except on West Country routes, a Champagne breakfast was regularly on offer in addition to the standard continental or cooked versions. Both the at-seat and the Express Diner menus offered a range of cuisines – Italian, Greek, Indian and Mexican – demonstrating the greater flexibility available with 'cook-chill' techniques. The Pullman First dinner menus had an even wider range, including Chinese and Provençale dishes, and demonstrating a return to *haute cuisine* traditions both in such dishes as Poached Asparagus with Hollandaise Sauce, Baked Salmon with Lobster Butter, or Irish Coffee Savarin, and in offering detailed descriptions of each dish and assigning the dish to its *chef de création*. The wine list was equally discerning, including a Pouilly Fumé 1989 and a Chateau Cissac Cru Bourgeois 1987.

Maintaining consistent quality across such a large range of services and geographical areas was not easy. Staff were trained at OBS's own training school, using a mock-up catering car, and chefs attended a course at Westminster Catering College prior to the introduction of new menus.[23] Menu quality was controlled by central design, and food quality was controlled by the 'cook-chill' process itself. The key issues, therefore, were quality control of train supply, on-train finishing and presentation to the customer.

The chief instrument for achieving this was the On-Board Services Menu and Tariff Guide and Chef's Manual, re-issued with each new six-monthly menu schedule. It listed the range of menus, the four-weekly cycles with change dates and any special notes, and for each dish on the menu the Chef's Manual gave the ingredients the chef should have had delivered on his trolley, how they should be finished on-train and how they should be presented to the customer. By the 1993 editions, the 'recipe' items were grouped in sections, with the menu to which they referred printed at the start of the section

exactly as it would appear on the dining car table, and for the main courses and some desserts a drawing was also included showing how the product should appear when it reached the customer's plate. This system has continued, with some modifications, through the diversity resulting from privatisation and up to the present day.

Mainland Europe: speed comes first?

In mainland Europe much less diversity of provision evolved than in UK.[24] (Indeed, there are only three basic models of contemporary high-speed on-board catering in use across the continent.) Historically, the key element in the TEEs' success was speed; dining, like other services, was an 'added value' rather than fundamental to the experience. As Claudia Wessner puts it in *Modern Trains and Splendid Stations*:

> '…high-speed trains are a vital lifeline for railroad companies. Train travel becomes competitive on a journey of between 100 kilometres and 600 kilometres from city center to city center. If we include travel to and from stations at either end, the train is quicker than the plane or the car…'[25]

Subsequent European rail developments have followed on from this understanding that the salvation of rail travel lay in high speed, but because the major target group of travellers was businessmen and Eurocrats, it was also essential for the new high-speed services to offer a whole raft of added-value provisions conducive to business travel. Thus increasingly as time went on catering was only one element out of many – telephones, laptop sockets, fax machines, conference compartments. Even more than in the UK, therefore, meals service is now and long has been only a small part of the high-speed train offer. Because of this, and because mainland European developments did not change dramatically in 1996-97, as UK developments did, we shall consider all mainland European developments since 1980 together, in the next and final chapter.

US on-train dining: Amtrak 'walks a crooked mile'

During the 1950s and '60s road and airline competition eroded US railroad passenger ridership, and with it both train services and catering provision; the final blow came in 1967, when almost all mail carriage contracts were moved from rail passenger to airline services.[26] However, it was realised that if there was no passenger railroading at all, the effects would be disastrous.

Thus, on 30 October 1970 Congress created the National Railroad Passenger Corporation, a federally subsidised train operating company, with services marketed under the name of 'Amtrak'. Technically it was a 'semi-public for-profit corporation': it could issue common and preferred stock, and common stockholders were represented on its Board of Directors, though there was an automatic majority of Government and ex-officio directors.[27] Amtrak is required to keep within its 'financial resources', but there is nothing to state how these resources are calculated, or to forbid federal funders from suddenly requiring the company to break even, with passenger receipts fully matching its expenses. This virtually gives carte blanche to any particularly parsimonious administration to set financial requirements for Amtrak that it is not able to meet, then require it to cut routes and services in order to meet them. It is this one simple issue that is at the back of many of the twists and turns that have dogged Amtrak throughout its 30-year history.

Amtrak has suffered a cash crisis roughly once every ten years – in 1981-82, in 1995-97, and in 2003-04. Superficially, the crises had separate origins, but ultimately they can all be traced back to a misperception by Government about the logistics of railway improvement; when Amtrak took over US passenger services, it did so not only with nearly empty balance sheets and roads that were seriously run down, but with rolling-stock, including the catering cars, that was antiquated, repair-heavy, and exceedingly uneconomic to run. As Bob Johnston of *Trains* magazine put it:

'Putting red-white-and-blue striping and the arrow logo on second-hand cars and locomotives was the easy part. The hard part was that Amtrak's managers had to choose between continuing to pay the ever-increasing maintenance costs on their rail relics, or finding the capital to buy new equipment.'[28]

Amtrak perforce took the second road, of investing in new equipment. But the benefits of such new equipment take some considerable time to work through; Claudia Wessner indicates a minimum design and development period of three years, followed by a further 18 months to make specific client-related adaptations and 'debug' the system.[29] Thus during at least 4½ years, the railroad operator will have to field the increasing maintenance costs of the old stock *and* the capital costs of developing and purchasing the new stock. Costs will inevitably go up before they go down – and the benefits will not follow through immediately, because it takes time for old stock to be phased out and its replacements delivered.

It was in large part Congress's inability to understand this process that led to the 1981-82 cash crisis; the Reagan administration saw the rising costs as management inefficiency, and demanded cutbacks. And it was largely Claytor's fixated belief that, after the 1981-82 cuts had been reversed, Congress now *did* understand the problem and *would* now come up with the additional sums involved that led him to go on authorising the purchase of new sleeping cars, 'Superliners' and locomotives, despite everything, right up to the retirement that preceded the financial crisis of 1995-97.

Amtrak started life with catering vehicles inherited from the private railroad companies. In addition to straight diners of all ages from 1937 to 1959, they included a wide range of café-type vehicles with an equally wide and bewildering set of names – bar-lounges, pub-cars, coach-snack-bar-lounges, and many more.[30] At their best they were splendid vehicles; at their worst they were time-expired, uneconomic to run, and only just able to cope. By 1973, therefore, the need for modern standardised catering stock was becoming urgent. To minimise maintenance costs, the catering vehicles simply involved internal modifications within the basic 85-foot stainless 'Amfleet' body-shell created by the Budd Company. These came in several different versions, but none of them were true 'diners' in the traditional sense. Bob Johnston has described them as follows:

'Imagine the snack bar in the center of the car. From this basic plan there was:
Amcafé – coach [ie Standard Class] seats on both sides
Amdinette – coach seats on one side, tables on the other *or* tables on both sides
Half Club – coach seats at one side, 1+2 First Class Club seating [at the other] (with meals at seats)
Full Club – 1+2 seating on both sides.'[31]

Initially put into service on the East Coast routes, by May 1976 they had reached all Amtrak routes – even

Capturing the essence of the Amtrak 'Superliner' dining car interiors, this shot of the place setting for breakfast on the 'Sunset Limited' against wooded countryside shows both the elegance of the table arrangements (note particularly the floral decoration) and the great height of the elevated dining saloon. *Bob Johnston collection*

The curved bistro of the 'Cascades' 'Talgo': note the elegant painted ceiling, reminiscent of the Santa Fé 'Chief'. *Bob Johnston collection*

those in California. A second series followed in 1980.

To the same period (1972-76) belong the 'Metroliners' that operated the 3-hour New York-Washington service, one of the few US runs directly competitive with the airlines. The 'Metroliner' cars were similar to Amfleet cars, except for having electric traction and being multiple-unit. Again there were two main varieties – snack-bar-coach and 'Metro-club'[32]. A typical 'Metroliner' train consisted of six coaches, including one club and one dinette.

So far, however, Amtrak had not invested in any new diners proper, and the stock taken over in 1971-72 was steadily getting older. The answer, when it came, was spectacular – the double-decker 'Superliner' design, ordered from Pullman-Standard from April 1975, and in revenue-earning service from April 1979. These cars again used a common body frame for passenger cars, diners and sleepers: once again it was to the 85-foot length, but this time to the very maximum height the US loading gauge would permit, 16ft 2in. In all, 283 cars were ordered,

39 of them diners. Tall and elegant, the diners seated 72 patrons on the upper floor, with the kitchen underneath; food was sent up by dumb waiter.[33]

In terms of ride quality and public interest the decision to go for an extra-tall car was successful. But it also resulted in some logistic problems; the 'Superliners' couldn't work the long-distance Chicago-New York services, which were every bit as much in need of full dining car services as those west of the Windy City. The answer was found in substantial (and expensive) modernising upgrades of the best of the old stock, which in its renewed state became the Heritage Fleet. This included 25 single-level diners and 26 cafeteria-lounge cars[34]; they not only included modern upgraded facilities, but in many cases also retained classic period features.

However, a genuine high-speed service was still missing. In part this was because the permanent way, with very few exceptions, would not support it. In the Washington-New York-Boston North East Corridor, of course, the 'Metroliners' had been intended to give such a service, at any rate over the southern part of the route, but technical problems had limited their speed to 90mph. West of Chicago, the main reason for a high-speed service, competition with air travel, was not valid, for reasons of distance, even though the Santa Fé permanent way might well have sustained one. There was, however, one other route on which a high-speed service was a possibility – the 'Cascades Corridor', linking Eugene, Oregon with Vancouver, British Columbia – and in 1999 a 125mph 'Talgo' train was put in service on this route, aimed primarily at the business traveller. Each train seated 268 passengers overall, and had both a bistro car with a curving counter, and a dining car next door to it.[35]

High speed finally arrived on the North East Corridor with the start of the 150mph Washington-Boston 'Acela Express' service in July 2000. Each six-car consist included one First Class car, four Business Class cars and one diner; services included telephone, fax, video, and computer outlets, and groups of seats could be reserved for business meetings.[36] The First Class passengers have an at-seat meal service prepared behind a curtain in a small galley at the end of the car; the 'diner' – a bistro, purposely sparse in furnishing to prevent computer-users taking it over for the entire journey – serves the four business cars.[31]

So much for the cars – what's the food like?

Thus, despite its recurring cash crises, Amtrak had by late 2000 acquired a modern – or modernised – catering vehicle fleet. But what of the quality of the food and menus offered to its patrons across this period? How did that relate to the state of affairs immediately before 1971? Bob Johnston has divided the sequence of events into six major periods, and, as an overall summary, his notes can hardly be bettered[31]:

'1971-73: Except for Penn Central on the 'Broadway Limited' (New York-Chicago) and North East Corridor, dining car departments maintain what they were doing prior to the Amtrak take-over. Quality varies widely between operations.
1974-79: Amtrak takes over all dining car operation. Tries to provide full meal service on most long-distance trains using old equipment. Quality is steady, but gradually improves, although cars are about at the end of their useful lives and this causes problems. Ridership increases due to energy crises.
1980-82: New "Superliner" equipment arrives in

the west, single-level equipment gets converted to head-end power, new crockery ordered. Everything gets more appealing. However, President Reagan tries to zero out Amtrak in 1981 and 1982 budgets, so at the end of October 1981 the company switches to spartan menus and paper plates so it can cut service staffs. 1982 was rock bottom.'

When Johnston says that 1982 was 'rock bottom', he really means it; in his June 2001 Amtrak review for *Trains* magazine, he describes a 'dinner from Hell' on the 'Lake Shore Limited' in November of that year:

'Bare bones, please, and while you're at it, hold the courtesy … steak was on the menu, but mine was tough, overcooked, and served on a wafer-thin paper plate that disintegrated under the plastic knife supplied with the plastic fork whose tines broke off in the meat. All this was brought to my table on a tray, and "Mister, you'd better pay me now while I'm here, because I'm only allowed to drop this off, not ask you if you want anything else. And pick up your trash when you get out."

By contrast, however, and to show how far things later improved, he also recounts in the same article a summer 1996 journey from Chicago to Seattle on the 'Pioneer' during the recovery period under Tom Downs described below:

'It featured smoked salmon and souvenir wine glasses in the sleeper, checkered tablecloths in the dining car, and another diner converted to be a "Horizons West Lounge" with a fun Western motif – a cross-country delight not seen since the Ranch Car on GN's "Empire Builder" or the "Traveler's Rest" on NP's "North Coast Limited".'[37]

He continues his summary:

'1983-94: W. Graham Claytor Jr becomes President of Amtrak and dining car service is put on a sounder [financial] footing by making "meals included" with all sleeping car accommodations. Company goes to menu cycles so people don't have to eat the same thing all the time; gradually upgrades all the food quality.
1995-98: Claytor leaves in cash crisis (then passes away from cancer). New President Tom Downs establishes three business units, Northeast, Amtrak West and Intercity (all long-distance trains except West Coast)). Everything is notched up. The "Coast

Starlight" (Los Angeles-Seattle) on Amtrak West offers wine-tasting, extensive menus. Real regionalization sets in – catfish on the "City of New Orleans", barbecue on "Texas Eagle", etc. Also, full diners make appearance for first time on non-overnight trains in North Carolina, California and state of Washington thanks to state involvement and funds.'

Johnston subsequently expanded on these sections in the following notes[31]:

'After the mid-'70s ... day trains always had snack bars serving sandwiches, pop, drinks, etc... In the North East corridor, First Class "club service" featured meals at seats, but there were no diners... Except for that First Class at-seat club service ... introduced in the early 1980s, no "cook-chill" technology was established until the late 1990s... Everything in the diners was cooked to order.'

In conclusion:

'**1999 to present:** Re-centralization but so far hasn't killed the flair started in the mid-1990's on long distance trains. Regionalization still exists [however] because the guy running the show came from the "Coast Starlight"... Beautiful dining car on the new Talgos.'

The details of how Amtrak's food service 'walked a crooked mile' can be seen by following the menus of the 'South West Chief' (originally the 'Super Chief'). Six menus in all are involved.

The original train was one of those on which standards were kept as high as possible. The menu for luncheon on 1 June 1972 (reproduced here) demonstrates how in Amtrak's earliest days, local policies and traditions simply carried on. Though shorter than the pre-war 'Super Chief' offerings, it has not degenerated into the all-sandwiches-and-burgers of some late 1960s menus; there is a nice balance between table d'hôte choices, salads, and quite special sandwich offerings. Clearly the standards of the 'Chief' are still being upheld

However, by 1973 a decline has set in. A typical luncheon menu (not illustrated) is very different from only a year earlier. The train name is no longer shown, and while one cooked 'old time Super Chief favourite' appears on the card, sandwiches and burgers now dominate. Our third example (again not illustrated) jumps a decade, to 1985. The train is now once again the 'Southwest Chief', and the menu bears the war bonnet and arrows sigil. However, it is still quite severely limited – four breakfast choices, four lunch choices, only one (Albacore tuna) a true entrée, and five dinner choices. The dinner dishes, however, show some improvement in culinary quality: Spanish chicken on a bed of wild rice, for example, sounds particularly attractive.

The fifth in our 'Southwest Chief' menu series takes us on another ten years, to 1995, and the improvement is truly remarkable. This menu in a 'generic' menu, but, as we can see, with a distinct regional flavour – catfish with tomato salsa, steamed vegetables with brown rice, and a green pepper topping to the beefburger. The range is not all that much greater than ten years earlier, but the stylish presentation and the more varied cuisine make it a completely different experience.

Most important, perhaps, Amtrak has now

This 'Super Chief' menu from the early Amtrak period, in a brown and beige colourway with regional paintings on the outside covers (not shown), is still being produced, as is the food, to the standards of the old Santa Fé line. *Bob Johnston collection*

introduced menu cycles, with certain dishes being varied to ensure patrons do not get 'flavour-tired'. This menu is the second one of its cycle; its predecessor had Spanish omelette as a breakfast choice, at lunch it had mushroom and mozzarella topping on the burger, a grilled cheese club sandwich instead of a hot turkey open one, a different salad, and sesame oriental noodles instead of fettuccini marinara. At dinner there was a different sauce on the steak, a different finish to the chicken, and salmon fettuccini instead of catfish; the vegetarian option was cheese tortellini with pesto. The children's menu and the cake were different too.

By 2001, the date of our final menu, recovery to old 'Super Chief' excellence is virtually complete. Presented in a cover replete outside with spectacular desert scenes, and with the train route mapped out on the inside, this menu illustrates that although Amtrak is centralised as a business, food and style regionalisation is most certainly not dead. 'Cook-chill' technology has now arrived, but much is still finished – or even completely cooked – on-train, as the Omelette Bar service added to the breakfast menu. That menu has got longer, too, and even returned to something like its pre-war 'heartiness', with a steak and eggs option. The luncheon selection is much more varied, and also more regional, including a chicken fajita and a stunning lobster ravioli, while the dinner selection (illustrated here) – half as long again as before – is both thoroughly regional (with jambalaya and red snapper) and elegantly *haute cuisine*.

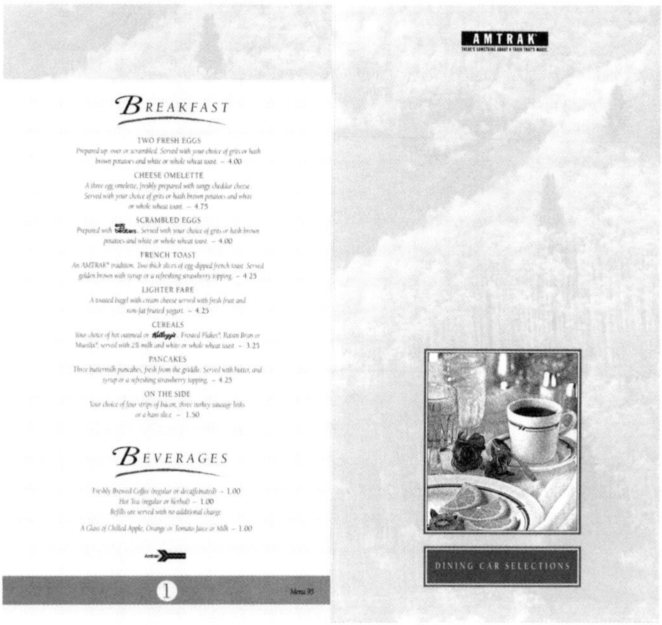

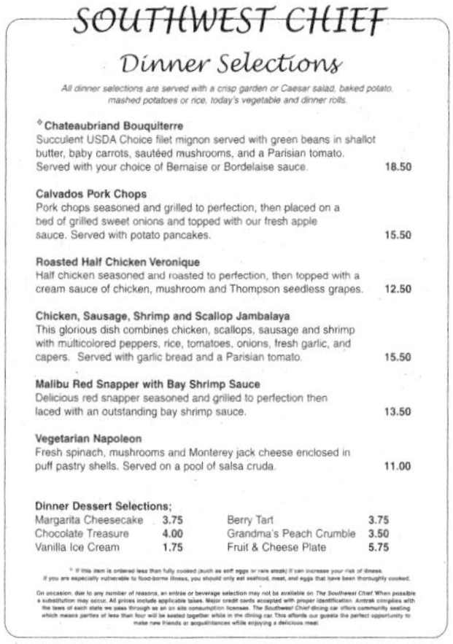

It took time, and the prices had to go up, but Amtrak got there in the end. It is, in fact, probably no exaggeration to say that of all the train companies, Amtrak had, until the 2003/4 financial reverses (discussed in the next chapter), come closest to re-establishing the old idea of 'dining at speed' as a form of luxurious magic.

Below **The cuisine and presentation of this 1995 menu are much more interesting than the one ten years before. Most important, it is now one of a cycle rather than being endlessly repeated.** *Bob Johnston collection*

BREAKFAST

TWO FRESH EGGS
Prepared up, over or scrambled. Served with your choice of grits or hash brown potatoes and white or whole wheat toast. – 4.00

CHEESE OMELETTE
A three egg omelette, freshly prepared with tangy cheddar cheese. Served with your choice of grits or hash brown potatoes and white or whole wheat toast. – 4.75

SCRAMBLED EGGS
Prepared with egg beaters. Served with your choice of grits or hash brown potatoes and white or whole wheat toast. – 4.00

FRENCH TOAST
An AMTRAK® tradition. Two thick slices of egg-dipped french toast. Served golden brown with syrup or a refreshing strawberry topping. – 4.25

LIGHTER FARE
A toasted bagel with cream cheese served with fresh fruit and non-fat fruited yogurt. – 4.25

CEREALS
Your choice of hot oatmeal or Kellogg's Frosted Flakes®, Raisin Bran or Mueslix® served with 2% milk and white or whole wheat toast – 3.25

PANCAKES
Three buttermilk pancakes, fresh from the griddle. Served with butter, and syrup or a refreshing strawberry topping. – 4.25

ON THE SIDE
Your choice of four strips of bacon, three turkey sausage links or a ham slice – 1.50

BEVERAGES

Freshly Brewed Coffee (regular or decaffeinated) – 1.00
Hot Tea (regular or herbal) – 1.00
Refills are served with no additional charge

A Glass of Chilled Apple, Orange or Tomato Juice or Milk – 1.00

1 Menu 95

AMTRAK

DINING CAR SELECTIONS

Below **This final 'Southwest Chief' menu is longer, more regional, and more *haute cuisine*-oriented than perhaps anything since the days of Fred Harvey.** *Bob Johnston collection*

SOUTHWEST CHIEF

Dinner Selections

All dinner selections are served with a crisp garden or Caesar salad, baked potato, mashed potatoes or rice, today's vegetable and dinner rolls.

***Chateaubriand Bouquiterre** Succulent USDA Choice filet mignon served with green beans in shallot butter, baby carrots, sautéed mushrooms, and a Parisian tomato. Served with your choice of Bernaise or Bordelaise sauce.	18.50
Calvados Pork Chops Pork chops seasoned and grilled to perfection, then placed on a bed of grilled sweet onions and topped with our fresh apple sauce. Served with potato pancakes.	15.50
Roasted Half Chicken Veronique Half chicken seasoned and roasted to perfection, then topped with a cream sauce of chicken, mushroom and Thompson seedless grapes.	12.50
Chicken, Sausage, Shrimp and Scallop Jambalaya This glorious dish combines chicken, scallops, sausage and shrimp with multicolored peppers, rice, tomatoes, onions, fresh garlic, and capers. Served with garlic bread and a Parisian tomato.	15.50
Malibu Red Snapper with Bay Shrimp Sauce Delicious red snapper seasoned and grilled to perfection then laced with an outstanding bay shrimp sauce.	13.50
Vegetarian Napoleon Fresh spinach, mushrooms and Monterey jack cheese enclosed in puff pastry shells. Served on a pool of salsa cruda.	11.00

Dinner Dessert Selections;

Margarita Cheesecake	3.75	Berry Tart	3.75
Chocolate Treasure	4.00	Grandma's Peach Crumble	3.50
Vanilla Ice Cream	1.75	Fruit & Cheese Plate	5.75

* If this item is ordered less than fully cooked (such as soft eggs or rare steak) it can increase your risk of illness. If you are especially vulnerable to food-borne illness, you should only eat seafood, meat, and eggs that have been thoroughly cooked.

On occasion, due to any number of reasons, an entrée or beverage selection may not be available on *The Southwest Chief*. When possible a substitution may occur. All prices include applicable taxes. Major credit cards accepted with proper identification. Amtrak complies with the laws of each state we pass through as an on site consumption licensee. *The Southwest Chief* dining car offers community seating which means parties of less than four will be seated together while in the dining car. This affords our guests the perfect opportunity to make new friends or acquaintances while enjoying a delicious meal.

8
PRIVATISATION AND AFTER

Has the idea run its course?

For most of the time from its initial origins, the main characteristics of the idea of 'dining at speed' – social inclusiveness but not classlessness, comfort, fine cooking, and the achievement of a sense of 'train magic', a relaxing well-being on the part of the diners – remained constant. But with the coming of an age of air and road competition, in which time is valued very differently, and the development of new culinary technologies, those characteristics have changed more in the last 30 years than they had in the previous hundred. Does this mean that the day of the on-train 'dining experience' is now over? How has it been affected by the 1996-97 privatisations? What are the portents for the future?

From InterCity to TOCs

UK rail privatisation in 1996-97 had two effects on the situation described in Chapter 7. First, except for trolley and buffet services in the old Southern Region, the catering staff became Train Operating Companies' employees, leaving OBS – now privatised as Rail Gourmet – dealing with the menu development, procurement and food supply logistics. Second, instead of procurement, supply and quality control policy being centralised, Rail Gourmet now worked to the quality specifications of each TOC, though the 'cook-chill', procurement and delivery control *processes* remained centrally managed.

But there have been two major additional effects of privatisation. One is that Rail Gourmet now provides catering support services in other countries as well as Britain, in particular Spain (where Rail Gourmet España has the on-board service contract as well as those for production and logistics[1]), Denmark, Holland and Belgium. The other is the very much greater diversity of offers from one train company to another – far beyond the range in former InterCity days.

There are several reasons for this diversity. First, each TOC operates routes of particular lengths with particular major competitors, affecting their strategic decisions as to what to offer in order to attract and retain custom. Second, the offer may be intended to produce an unique brand image; thus both GNER and Virgin run between London and Glasgow, but GNER deliberately cultivates the 'traditional' image of on-board dining as a walk-in sit-down service for all, while Virgin equally deliberately cultivates the airline-related image of at-seat meals included in the premium ticket price. As David Small says, 'every train operator has different values.'

The nature of the offer may also depend on expected loadings and available rolling-stock and on what solution the company takes to the problem of on-train catering profitability. But especially, the diverse range of post-privatisation offers depends on the social trends that mean there is now not one consistent on-train dining market, but rather a complex segmented market, in which the fluidity of contemporary attitudes both to simply eating and to the more special event called 'dining' mean that customer desires are almost individualised. This diversity makes it very difficult to give a simple answer to the question 'How far does the historical idea of "dining at speed" still survive?'

Those TOCs that offer dining car or at-seat services, however, seem to have a number of elements in common. First, they all appear to see their offers as 'added value' – a means of attracting customers to use the train rather than the car, or their trains rather than others. They all also claim that the particular kind of service they offer is what their customers want:

'The consumer does demand that there are refreshments available on the train, particularly our business travellers and First Class passengers, so we … offer it the best way we can.'[2]

Second, while all talk about adding value, they all shy away from the notion of offering anything resembling 'luxury' – possibly a carry-over from the attitudes described in Chapter 7. This is true even when the offer is described in terms that most listeners would associate with luxuriousness, as in this example from David Crome of First Great Western:

> 'Luxury is not a very 2001 word, is it? I think we're talking about a high standard of service, a high standard of product, added value. Luxury? Not in the historical sense, but I think we are cosseting people. I think we're talking premium rather than luxury, so the quality is high, the level of service is high, people are cosseted, looked after, they're well fed; as a consequence they feel good about this as a mode of travel, and it'll become a habit.'[3]

Third, all see their offers in very much more hard-nosed cash-flow terms than has commonly been the case in the past. Thus, financial and logistic constraints are cited to account for such different policies as First Great Western's restriction of full dining-car services to its main West of England business trains, Anglia's 'light lunch' offers on its midday diners, and Midland Mainline's failure to open its First Premier cars to Standard passengers at times when they are running almost empty (the point here is that at other times of the day they are filled by full-fare-paying passengers).

In terms of their detailed offers, however, though the companies vary considerably, they fall into two major groups – those that offer a traditional walk-up dining car service on at least some of their trains, available to both First and Standard passengers subject to capacity (Anglia, First Great Western, GNER), and those that offer a fare-inclusive at-seat catering service to First Class passengers only (Eurostar, Midland Mainline in First Premier, Virgin Trains). Broadly speaking, the first group offer a service that at its best is almost indistinguishable in quality from the traditional 'dining at speed' offer, while the second group do not.

The 'dining companies': Anglia, Great Western, GNER

These companies pride themselves on the quality of their food and their menus. GNER probably operates the largest number of full dining services, and FGW, as noted above, the fewest. All three stress their commitment to fresh, locally sourced produce…

> 'We're not like the West Coast. We've still got chefs on board, we source a range of products, we then pass those now on to a third party middleman [Rail Gourmet] who then looks after the logistics to get it to train-side, where we take it back again. We make a lot of use of regional food: we source our sausages from Thirsk, our meat supplies all come from the Vale of York. We make a big issue about our local suppliers.'[4]

…and to high-quality on-board finishing:

> 'Without wanting to boil up bones for soups on board, we can say quite legitimately that everything is freshly cooked… Any of the meats we buy in a fillet form or a cut that's going to be very quickly finished off, so any starter can be made in 10 minutes, a main course needs to be a 20-minute maximum … the main product is recognisable as freshly cooked.'[5]

The result in practice is demonstrated by the FGW 'Golden Hind' dinner menu, in which the blend of international cuisine (Thai prawn kebabs, fillet of escolar) and regional specialities (West Country steaks and cheeses) is both distinguished and distinctive

All three companies also make the point that a formal dining offer, in today's segmented market, is not sufficient to attract everyone, particularly among leisure travellers and particularly at lunchtime, where the by now 'traditional' dining car patrons – the business persons – are almost totally absent. Anglia and GNER offer special light lunch

Top right The cover of First Great Western's Pullman Restaurant menu for 16 February 2001. Note the unusual layout (and the use of the word 'Pullman' for what is actually a classic dining car service). The menu comes at an all-in price of between £15 and £25.50, depending on the number of courses taken. Coffee is inclusive in all cases. *Author's collection, courtesy of David Crome*

Rest of page One of the pioneering Pullman Bistro menus: patrons can order any item(s) from the menu, from soup or a baguette to a freshly cooked sirloin steak, singly or in combination, though a simple three-course set lunch is also available. This service gives a quite different meaning to the word 'Bistro' from that offered on Eurostar! *Author's collection, courtesy of David Crome*

STARTERS AND BAGUETTES

Onion Soup with Parmesan crumpets
£4.25

Freshly Prepared Baguettes
• Smoked Salmon
• Bacon and Cheese
• Steak and Onions
Served with side salad
£6.95

MAIN COURSES

West Country Sirloin Steak
with Mustard Butter
£11.95

Chicken Olives
with a Savoury Fruit Stuffing and an Orange Jus
£11.95

Potato and Caramelised Red Onion Tart
with Carrot and Coriander Cream
£10.95

All Main Courses are Served with Vegetables and Potatoes

DESSERTS

Bitter Chocolate Marquise
with White Chocolate Sauce
£3.95

A West Country Cheese Board
£4.75

Coffee and Chocolate

SPECIAL 3 COURSE SET MENU AT £9.95

Garlic Bread

Corned Beef Hash

Chocolate Tart with Crème Fraiche

Coffee

menus to attract custom at this time (though this makes stocking rather more complex); FGW has recently developed an even more radical offer, the 'Pullman Bistro', which involves refurbishing the buffet and trolley services so that customers can get espresso or cappuccino coffees, gourmet sandwiches or fresh, non-microwaved hot snacks. This upgraded buffet service would also be able to offer light, informal meals in the restaurant section of the catering car. One of the new Bistro menus is illustrated here.

Another 'more modern' mode of service, launched on FGW in February 2001 on four trains but intended eventually to operate on 300 trains a week, is an innovation to be called the 'Travelling Chef', which David Crome described as follows:

'Now these Travelling Chefs … make quality snack food for people. It's served at-seat to people in First Class by the First Class Service Host, and it's sold packaged up over the bar to people who walk up to the counter. The principle of this is that people aren't necessarily in the market for the £15-£20 meal, particularly outside of the real niche business traveller, [but] there's a … leisure commuter customer who maybe wants to spend three, four, five, six pounds on a quality snack that's *made for them*, and this is absolutely made to order. That's where I see the future of freshly cooked food on trains. This will reach a much wider audience.'[3]

For these companies, then, 'dining at speed' is most certainly alive and well, and likely to continue, both in its traditional form (though increasingly business-market-oriented) and in a number of more informal new variations, designed to reach segments of the leisure or Standard Class market who for whatever reason seem to believe the conventional restaurant car meal is 'not for them'.

There is, however, one complicating factor – the uncertain nature of TOC franchises. Even as this book was being readied for press, the Strategic Rail Authority announced that from April 2004 the Anglia franchise discussed above would be offered to the parent company of Midland Mainline. Theoretically, this could mean the new 'Greater Anglia' moving from its traditional walk-up dining service to an at-seat service of the sort described below – though since the SRA also announced that all existing 900 Anglia staff (presumably including managers) would transfer to the new company, it may be that the existing policy will after all continue.

The 'at-seat purveyors': Eurostar, Midland Mainline, Virgin Trains

All three of these companies decided to go down a quite different road, offering a fare-inclusive at-seat catering service to First Class only (in MM's case, initially to First Premier only) and making no provision for Standard Class dining other than via purchases from the buffet/bistro. In at least two cases – Virgin and Eurostar – this was occasioned by a deliberate decision to offer 'added value' directly analogous to that of their main competitor airlines; but other reasons were also adduced – in Virgin's case that of what the added First Class ticket actually gave in return.

'We happen to believe that the provision of … food is an added value that the customer pays for with a First Class ticket. You pay your ticket price, and then you have a wallet-free zone in First Class, which means you can have your breakfast, tea or coffee, and your snack food and drinks all day long.'[5]

And associated with this, for Eurostar and MM, a sense of what the hurried businessman actually needs by way of catering:

'We do not aim to provide a "dining experience": we aim to provide an efficient food service – fuel for the businessman.'[6]

'Bearing in mind that today's business era is so fast, so hectic, people have to eat at some stage, and they find it a lot easier to eat if they're travelling on a train. They don't have to stop, they're still moving, they can work. They have a table, they've got their laptop, they've got their telephone … if they can get a meal at the same time, and it's cleared and they can carry on working, they're still "working" even when having a chance to eat.'[7]

The sheer volume of catering that this involves, when at full stretch, implies a very high dependence on 'cook-chill' regeneration (standard on the French TGVs, on which Eurostar design was based), and this in turn, at least initially, led to the offers by these three companies being noticeably different from the traditional dining car meal (except perhaps for the 'Great British Breakfast'). Thus on Virgin, once breakfast was over, there was effectively only an at-

The Virgin West Coast offer menu starting 29 August 2001 was styled with a 'Mediterranean' theme, including dishes with a Provençale, Italian and Moroccan flavour. Note the staff guide to pronunciation, and the precise instructions as to how to present the food on the trolley – and on how much to give each customer! *Author's collection, courtesy of Rail Gourmet and Virgin Trains*

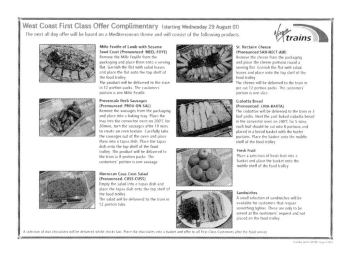

seat snack service, though that could be quite sophisticated and was often 'themed' to create variety, as in the sample Chef's Guide Card illustrated here.

Midland Mainline's menus likewise offered an interesting variety of ethnic food, including some hot dishes, but one could not make up a conventional dining car meal from the selection; the assumption was that the customer would at most request a series of substantial snacks. Eurostar, however, did provide a menu offer laid out as a formal lunch or dinner menu, with dishes such as Hoi Sin duck, steamed salmon in hollandaise sauce, veal Marengo, or bitter cherry mousse with meringue, that certainly looked from the page to be evidence of *haute cuisine*. But the problem in this case was the actual at-seat service, which because of the volume of meals concerned inevitably involved high-speed delivery in pre-packed format from trolleys, and downgraded the entire experience to the level of a not-too-good Economy Class airline meal. These three providers, then, were certainly providing something their customers wanted, but it equally certainly wasn't a traditional dining experience.

However, things, as always, are not as simple as that, and in the past couple of years these offers, too, have begun to change. Midland Mainline and Virgin are both in the process of acquiring new rolling-stock, and Eurostar has announced an upgrade and re-launch of its London-Paris and Brussels service, and a new service direct to Avignon. In each case, this has led to a proposal to change the company's catering offer.

In the case of Eurostar, neither stock nor offer style

is likely to change, but the company is currently looking at including a variety of catering upgrades, such as an 'extended meal service' in Club Class for travellers interested in on-train fine dining, which could be booked and paid for in advance, and a complimentary Tapas bar service in Premium First as an alternative to the regular meal.[6]

Some pointers as to these changes are already visible. In January 2002 Eurostar issued a new menu series aimed at providing 'seasonal dishes with a regional twist'. One of the winter menus is reproduced here: the game casserole and the North African starter demonstrate a real attempt to produce a themed menu appropriate to the time of year. The Premium First menus (not shown) have a choice of starters and an additional alternative main course (roast guinea fowl stuffed with grapes and pine kernels), and include finer wines. In summer 2002 Eurostar also started a new London-Avignon service with new menus and catering arrangements.[8] The standard of cuisine on these new menus is now reported to be very good indeed.[9]

Midland Mainline is revising its catering strategy to fit a fleet of 28 new 'Voyager' sets, to be marshalled in four- or nine-car consists, due for delivery in 2004. Each driving car will also contain a galley, and on the nine-car sets these galleys will be capable, working in combination, of providing 100 breakfasts inside 45 minutes. There will also be a buffet towards the centre of the train. Duncan Fraser, in interview, commented on the changes to MM's catering offers that this development would be likely to bring about as follows:

'We currently have First Premier and First, but the number of First seats on the new train will

Lime and ginger grilled Haloumi cheese served
with tabbouleh salad and a green sweet chilli dressing

A mixed winter casserole of game,
consisting of venison, pheasant, rabbit and pigeon
served with roasted root vegetables and a herb dumpling
or
Tuna, lime and coriander rosti cake
served with lemongrass and coriander flavoured rice,
sugarsnap peas and a julienne of peppers

Caramel mousse with caramelised apples

Worcester Gold is a rich, strong tasting
Jersey milk cheese

Haloumi grillé au citron vert et au gingembre,
taboulé sauce au piment vert doux

Daube de gibier d'hiver,
comprenant chevreuil, faisan, lapin et pigeon
avec légumes grillés et quenelle aux fines herbes
ou
Galette rösti au thon, au citron vert et à la coriandre,
riz aromatisé à la citronnelle et à la coriandre,
pois gourmands et julienne de poivrons

Mousse au caramel et pommes caramélisées

Worcester Gold est un fromage de caractère fort
fait à partir de lait de vache jersiaise

Met limoen en gember gegrilde haloumi-kaas geserveerd
met tabbouleh-salade en een zoete groene chilidressing

Een gemengde winterschotel met hertenvlees,
fazant, konijn en duif, opgediend met geroosterde
wortelgroenten en een kruidenballetje
of
Rösti met tonijn, limoen en koriander,
geserveerd met citroengras-korianderrijst,
sugarsnaps en paprikajulienne

Karamelmousse met gekarameliseerde appels

Worcester Gold is een rijke en scherpe
kaas van Jerseymelk

01/2002 - LWO - F - DNR - 1

Eurostar's new Winter 2002 menu range, revised and
upgraded to offer some degree of themed dining. This is
the dinner menu, identical with lunch except for the
cheese course. Reports by colleagues label the food as
excellent. *Author's collection, courtesy of Rob Mulder and
Eurostar*

be 102. We want to offer all of those First seats
a meal option – our Premier option. So every
one of those 102 seats on an eight-coach train
will be able to have a meal, and it will be
inclusive.'[10]

This sounds like a simple increase in availability –
'more of the same'. Virgin's new 'Voyager' and
'Pendolino' stock, however, will actually involve a
substantial change in the offer. Indeed, a recent
article by Brian Perren for *Modern Railways* describes
it as no less than 'Virgin's catering revolution'[11].

First, what Perren calls the 'cramped and
claustrophobic takeaway bars' of existing HST stock
will be replaced by a 'retail shop [that] will carry a
wide range of food and beverage items ... as well as
books and CDs', and will be positioned so that no
Standard Class passengers are more than two or three
carriages' walk away instead of right at the First Class
'barrier' end of Standard, as on the present HSTs.
Virgin Trains' press release of February 2003
indicates the increased range of food on offer:

'Selections [of sandwiches] include tuna and
peppers on mixed pepper bread, chicken Caesar
salad in Parmesan bread and smoked salmon
with lemon and cream cheese in a dill bagel...
For a more substantial snack customers can
choose an Aberdeen Angus cheese-topped
ciabatta burger with caramelised onions or wild
mushroom risotto, while those with a sweet
tooth might like to try Papa Haydn's Pecan Pie.'

It is in the at-seat service to First Class, however, that
the biggest revolutions are due to appear. On cross-
country, a 'Club Class' coach in each 'Voyager' unit
provides at-seat drinks and light snacks from 'a small
galley at the end of the coach'. Each coach
accommodates 26 passengers under the charge of a
dedicated hostess, rather in the manner of Premium
First on Eurostar. Inevitably, the small size of the
'Voyager' galleys means that only pre-prepared tray
snacks are available, but this is still a vast
improvement on the coffee-and-sandwich offer
previously available in First on those routes!

On the main West Coast routes, however, the
'Pendolino' sets are designed to serve hot breakfasts
at-seat to up to 150 First Class passengers from a
galley at the *forward* end of the train, immediately
behind the driver's cab and luggage space. As the
position of this galley means that no corridor space is
required, the kitchen area extends the full width of
the vehicle, allowing the kitchen designers to
include a four-ring boiling plate, a large grill, and a
convection oven. There is also a dishwasher, a large
freezer, and an integral refrigerator, which largely
overcomes the hitherto major cost problem of
keeping food. The storage space holds 16 trolleys –
seven each for food products and meal service, two
each for drinks and food warming.

This vastly enlarged kitchen design has enabled
Virgin to radically overhaul its First Class at-seat
dining experience in two main ways. First, the ever-
popular full English breakfast will be supplemented by
lighter alternatives to provide a wider range of choice

– sausage and bacon butties, continental pastries and toast. Second, and perhaps even more important, the post-breakfast snack meal option will now be able to be changed a further four times each day – a brunch cycle (continuing the bacon butties) from 9.30 to 12 noon, a lunchtime offer (12.00 to 16.30) of filled rolls, nibbles, cakes and pastries (not unlike the original HST service), an aperitif service with nibbles, a choice of three light snacks, and tea and coffee from 16.30 to 20.30, and after 20.30 and at weekends a late-night 'clip box' offer of four separate food items delivered to your seat. Thus the return business passenger will be assured of a different meal experience in each direction – and the same enlarged kitchen capacity means that the menu can be rotated every two weeks rather than every four as at present.

Thus as far as the UK train operating companies are concerned, the idea of 'dining at speed' if anything seems to be increasing its comeback overall, but still in a much more diversified form than prior to privatisation.

Mainland Europe

As I said in Chapter 7, developments in mainland Europe are much more of a 'seamless robe' both before and after the 1990s than in either Britain or the USA. Accordingly I have delayed discussing them all until this final chapter. As we shall see, there are essentially just three contemporary on-train dining paradigms in mainland Europe – the French, the German and the Spanish.

The post-war concept of high-speed travel in mainland Europe can be dated to the TEEs, but the first serious technological embodiment of those ideas was the French TGVs (*Trains à Grande Vitesse*). The first tranche of these began working on the Paris-Lyons route in 1981. Cruising speed on the special high-speed track was 260kmph (160mph), and Lyons was reached from Paris in just 2 hours. Like the 125s, the trains were an immediate success; by November of their year of introduction they had carried more than a million passengers and were running at full capacity.[12]

Catering on the TGVs was – and indeed still is – in many ways similar to catering on Eurostar. Second Class has no meals service, though it does have what Behrend called a 'bar car' (Wessner refers to it as a 'bistro'). First Class has an at-seat meal service, served airline-style from a small galley in the end trailer. Space, as on Eurostar, limits the equipment strictly to that for regenerating 'cook-chill' food. Behrend quotes a typical 1982 lunch offer as

'…a cold entrée such as ham or smoked salmon, a hot *plat du jour* with vegetables or a steak … followed by cheeses and a patisserie… The TGV has a repertoire of 28 different four-course table d'hôte luncheons, to provide a different one daily, but supper is à la carte.'[13]

One important difference between that meal and those on Eurostar would appear to be the service quality, 'real china and Christofle silverware'. Another was that the meal was not included in the ticket price: the four-course lunch described cost 95 francs, supper, being à la carte, varied in cost, but was usually in the same overall region. Wines – Behrend lists the choices as Rosé, Beaujolais Villages, Côtes du Rhône and St Emilion –were 16-24 francs a half bottle. Until recently, TGV catering was still charged separately, though it was more usual to pay for it in advance when buying your ticket[29]: but now it too is included in the ticket price, provided since November 2002 by CIWL to what Brian Perren describes as 'good value for money … superior to what you normally get on short-haul "Club Class" airlines'[14].

The quest for high-speed trains, and the construction of dedicated high-speed lines, was also going on during this period elsewhere in mainland Europe, most notably in Germany. Meanwhile some other EU member states, particularly Italy and Spain, developed trains (the 'Pendolino' and the 'Talgo') that could run at high speeds on suitably upgraded normal lines. The various projects were coordinated under the European High Speed Rail Network document of 1989, which

'called for … 9,000 kilometres of new track and 15,000 kilometres of upgraded track … [to] increase ridership fourfold between 1995 and 2025.'[15]

Catering on the various other new high-speed trains, however, did not necessarily follow the TGV model. Germany in particular was loath to give up its 'unclassified' Speisewagen policy, and on its various marques of ICE (*Inter-City Europ*) it retained a walk-down restaurant car service open to all.

This tradition has been continued on the latest ICE3 sets put into service from 2000; the *Modern Railways* report on the multi-current version purchased by Netherlands Railways in May that year lists the eight-car consist as 'three First Class, four Second Class and a bar-restaurant car'[16]. Italy's 'Pendolinos', though initially offering only a 'bistro' in the ETRY500 series of 1990-92, which was severely influenced by airline styling, have, since the ETR460 series of 1993, also offered a kitchen/restaurant car.[17]. On the 'Pendolino', snacks are complimentary in First Class.[18]

The third version of contemporary European high-speed catering is that provided on board the Spanish 'Talgos'. Operated as well as serviced by Rail Gourmet España, this has been claimed to be the best train food currently available on regular passenger services in Europe.[1] There are three classes – Club (First), 'Preferente' (Business Class), and Tourist. Club and Preferente meal service is at-seat and included in the ticket price, though the menus are different. Tourist passengers do not have a fare-inclusive meal service; as on Eurostar, 'they should visit the cafeteria coach'[19]. In Club and Preferente, meals are trolley-served, though the desserts are served separately. All food is 'cook-chilled' on shore and regenerated on board. But what is offered is a substantial four-course meal with several 'Entremeses' (something like our 'hors d'oeuvres') and a choice of main dishes and dessert. Menus are themed: they remain the same for lunch (Almuerzo) and dinner (Cena), but the themes change weekly, and within each theme three menus operate during that week. Menus are also route-specific for Madrid-Seville ('Club Al Andalus') and Madrid-Malaga-Algeciras.

The menu illustrated is the third of the 'Club Al Andalus' (First Class, Madrid-Seville) cycle for 10-16 April 2002. The cover is headed 'Semanas Gastronómicas' ('Themed Gourmet Weeks'), and this is Semana Regional Madrileña (Madrid Regional Cookery Week); the back cover has a note by Rail Gourmet's senior chef on the region's cuisine. Soup and dessert remain the same on both menus, but there is a complete change of 'entremeses' – a tapas-like selection of several salads, patés and smoked meats or fish – and main dishes, which in each case offer a choice of white meat or fish in authentic Madrilenian recipes; the millefeuille of salmon sounds particularly stylish.

Food quality thus currently seems assured on European services. The questions for mainland Europe are, will this quality be maintained in the future? And will the old-style Speisewagen survive, or will the less sociable at-seat tray-service provision win out through sheer cost-effectiveness? One thing about which there is no question is that the number and journey length of high-speed trains and links will continue to increase – Amsterdam-Brussels will be completed in 2005, Karlsruhe-Basel in 2007, and further ahead still there is the prospect of Amsterdam-Hannover-Berlin.[20]

For the answers to the two catering questions, signals appear to be mixed. In terms of the immediate

This menu is from the 'Club Al Andalus' (First Class, Madrid-Seville) menu cycle for 10-16 April 2002, themed around Madrid regional cookery in the 'gastronomic weeks' series. Note the tapas-like 'Entremeses' and the offer of 'café 100% natural'. The English menu to the left is part of the original – 'Club Al Andalus' menus are multi-lingual, and English has been selected as the EU language non-speakers of Spanish are most likely to be able to read. *Author's collection, courtesy of Rail Gourmet España*

situation, Tim Locke of 'Europe 2002' returned an answer that is more self-contradictory than reassuring…

'Most long-distance trains in Europe have dining cars serving full meals and/or buffet cars selling drinks and snacks. There is an increasing tendency for refreshments to be served from a trolley wheeled through the train… Quite a few services serve full meals only to First Class passengers. In some countries, especially in Spain, the cost of a meal is included in the First Class fare. Dining cars often have set times for full meals. Buffets are usually open to both classes and food is served for longer periods…'[21]

… while David Small sees at-seat provision firmly taking over, despite its less sociable ambience, not only for cost-efficiency but also for company-customer relations:

'Certainly there's restaurant meals, but for the most part they're actually served at-seat and therefore I think the idea of a restaurant car as such is probably going to be history. You can have an interaction with the customer much more readily if you build something into the ticket, or it's payable in advance or whatever. Reaching out to more people and actually having that staff-customer interaction in some respects is more important than what you do with it. So instead of saying "We've got this restaurant car and you can only come in if we've got seats", we're actually saying that every seat can be a restaurant, and serving something up that is restaurant standard.'[22]

But there are signs that the old-style dining car may be due for a revival. The proposed German ICE4 would have 180 more passenger seats than ICE3, but in other respects would retain the same general consist plan, which still includes an unclassed Speisewagen.[23] And even more significantly, *Today's Railways* reported in December 2001 that the existing EuroCity service between Berlin and Warsaw was about to be 're-branded as the Berlin-Warsaw Express, in a new blue/grey livery'. It would run three times a day and would have a six-car consist – one First, one diner, and four Third.[24] With such a consist structure, the diner clearly could not possibly be going to be open to First Class passengers only. Finally, *European Railways* for October-November 2002 reported (pp45-46) that a 'new

commercial offensive' by Austrian Railways will include marshalling a dining car in the middle of each long-distance train; withdrawn diners will be re-instated and upgraded, and others purchased from Germany, to make up the numbers required.

United States

The USA entered 2002 with its North East Corridor trains at last benefiting both from high speed and a 'cook-chill' technology at-seat meals service, its long-distance dining services almost completely restored to their former glory and its passenger operator, Amtrak, perhaps the most committed of any operator to the 'traditional' idea of the romance of on-train dining. On all these counts, therefore, one would expect the idea's future in the States to be good. However, the signals are a good deal more mixed than these comments may suggest.

Amtrak ridership and public approval have both risen substantially, particularly since 11 September 2001; following that dreadful event, the 'Lake Shore Limited' booked 500 passengers from Chicago to New York and Boston, long-distance ridership went up generally by 35% (and appears to be staying up), and on the North East Corridor 'Acela Express' and 'Metroliner' ridership rose by 13% and again seems to be holding.[25] The 'Acela Express' was already proving a success, arousing excitement in bystanders and spontaneous customer care in staff. Significantly, one of the aspects given the 'thumbs up' in Johnston's 'Acela' review for *Trains* magazine is the at-seat meals service in First Class – 'A cut above "Metroliner" fare. Creatively prepared and presented. Cannot be confused with airline food' – though the Business Class Bistro is faulted for being too spartan and understaffed.[26]

However, from 1 May 2002 Congress once again placed severe financial restraints on Amtrak. The service won't be closed down, but several route cutbacks and space reductions were scheduled as of January 2003 – though there have also been some schedule increases, for example a new midday 'Acela Express'. There have also been reductions in service advertising: Johnson quotes a 'City of New Orleans' passenger as saying, 'I'm here only because a friend told me about it.'[27]

The constraints have also once again brought about cuts in dining car menus and services. From 1 May 2002, new official regulations require that

'the menu on every long-distance train will be the same, with the exception of three different fish selections – salmon, catfish and halibut… No regional speciality desserts or entrees. No separate cycles across the country or on the way back … you get a choice of center cut pork chop, New York strip steak with sherry mushroom sauce, chicken a l'orange and vegetarian penne pasta. Lunch is veg stir fry, SW chicken salad, Reuben and sirloin burger. Once again, Amtrak's dining cars have become the whipping boy.'[28]

Menu quality does appear during 2002/3 to have been fighting back on some trains, though. The policy directives mean that the 'City of New Orleans' cannot serve its red beans and rice and bread pudding, although they turn a higher profit margin than the national selections and encourage coach passengers into the diner, but because fish is exempt from the 'one size fits all' rule, the 'City' can still serve its catfish and the 'Empire Builder' Pacific salmon, and they do. But in general terms the change has set Amtrak menu quality right back to 1985 – even 1975. So, once again it seems, Amtrak's dining services will have to 'walk a crooked mile'.

How, then, do we sum up overall the future of 'dining at speed'? It has not yet 'run its course' – but it is still under change, under diversification, and – if the Amtrak experience is anything to go by – under threat. Perhaps the best summing up is to be found in the ending of David Crome's paper to the Transport 2000 conference:

'It's time then to stop thinking in a linear fashion.

A typical 'Acela' First Class at-seat tray meal, in this case fillet steak with broiled tomato. *Bob Johnston collection*

There is no straight-line graph that can be applied to the on-train dining market as growing or declining. Only changing and adapting to demand, needs and opportunities fits.'[29]

TIME LINE

Decade	Britain	Mainland Europe	USA
1800	1802 Edgeworth proposes 'Railtrack-style' common carrier railways		
1810	1812 William Chapman's UK bogie suspension patent		1819 Dearborn proposes refreshment facilities on future US railroads
1820	1829 Liverpool & Manchester Railway's promoters stress it as a *freight* line		
1830	1830 L&MR opens (with many passengers!) 1831 Brunel rides on L&MR and considers 'taking coffee at 45mph' 1837 Rules against itinerant food hawkers on trains 1838 Brunel designs 'grand saloon'; L&B opens Curzon Street Royal Station Hotel; Darwin's first two 'railway letters'		1831 Birth of George Pullman 1834 Ross Winans patents bogie suspension in US 1835 First open saloon carriages (on B&O); Philadelphia & Columbia builds 'food service car' 1836 First (very primitive) US sleeping cars
1840	1840 Refreshment room stops on most long journeys 1841 Brunel allows Rigby Bros monopoly on Swindon refreshment catering; Thomas Cook organises first excursion 1844 Joseph Wright's patent for four-, six- or eight-wheel bogie suspension in UK; Disraeli's *Coningsby* 'feminises' lunch 1845 Many lines' passenger takings exceed freight 1846 Eastern Counties Railway builds smoking saloons; *Punch* proposes 'a portable refreshment room on every train'; Dickens serial *Dombey and Son* starts 1847 'Locomotive larder' proposal (possibly by *Bristol Gazette*) 1849 Ruskin stresses inherent 'misery' of rail travel		1848 Pullman enters cabinet-making business
1850	1852 Measom's *Guide to the Great Western Railway* 1853 James Allport becomes Midland Railway General Manager 1858 Trollope's *Dr Thorne* presents rail travel as comfortable		1853 Pullman's 'overnight journey from Hell'; B&O serves food (prepared off-train) on two specials

Decade	Britain	Mainland Europe	USA
1860	1861 Mrs Beeton describes portable cooking stoves 1862 The *Railway Traveller's Handbook* advises avoiding overcrowded refreshment halts 1863 Café Royal opens 1864 *Punch* prints 'Wonders of Modern Travel' 1867 MR London extension opens 1869 Mrs Beeton (2nd edition) re-legitimises lunch	1863 Waldegg builds first corridor carriages 1864 'Luxury class' diners on Odessa-Kiev service 1868 Georges Nagelmackers visits USA 1869 Nagelmackers proposes CIWL	1858 Pullman working as building contractor for Tremont Hotel, Chicago 1859 Pullman's initial car conversions for C&A 1861 American Civil War: Government commandeers all C&A rolling-stock 1862 Enabling Act offers land grant to railroads 1863 Philadelphia, Wilmington & Baltimore steam bath refreshment car 1864 Pullman builds 'Pioneer' (initially out of gauge) 1865 Lincoln assassinated; 'Pioneer' used for funeral, Pullman becomes a household name 1867 Pullman has contracts with seven railroads; Andrew Carnegie invests $100,000 in Pullman; policy of employing 'Negro porters' begins; Pullman's first 'hotel car', 'President' 1868 Pullman's first dining car 'Delmonico' built
1870	1871 Spiers & Pond market refreshment hampers 1872 MR provides Third Class coaches on all trains; Allport visits USA and meets George Pullman 1873 James Clayton becomes MR carriage superintendent; MR Third Class carriages get upholstered seats; Allport invites Pullman to address MR Board 1874 Great Northern builds bogie 'special stock'; MR operates Pullmans London-Bradford (press run has cold catering by Spiers & Pond) 1875 MR under Allport abolishes Second Class and upgrades Third; MR markets first railway-run refreshment hampers from Derby; GNR operates Pullmans; LCDR Mann pantry boudoir car, London-Dover 1876 LNWR markets two-price refreshment hampers;	1870 Franco-Prussian War stops CIWL project 1873 Nagelmackers restarts CIWL with support from Mann and King Leopold of Belgium 1875 Pullman signs contract with Northern Italian Railway; 'trade war' between Pullman and CIWL 1879 CIWL gets 'Indian Mail' contract, but Pullman blocks Brindisi end	1870 Centralised signalling adopted 1872 C&A operates five dining cars Chicago-Kansas City 1873 Major financial crisis in US severely affects railroad finance; Henry Villard involved in rescue package schemes 1876 Fred Harvey's first AT&SF lunch counter; NP serves food on specials and hunting trains; Henry Villard's fund involved in NP rescue package 1878 First 'Harvey House' (Florence, KS); Pullman diners on most roads ex-Chicago, with standard bill of fare; AT&SF, Burlington and UP form

Decade	Britain	Mainland Europe	USA
	1878 refreshment stop times increase to 30 minutes; MR opens Settle & Carlisle route to Scotland via 'Waverley' route; Food cooked on-train on MR private hire, London-Wick 1879 First dining car service, GNR 'Prince of Wales' Pullman, Leeds-London		'cartel' not to operate dining cars west of Kansas City
1880	1880 Allport retires; John Noble succeeds him 1881 First Brighton Pullman service on LBSCR 1882 MR begins operating Pullman diners, London-Manchester-Liverpool 1883 MR buys out its Pullman diners 1884 MR markets hot refreshment hampers 1885 GNR buys out 'Prince of Wales' 1888 First 'Race to the North' 1889 LNWR puts diners on Euston-Manchester/Liverpool services	1880 CIWL temporary diners on summer Berlin-Frankfurt service 1881 CIWL first purpose-built diner, Nice-Marseilles 1882 Diner on Paris-Vienna 'Train éclair de luxe'; national dining car services start in Europe; Thomas Cook Rome excursion still uses refreshment stops 1883 First run of 'Orient Express' 1889 Paris Exhibition	1881 Henry Villard becomes President of NP 1882 Villard orders dining cars from Pullman, despite Transportation Supt's objection 1883 NP 'cartel breaking' dining service starts 1884 19 'Harvey Houses' in operation on AT&SF 1887 Interstate Commerce Act bans 'rate cutting' 1889 AT&SF 'Coronado' diner offers wide-choice menu; C&O starts 'Fast Flying Virginian' (Pullman)
1890	1891 GER provides Second and Third Class diners on Harwich-York service; LSWR Pullmans on London-Southampton-Bournemouth service 1892 GER diners on London-Harwich service 1893 LNWR launches 'The Corridor'; dining services begin on all Anglo-Scottish routes 1894 Queen Victoria still using refreshment stop at Preston en route to Balmoral 1895 GWR buys out Swindon refreshment rooms contract 1896 GWR begins dining services to South Wales and West Country 1897 MR dining set on Bradford-Bristol service; GWR begins dining services Bristol-London 1899 GER diners on London-Cromer service; GCR opens London Extension	1890 Diner on 'Indian Mail' (now CIWL-operated throughout) 1896 First run of 'Nord Express' (Ostend-Moscow) 1897 Dining cars on 'Rome Express' 1898 DSG formed for CIWL services in Germany	1890 C&O takes over 'Fast Flying Virginian' dining from Pullman; Chicago-Omaha route Christmas menu sports 45 dishes in 12 courses 1891 'Cartel companies' end dining car embargo 1892 Diners run on AT&SF west of Kansas City 1897 George Pullman dies
1900	1900 Restaurant cars on 'Flying Scotsman' 1901 LSWR begins diners on West Country routes 1902 NER begins breakfast/tea cars on Scarborough-Leeds run; diners on Newcastle-Bournemouth service	1905 Nagelmackers dies; Dalziel becomes Chairman of CIWL 1906 'Simplon Express' (Calais-Trieste only)	1900 NP starts 'North Coast Limited'

Decade	Britain	Mainland Europe	USA
	1903 Dining cars on MR overnight expresses		
	1905 MR diners on Leeds–Bristol service		
	1906 LNWR runs dining and tea cars, Euston–Birmingham; refreshment hamper sales reach peak		
	1907 LYR runs diners on Newcastle–Liverpool and Leeds–Fleetwood services; Dalziel buys Pullman Co		
	1908 LBSCR Brighton Pullman becomes 'Southern Belle'		
	1909 GWR begins dining services to Birmingham		
1910	1910 LSWR diners running to Bournemouth; Pullman buffet cars on Metropolitan Railway	1910 'Ostend-Vienna Express' begins operation	1910 NP builds major tranche of dining cars
	1913 GWR dining car on Taunton–Ilfracombe slip	1914 'Orient Express' (and other trans-front-line services) suspended	1911 NP operates own food production firms; AT&SF starts 'Santa Fé De Luxe' service
	1914 First World War: Railways Executive Committee takes over all main lines	1916 Mitropa formed, using 'stranded' CIWL cars	1917 War Board/USRA takes over railroad scheduling; 'De Luxe' discontinued
	1915 'Competitive' dining car services restricted; Third Class Pullmans start		
1920	1921 GCR begins through Penzance-Aberdeen dining/sleeper service	1922 'Le Train Bleu' introduced	1921 'North Coast Limited' receives stock upgrade
	1923 'Big Four' railway companies formed; 'Harrogate Pullman' (actually to Newcastle!) starts operation	1923 Mitropa Berlin-London express starts via Hook	1925 NP upgrades 'Yellowstone Comet'
	1925 New stock for 'Cornish Riviera Limited'	1925 Dalziel orders Pullman stock for CIWL	1926 Santa Fé 'Chief' starts
	1926 SR introduces 'Atlantic Coast Express'	1927 CIWL admits Second Class; 'Anatolia Express' starts	1927 NP café cars introduced
	1927 'Royal Scot' and 'Irish Mail' introduced on LMS	1928 Mitropa starts 'Rheingold', particularly popular with British market	1929 US railroad grouping proposed (abandoned); 1 in 5 Americans owns a car by end of year
	1928 'Harrogate Pullman' renamed 'Queen of Scots'; 'Flying Scotsman' non-stop London-Edinburgh	1929 'Flèche D'Or' ('Golden Arrow') London-Paris service starts	
	1929 Swing service in general operation on peak trains; plated service on GWR; LMS begins menu simplification		
1930	1932 Gresley buffet cars for Cambridge 'beer trains'; Stanier builds 'cafeteria-style' LMS buffet car for Liverpool-Leeds service	1930 Six variants of 'Orient Express' shown on maps; 'Taurus Express' links to Baghdad and Cairo	1930 NP advertises dining services via recipes; C&O introduces 'Sportsman'
	1933 Gresley 'Tourist stock' includes buffet car; 'Southern Belle' electrified (as 'Brighton Belle')	1931 'Trains de luxe' admit Second Class	1932 C&O introduces 'George Washington'
	1934 Gresley buffet cars on Newcastle-Carlisle route; GWR introduces 'quick lunch cars'; GWR diesel railcars with buffets for Birmingham-Cardiff service; Railway Air Services formed	1932 International services admit Third Class; 'restaurant-cum-bar' buffet cars begin	1934 Union Pacific 'City' and Burlington 'Zephyr' high-speed buffet diesel sets
		1933 Germany introduces 'Fliegende Hamburger' high-speed diesel train	1936 AT&SF introduces 'Super Chief'
		1934 French Bugatti twin-car diesel sets	1937 Price war between Southern Pacific and AT&SF; SP 'coffee shop-diners', swing and plated service; New Haven grill cars

Decade	Britain	Mainland Europe	USA
	1935 LNER introduces 'Silver Jubilee'		1938 introduce tray meals; SP introduces 'tavern cars'
	1936 Stanier buffets rebuilt closer to Gresley design		
	1937 LNER runs 'Coronation' to Edinburgh and 'West Riding Limited' to Bradford; LMS runs 'Coronation Scot' to Glasgow		
	1938 Bulleid buffet cars for Bognor line; second group of GWR buffet cars	1939 'Orient Express' ceases for duration	
	1939 Second World War begins in Europe; all lines under National Railway Executive; all restaurant cars cease; Pullman cars stored for duration		
1940	1940 Some restaurant services re-instated	1940 Fall of France; CIWL continues to run on 'as and when' basis	1940 Anti-trust legislation splits Pullman operating from car construction
	1941 426 restaurant car runs per day (many with LNER buffet cars replacing diners)	1945 'Orient Express' re-starts (to Innsbruck only)	1941 Pearl Harbor; Second World War begins for USA; red meat, sugar and coffee rationed
	1942 Restaurant car runs reduced to 65 per day	1947 Post-war 'Orient Express' reaches Bucharest	1942 US passenger mileage at three times 1930 level; substantial strain on dining car services
	1944 All restaurant cars withdrawn from April	1949 'Simplon Orient' now preferred route; 'Tauern Orient' begins	1943 SP serves 23 million meals
	1945 Some restaurant cars re-instated from October; many foods still on ration (meat, bread, etc)		1944 Railroads handle 80% of inter-city traffic; first transcontinental flight, 17 April
	1946 'Golden Arrow', 'Brighton Belle' and 'Bournemouth Belle' re-start		1945 Santa Fé orders refurbished 'Super Chief'
	1947 'Devon Belle' begins, 'Frood' tried as way round rationing limits; 'Yorkshire Pullman' re-starts; railways nationalised; railway passenger travel market share 27.6%; Bulleid starts work on 'Tavern Cars'		1947 C&O plans to introduce 'Chessie'
	1948 British Railways takes over; dining cars come under Hotels Executive; 'Thanet Belle' and 'Tees-Tyne Pullman' begin; 'Queen of Scots' re-starts; two distinct on-train catering markets develop		1948 Chicago Railroad Fair opens; C&O engages DeZutter as executive chef and opens training school
	1949 Inman admits train food makes losses per serving; Bulleid 'Tavern Cars' go into service		1949 'Hamburger-grill' cars introduced on SP 'Daylight'
1950	1951 Festival of Britain; first BR catering cars; 'Thanet Belle' renamed 'Kentish Belle'	1957 TEE (Trans-Europ Express) network starts, First Class plus supplement, at-seat meals service	1950 Railroad share of inter-city passenger traffic falls to 47%
	1953 Transport Act restores dining car links with operating regions		1952 NP accelerates 'North Coast Limited' and starts 'Mainstreeter'
	1954 Meat ration finally abolished; BR buys out all Pullman ordinary shares; 'Devon Belle' taken off		1955 NP provides 'Traveller's Rest' lounge/snack bar on 'North Coast Limited'
	1955 'South Wales Pullman' begins (using 'Devon Belle' stock)		

Decade	Britain	Mainland Europe	USA
	1957 Changing social patters of on-train eating; building of BR Mark 1 standard stock begins 1958 Kent Coast electrification, 'Kentish Belle' taken off		1960 Railroad share of inter-city traffic falls to 29% 1961 SP converts surplus tavern cars to automats 1967 C&O and B&O merge; Pres Johnson gives support to fast New York-Washington link; US Post Office shifts mail contracts to air 1969 'Metroliner' trains enter service New York-Washington
1960	1961 Griddle cars built; business-oriented 'Blue Pullmans' begin 1962 BR buys out Pullman preference shares 1963 Pullman Co re-formed as division of British Transport Hotels 1964 'Queen of Scots' becomes 'White Rose' (terminates at Harrogate) 1966 West Coast electrification, traffic increases by 66% 1967 Pullman Co effectively ceases to exist; 'White Rose Pullman' and 'Bournemouth Belle' both taken off 1968 Transport Act, requires rail routes to pay their way	1961 CIWL menus still hand-written by *chef de brigade* 1962 'Arlberg Orient' and 'Tauern Orient' cut back to Vienna/Venice	
1970	1970 'Booth car' experiment 1972 'Brighton Belle' and 'Golden Arrow' both taken off 1973 Railway passenger travel market share only 7.8%; BR Catering renamed Travellers-Fare 1976 HST 125s introduced on Western Region 1977 'Night Ferry' food service reduced to MicroBuffet 1978 HST 125s introduced on East Coast Main Line; Prue Leith joins board of Travellers-Fare; Standard Class dining car abolished on HST sets; microwave ovens in Mark III kitchen cars 1979 Four standard levels of menu created across whole InterCity network	1977 Last run of 'Orient Express'; SNCF declares 'age of "trains de luxe" over' 1978 French 'Night Ferry' reduced to snack bar; TEE expresses admit Second Class	1970 Penn Central bankruptcy; railroad share of inter-city passenger traffic now only 7% 1971 Amtrak formed 1972 'Metroliner' stock include 'dinettes' 1973 New 'Amfleet' cars enter service on East Coast, include central snack-bar coaches 1976 Amfleet cars reach West Coast 1979 Amtrak 'Superliner' bi-level coaches enter service, dining car has restaurant upstairs, kitchen below; 'Heritage' rebuilds for East Coast
1980	1980 'Night Ferry' taken off 1982 BT Hotels privatised 1984 NUR agrees to trolley service operation 1985 BR launches 'New Pullman Concept'; first 'cook-chill' meals ('Cuisine 2000') made on shore, loaded by trolley and finished on-train 1986 Management buy-outs of Travellers-Fare station refreshment rooms; InterCity On-Board Services formed, four-weekly menu cycles and 'matrix' spread of dishes across equipment developed	1981 First French TGV service (Paris-Lyons), First Class at-seat meal service (charged extra), Second Class bistro 1989 EU sets out European High-Speed Rail Network proposal	1981 Pres Reagan cuts Amtrak budget, company moves to spartan menus, plastic cutlery and paper plates 1982 Amtrak catering 'hits rock bottom' 1983 Meals-inclusive sleeper fares introduced; menu cycles introduced

Decade	Britain	Mainland Europe	USA
1990	1987 InterCity rediscovers idea of 'train magic' 1988 InterCity moves into trading profit 1993 OBS issues Chef's Manuals with recipes grouped next to menus and describing *exactly* how each dish is to be received from shore-base and finished on-train 1994 InterCity regional routes become companies ready for privatisation; OBS becomes supply, logistics and development company only; on-board staff now work directly for TOCs 1997 Rail privatisation results in multiple train operating companies with varying dining car policies; OBS becomes Rail Gourmet and expands into Europe	1990 First 'Pendolinos' enter service in Italy (bistro service only provided) 1993 Second tranche of Italian 'Pendolino' series offer kitchen/restaurant car plus bistro, at-seat snacks complimentary in First Class 1996 France introduces third-generation TGVs with bi-level format 1997 OBS begins operations in Denmark, Holland, Belgium and Spain	1994 Second Amtrak cash crisis 1995 Amtrak divided into three business units; real menu and cuisine regionalisation 1999 'Cascades' 'Talgo' high-speed train begins, with bistro and dining car; dining car operations re-centralised
2000	2000 Hatfield disaster, large-scale disruption of dining services follows 2001 Anglia Railways re-introduces MicroBuffets; First Great Western introduces 'Travelling Chef' 2002 Eurostar introduces new 'regional' menus; Virgin mounts 'Pendolino' acceptance trials (version with full kitchen); GNER starts 'Go East' dining service, chef Peter Jordan wins Chef of the Year award 2003 Re-launch of Eurostar in autumn 2004 Midland Mainline Bombardier 'Voyager' sets due to be in service	2000 German ICE3 sets enter service – multiple extra on-board business facilities, but also unclassed restaurant car 2001 'Berlin-Warsaw Express' starts (Dec), facilities include 'unclassed' dining car; ICE4 design under discussion in Germany with same facility 2002 Rail Gourmet España offers at-seat meal service (themed menu cycles, four courses, fare-inclusive) to First and Second Class on Spanish 'Talgos' 2003 Austrian Railways 'new commercial offensive' – dining car to be marshalled in every long-distance train	2000 'Acela Express', New York-Boston high-speed service, begins, includes Business Class diner and First Class at-seat meal service 2001 11 September atrocity results in up to 35% increase in Amtrak ridership 2002 Third Amtrak cash crisis, menu choice drastically reduced across system 2003 Amtrak services and advertising cut, but some menu choices remain

BIBLIOGRAPHY

Austin, S. *Portrait of the Atlantic Coast Express* (Shepperton, Ian Allan Publishing, 1997)
Portrait of the Pines Express (Shepperton, Ian Allan Publishing, 1998)

Bagwell, P. J. *The Transport Revolution From 1770* (London, Batsford, 1974)

Baker, S. L. and Kunz, V. B. *The Collector's Book of Railroadiana* (New York, Hawthorn Books Inc, 1976)

Beddoes, K., Wheeler, C. and Wheeler, S. *Metro-Cammell: 150 Years of Craftsmanship* (Cheltenham, Runpast Publishing, 1999)

Beeton, Isabella *Mrs Beeton's Book of Household Management* (London, Ward, Lock & Co, 1861 (2nd edn, ed Beeton, S. O., 1869)

Behrend, G. *Grand European Expresses* (London, George Allen & Unwin, 1962)
Pullman in Europe (London, Ian Allan, 1962)
History of Trains de Luxe (Glossop, Transport Publishing Company, 1977, rev 1982)

Behrend, G. and Buchanan, G. *Night Ferry* (St Martin, Jersey Artists Ltd, 1985)

Booth, G. *The Tilling Group* (Shepperton, Ian Allan, 1998)

Boston, H. L. 'Kitchen Service', *Great Western Railway Journal*, 12, Autumn 1994, pp505-18

Bower, A. J. 'Dining on Wheels', *The Railway Magazine*, September 1979, pp422-26
Prince of Wales Pioneering Dining Car 1879 (original ts preserved in NRM boxed archive, York; contains substantial unpublished additional material)

Bradley, R. *Amtrak: The US National Railroad Passenger Corporation* (Poole, Blandford Press, 1985)

Bradshaw, Volume for May 1913

Brett, Gerard *Dinner Is Served* (London, Rupert Hart-Davis, 1968)

Bristol Gazette, Volumes for 1845, 1846, 1847 and 1848

Brogan, M. *Home Sweet Home* (Great Addington, Silver Link Publishing Ltd, 1999)

Brown, D. *Hear That Lonesome Whistle Blow – Railroads in the West* (New York, Holt Rinehart, 1977)

Bryant, K. L. Jr. *History of the Atchison, Topeka and Santa Fe Railway* (New York, Macmillan, 1974)

Burton, A. *The Orient Express* (London, Amber Books Ltd (David & Charles), 2001)

Campling, N. *Historic Carriage Drawings: LNER and Constituents* (Easingwold, The Pendragon Partnership, 1997)

Charman, M. *At Your Service* (Great Addington, Silver Link Publishing Ltd, 1999)

Cookridge, E. H. *Orient Express* (London, Allen Lane, 1978)

Cox, D. 'Dining Car Attendant Call Systems', *BackTrack*, 14, 10 (October 2000), pp610-11

Crome, D. 'Is Anyone Taking Dinner Tonight?', paper to Passenger Services Conference, London, May 2000

Darwin, Charles *Correspondence* (ed Burkhardt, F. and Smith, S.) (Cambridge, CUP 1987)

Des Cass, J. A. and Caracalla, J. P (trs Behrend, G.) *The Orient Express* (London, Grand Express Books, 1984)

Dickens, Charles *A Christmas Carol* (London, 1843), reprinted in Dickens, ed Farjeon, E., *Christmas Books* (Oxford, OUP, 1954)
Dombey and Son (1848; reprinted Oxford, OUP, 1982)
Our Mutual Friend (1864, reprinted Oxford, OUP, 1982)

Disraeli, Benjamin *Coningsby* (1844, reprinted London, J. M. Dent & Sons, 1928)

Doughty, G. H. *The New Haven Railroad's Streamline Passenger Fleet* (Lynchburg VA, TLC Publishing Inc, 2000)

Dow, G. *Great Central* (London, Locomotive Publishing Co Ltd, 1962)

Edwards, D. and Pigram, R. *The Golden Years of the Metropolitan Railway* (London, Midas Books, 1983, reprinted Baton Transport, 1985)

The Engineer, Volume for 1879

European Railways, issue for October-November 2002

Ferguson-Kosinski, L. *Europe by Eurail* (Guilford, Connecticut, USA, The Globe Pequod Press, 2000)

Fletcher, M. and Taylor, J. *Railways: The Pioneer Years* (London, Studio Editions, 1990)

Freeman, M. *Railways and the Victorian Imagination* (New Haven, Yale University Press, 1999)

Fryer, C. *British Pullman Trains* (Great Addington, Silver Link Publishing Ltd, 1992)

Gaskell, Elizabeth *Cranford* (London, Nelson's, nd)

Gourvish, T. R. *British Railways 1948-73: A Business History* (Cambridge, CUP, 1986)

Great Western Railway Magazine for 1934 (reprinted in Vol 2 Reprint No 5, March 1985)

Griffin, J. J. 'Birmingham (Snow Hill) Station Restaurant', *Great Western Railway Magazine*, 1909, p81 (reprinted at p29 of Vol 2 Reprint No 5, March 1985)

Hanger, E. S. *Chesapeake and Ohio Dining Car Recipes* (Clifton Forge, VA, Chesapeake & Ohio Historical Society Inc, 1995)

Harris, M. *British Main Line Services in the Age of Steam* (Sparkford, Oxford Publishing Company, 1996)

LNER Standard Gresley Carriages (Ottershaw, Surrey, Mallard Books, 1998)

'Britain's Titled Trains' 19: The "Merseyside Express"', *Steam Days*, 193 (March 2001), pp181-89

Haug, W. F. *Warenästhetik und kaptalistische Massenkultur* (*Consumer Aesthetics and Capitalist Mass Culture*) (Berlin, Aktion-Verlag, 1980)

Heaps, C., Hunter, D. and Le Jeune, B. 'Dutch Railways in the 21st Century', *Modern Railways*, Oct 2000, pp34-38

Hoole, K. 'The first British railway dining car – a case of mistaken identity', *Railway World*, Sept 1979, pp456-58

Hughes, G. *LNER* (London, Guild Publishing, 1986)

Hughes, Thomas *Tom Brown's Schooldays* (London, The Walter Scott Publishing Co Ltd, nd)

The Illustrated London News, Volume for 1879

ITV Teletext Service, Reports for 3 and 26 April 2001 and 26 August 2002

Jenkinson, D. *LNWR Carriages: A Concise History* (Easingwold, Pendragon, 1995)
British Railway Carriages (Easingwold, Pendragon, 1996)
Historic Carriage Drawings, Vol Two: LMS and Constituents (Easingwold, Pendragon, 1998)

Jenkinson, D. and Essery, R. *LMS Standard Coaching Stock: II – General Service Gangwayed Vehicles* (Sparkford, Oxford Publishing Co, 1994)

Johnston, Bob 'Brer Amtrak', *Trains*, June 2001, Vol 61 No 6, pp50-59
'Amtrak Responds, Reacts … and Hopes', *Trains*, December 2001, Vol 61 No 12, pp18-20
'Acela Report: Will Amtrak Prove Itself?', *Trains*, December 2001, Vol 61 No 12, pp52-57

Jordan, A. and Jordan E. *Away For The Day: The Railway Excursion in Britain* (Great Addington, Silver Link Publishing Ltd, 1991)

Kitchenside, G. *The Restaurant Car: A Century of Railway Catering* (Newton Abbot, David & Charles, 1979)

Laut, A. C. *The Romance of the Rails* (New York, Tudor Publishing Company, 1936)

Locke, T. (ed) *Europe 2002: The Inter-Railer's and Eurailer's Guide* (Peterborough, Thomas Cook)

McKenzie, W. A. *Dining Car Line to the Pacific* (St Paul, Minnesota Historical Society Press, 1990)

Metropolitan Railway, Pullman timetable leaflet for 1913

Mitchell, P. B. *Dining Cars and Depots* (Chatham, VA, Foodways Publications, 1992)

Modern Railways, issues for October 2000, December 2001 and April 2003

Morel, J. *Pullman* (Newton Abbot, David & Charles, 1983)

Nicholas, R. 'Dinner is Served', *The Railway Magazine*, November 1979, pp427-29

Nock, O. S. *British Locomotives of the 20th Century* (two volumes) (Cambridge, Patrick Stephens Ltd, 1984)

Palmer, A. *Movable Feasts* (London, OUP, 1952)

Parkin, K. *British Railways Mark I Coaches* (Easingwold, Pendragon Books, 1991, 2nd repr 1999)

Peacock, Thomas Love (ed Garnett, David) *The Novels of Thomas Love Peacock* (London, Rupert Hart-Davis, 1948)

Petchey, T. 'Railway Catering', in Kardas, H. (ed) *A Collector's Guide to Railwayana* (Hersham, Ian Allan Publishing, 2001), pp78-90

Perren, B. 'Virgin's Catering Revolution', *Modern Railways*, December 2001, Vol 58 No 639, pp56-58

Punch, Volumes for 1844/5, 1846, 1851, 1852, 1864 and 1918

Radford, J. B. *The American Pullman Cars of the Midland Railway* (London, Ian Allan, 1984)

The Railway Magazine, issues for April 2002 and May 2003

Reed, M. C. *The London & North Western Railway* (Penryn, Cornwall, Atlantic Transport Publishers, 1996)

Robotham, R. *The Great Central Railway's London Extension* (Shepperton, Ian Allan Publishing Ltd, 1999)

Rogers, A. E. *A Century of Meals on Railway Wheels* (1979, unpublished ts in archive collection of NRM, York)

Russell, J. H. *Great Western Coaches, 1903-1948* (Shepperton, Oxford Publishing Company, 1973, n.i. 1999)

Ryan, D. and Shine, J. *Southern Pacific Passenger Trains, Vol 2 (Day Trains of the Coast Line)* (La Mirada, CA, Four Ways West Publications, 2000)

Schivelbusch, W. *The Railway Journey* (Oxford, Blackwell, 1980)

Shackleton, J. T. *The Golden Age of the Railway Poster* (London, New English Library, 1976)

Sherwood, S. *Venice-Simplon-Orient Express* (London, Weidenfeld & Nicholson, 1983, 4th edn, 1996)

Simmons, J and Biddle, G. (eds) *The Oxford Companion to British Railway History* (Oxford, OUP, 1997)

Smalley, E. V. 'The Northern Pacific Opening', *The Northwest*, October 1883

Smith, D. N. *The Railway and its Passengers: A Social History* (Newton Abbot, David & Charles, 1988)

Smith, W. H. *Norfolk Railways* (Stroud, Sutton Publishing Ltd., 2000)

St John Thomas, D. and Whitehouse, P. *SR 150: A Century and a Half of the Southern Railway* (Newton Abbot, David & Charles, 1988)

Tayler, A. *Illustrated History of North American Railways* (London, Apple, 1996)

Thorne, M. (ed) *Modern Trains and Splendid Stations* (London, Merrell/The Art Institute of Chicago, 2001). Includes quotation from Ruskin's *Seven Lamps of Architecture* (London, 1849) on p11.

The Times, Volume for 1874

Today's Railways, issue for December 2001

Trains, issues for June and December 2001

Trollope, Anthony *Doctor Thorne* (London, 1858, repr Chatto & Windus, 1951)

Vaughan, A. *Isambard Kingdom Brunel, Engineering Knight-Errant* (London, John Murray, 1991)

Vincent, M. and Green, C. (eds) *The InterCity Story* (Sparkford, Oxford Publishing Company, 1994)

Weddell, G. R. *LSWR Carriages in the 20th Century* (Hersham, Oxford Publishing Company, 2001)

Wessner, C. 'Designing for their Needs', in Thorne, M. (ed) *Modern Trains and Splendid Stations* (London, Merrell/The Art Institute of Chicago, 2001)

Whitehouse, P. and St John Thomas, D. *The Great Days of the Southern Railway* (London, BCA, by arrangement with David St John Thomas, 1992)

Williams, R. *The Midland Railway: A New History* (Newton Abbot, David & Charles, 1988)

Winchester, C. and Allen, Cecil J. (eds) *Railway Wonders of the World* (two vols) (London, Amalgamated Press, 1936)

Wooler, N. *Dinner in the Diner: The History of Railway Catering* (Newton Abbot, David & Charles, 1987)

NOTES

Introduction

[1] Kitchenside, G. *The Restaurant Car: A Century of Railway Catering* (Newton Abbot, David & Charles, 1979)

[2] Wooler, N. *Dinner in the Diner: The History of Railway Catering* (Newton Abbot, David & Charles, 1987)

[3] Schivelbusch, W. *The Railway Journey* (Oxford, Blackwell, 1980), p114

[4] Vaughan, A. *Isambard Kingdom Brunel, Engineering Knight-Errant* (London, John Murray, 1991), pp41-42

[5] Wooler, op cit, Chapter 2

[6] *Punch*, 1846 Vol II, p136, 'Railway Luxuries'

[7] Charles Darwin, *Correspondence* (ed Burkhardt, F. and Smith, S., Cambridge, CUP 1987), Vol 2, pp119-120, Letter to Emma Wedgwood, 21 November 1838

[8] Bryant, K. L., Jr. *History of the Atchison, Topeka and Santa Fe Railway* (New York, Macmillan, 1974), Chapter 4

[9] Mitchell, P. B. *Dining Cars and Depots* (Chatham, VA, Foodways Publications, 1992), Chapter 5

[10] Morel, J. *Pullman* (Newton Abbot, David & Charles, 19830, Chapter 1

[11] Behrend, G. *Pullman in Europe* (London, Ian Allan, 1962), Chapter 2

[12] Radford, J. B. *The American Pullman Cars of the Midland Railway* (London, Ian Allan, 1984)

[13] Hughes, G. *LNER* (London, Guild Publishing, 1986), Chapter 3

[14] Harris, M. *LNER Standard Gresley Carriages* (Ottershaw, Surrey, Mallard Books, 1998), pp145-155

[15] Behrend, op cit (pp29ff)

[16] Fryer, C. *British Pullman Trains* (Great Addington, Silver Link Publishing, 1992), pp145-46

[17] Morel, op cit, p163

Chapter 1

[1] Kitchenside, op cit, Introduction

[2] Wooler, op cit, p8

[3] McKenzie, William A. *Dining Car Line to the Pacific* (St Paul, Minnesota Historical Society Press, 1990), p ix

[4] McKenzie, op cit, p21

[5] Fryer, op cit

[6] Fryer, op cit, pp9 & 11

[7] Behrend, op cit, p17

[8] Morel, op cit, p15

[9] ditto, p6

[10] Smith, D. N. *The Railway and its Passengers: A Social History* (Newton Abbot, David & Charles, 1988), p68

[11] Fryer, op cit, p20 (quoted from *The Railway Magazine*)

[12] Behrend, op cit, Foreword by Sir John Elliot

[13] Fryer, op cit, p212

[14] Radford, op cit, p13

[15] Freeman, M. *Railways and the Victorian Imagination* (New Haven, Yale University Press, 1999), p148

[16] Smith, op cit, p123

[17] Bryant, op cit, p111 (reproduced by permission of University of Nebraska Press)

[18] Hanger, E. S. *Chesapeake & Ohio Dining Car Recipes* (Clifton Forge, VA, Chesapeake & Ohio Historical Society Inc, 1995), p ii

[19] Dow, G. *Great Central* (London, Locomotive Publishing Co Ltd, 1962), Vol II, pp272 & 275 (reproduced by permission of Ian Allan Ltd)

[20] Cox, D. 'Dining Car Attendant Call Systems', *BackTrack*, 14, 10 (October 2000), pp610-611

[21] Shackleton, J. T. *The Golden Age of the Railway Poster* (London, New English Library, 1976), Introduction

[22] Haug, W. F. *Warenästhetik und kaptalistiche Massenkultur* (*Consumer Aesthetics and Capitalist Mass Culture*) (Berlin, Aktion-Verlag, 1980)

[23] Mitchell, op cit, p11

[24] Schivelbusch, op cit, pp113 & 201, note 56

[25] ditto, p28

[26] ditto, pp111-117

[27] Vaughan, loc cit (The original is in the Bristol University special collection.)

[28] Winchester, C. and Allen, Cecil J. (eds) 'The Railway Carriage', *Railway Wonders of the World* (London, Amalgamated Press, 1936), Vol 1 Part 16 (17 May), p488

29 Vaughan, op cit, pp100-101

30 ibid, p141

31 Wooler, op cit, p21

32 ditto, p29

33 ditto, p20

34 Punch, 1846, Vol I, p215

35 The Bristol Gazette, 10 Sept 1846, p2 col 4

36 Punch, 1846, Vol II, p118.

37 ibid, p137

38 ibid, p136. Wooler (op cit p29) omits the two sentences marked *, and does not quote anything after the mark **.

39 Freeman, op cit, p86

40 Jordan, A. and Jordan, E. Away For The Day: The Railway Excursion in Britain (Great Addington, Silver Link Publishing Ltd, 1991), p24

41 Wooler, op cit, pp108 & 109

42 Schivelbusch, op cit, pp88-92 and notes p197

43 Williams, R. The Midland Railway: A New History (Newton Abbot, David & Charles, 1988), p125

44 Behrend, op cit, p15

45 Morel, op cit, pp11-12

46 Bryant, op cit, pp106-118 (quotation courtesy of University of Nebraska Press)

47 Mitchell, op cit, pp17-20

48 Wooler, op cit, p99

49 McKenzie, op cit, p28

50 Bryant, op cit, p114, says '$17.50 per week', but is almost certainly mistaken.

51 Beeton, Isabella Mrs Beeton's Book of Household Management (London, Ward, Lock & Co, 1861; 2nd Edn, ed Beeton, S. O., 1869), p7

Chapter 2

1 McKenzie, op cit, p25

2 Wooler, op cit, p20

3 Kitchenside, op cit, Chapter 1 captions

4 Fryer, op cit, pp18-23 (Kitchenside and Wooler both also acknowledge Pullman)

5 Mitchell, op cit, pp9-11

6 Schivelbusch, op cit, pp100-102 and accompanying figure

7 Beddoes, K., Wheeler, C. and Wheeler, S. Metro-Cammell: 150 Years of Craftsmanship (Cheltenham, Runpast Publishing, 1999), pp5 & 87

8 Beeton, op cit, pp50-56

9 Wooler, op cit, p34

10 ibid, p37

11 Schivelbusch, op cit, pp16 & 191, n23

12 Freeman, op cit, p40

13 Schivelbusch, op cit, p58

14 Freeman, op cit, p11

15 ibid, p18 & plate 22

16 ibid, p10

17 quoted in Thorne, M. (ed) Modern Trains and Splendid Stations (London, Merrell/The Art Institute of Chicago, 2001), p11

18 Darwin (ed Burkhardt & Smith), op cit, pp94-95 (letter to Emma Wedgwood, 7 August 1838), quoted by permission of Cambridge University Press

19 ibid, pp119-120 (letter to Emma Wedgwood, 21 November 1838), quoted by permission of Cambridge University Press

20 Gaskell, Elizabeth Cranford (London, Nelson's, nd), p1 (the original was published in Household Words, 1851-53)

21 ibid, p5

22 ibid, pp24-25

23 Dickens, Charles Dombey and Son (1848, repr Oxford, OUP, 1982), p53

24 ibid, pp184-85

25 Disraeli, Benjamin Coningsby (1844, repr London, J. M. Dent & Sons, 1928), p128

26 Dickens, op cit, pp236-37 (passage abridged)

27 Freeman, op cit, pp80-81

28 Dickens, op cit, pp652-53

29 Punch, Vol XXIII (1852), p157

30 Trollope, Anthony Doctor Thorne (London, 1858, repr Chatto & Windus, 1951), p477

31 Punch, Vol XLVII (1864), p217. I place a different interpretation as to the level of anxiety it portrays from Freeman, who also quotes it, op cit, pp82-83

32 Smith, op cit, p11

33 Williams, op cit, p14

34 Freeman, op cit, pp112-114

35 ibid, pp109-110

36 Simmons, J. and Biddle, G. (eds) The Oxford Companion to British Railway History (Oxford, OUP, 1997), p358

37 McKenzie, op cit, pp24-27

38 Wooler, op cit, p14 (quotation from the Manchester City News for 1830)

39 Palmer, Arnold Movable Feasts (London, OUP, 1952), pp52 & 59

40 Bagwell, P. J. The Transport Revolution From 1770 (London, Batsford, 1974), p54

41 Hughes, Thomas Tom Brown's Schooldays (London, The Walter Scott Publishing Co Ltd, nd), Chapter IV, esp pp62-71 (the novel is set in the 1830s)

42 Beeton, op cit, pp1322-1324

43 Bristol Gazette, 30 September 1847, p6 col 2

44 Smith, op cit, p15 (Smith also gives the 'inside' stagecoach rate as 6d. per mile)

45 Freeman, op cit, p20

46 Bryant, op cit, p116

47 Quotation from He Knew He Was Right, cited in Wooler, op cit, p27

48 Smith, op cit, pp57-58& p178 n 26

49 Darwin, ed Burkhardt & Smith, op cit, p165, reproduced by permission of Cambridge University Press. (The italics at the word 'home' are in the original.)

50 Palmer, op cit, p80

51 Disraeli, op cit, p132

52 Palmer, op cit, p41

53 ibid, pp35-36

54 Brett, Gerard Dinner Is Served (London, Rupert Hart-Davis, 1968), pp107-108

55 Beeton, op cit, p1325

56 ibid, p1327 (figure also reproduced in the text)

57 Peacock, Thomas Love (ed Garnett, David) The Novels of Thomas Love Peacock (London, Rupert Hart-Davis, 1948), quoted in Introduction, p xiv

58 Dickens, Charles Our Mutual Friend, 1864, Bk I Ch XI, quoted in Palmer, op cit, pp92-93

59 Disraeli, op cit, pp17-19

60 Quoted in Palmer, op cit, p77

61 For further analysis, see Palmer, op cit, p67

62 Dickens, Charles A Christmas Carol (London, 1843, reprinted in Dickens, ed Farjeon, E. Christmas Books (Oxford, OUP, 1954), p59

63 Palmer, op cit, p81

64 Quoted in Wooler, op cit, p25. 'Sherry cobbler' was a popular Victorian sherry-based long drink

Chapter 3

1 Freeman, op cit, pp203 & 257, nn 38 & 39

2 Palmer, op cit, p146

3 *Illustrated London News*, 22 November 1879, quoted in Wooler, op cit, p33

4 Palmer, op cit, p85

5 ibid, p80

6 ibid, pp131-32

7 Beeton, op cit, p1330

8 *The Engineer*, 24 October 1879, p309, col 1

9 Wooler, op cit, p34

10 Bower, A. J. 'Dining on Wheels', *The Railway Magazine*, September 1979, p426

11 Palmer, op cit, pp123-24

12 ibid, pp106-114

13 ibid, pp127-28

14 Jenkinson, D *British Railway Carriages* (Easingwold, Pendragon, 1996), ibid, p54

15 Smith, op cit, p60

16 Schivelbusch, op cit, pp91-2 & 197 n 34

17 Simmons & Biddle, op cit, p77

18 Schivelbusch, op cit, p119 n 28

19 Radford, op cit, p18

20 Williams, op cit, p127

21 Quoted in Wooler, op cit, p99

22 Brown, D. *Hear That Lonesome Whistle Blow – Railroads in the West* (New York, Holt Rinehart, 1977), p144

23 Wooler, op cit, pp27-28

24 Palmer, op cit, p80 n 1

25 Wooler, op cit, p101

26 ibid, pp99-102

27 Freeman, op cit, p4

28 Tayler, A. *Illustrated History of North American Railways* (London, Apple, 1996), p32

29 Bryant, op cit, p123 (reproduced by permission of University of Nebraska Press)

30 Williams, op cit, pp67-68

31 Tayler, op cit, p85

32 ibid, pp44-45

33 Simmons & Biddle, op cit, p465

34 ibid, p464

35 Smith, op cit, p16

36 Williams, op cit, p85

37 Brown, op cit, p233

38 Tayler, op cit, pp81-83

39 ibid, p72

40 Bryant, op cit, pp327-33

41 Fryer, op cit, p18

42 Behrend, op cit, p16

43 Morel, op cit, p12

44 Behrend, op cit, p15

45 Radford, op cit, pp6-8, documents the venue

46 Radford, op cit, p8. Behrend, op cit, p17, claims that the car had 'two eight-wheel bogies', but pictorial evidence from the Pullman archive supports Radford.

47 Morel, op cit, p13

48 Fryer, op cit, p19

49 Baker, S. L. and Kunz, V. B. *The Collector's Book of Railroadiana* (New York, Hawthorn Books Inc, 1976), pp128-29

50 Morel, op cit, pp14-16

51 ibid, p17

52 McKenzie, op cit, p27

53 ibid, p28

54 Quoted in Smith, op cit, p60

55 Quoted ibid, p62

56 ibid, p61

57 Radford, op cit, p13

58 Behrend, op cit, p26

59 ibid, p22

60 ibid, p25. Radford (see reference below) concurs. *The Times*'s report of 23 March, however, states that there were two sleepers and two parlour cars.

61 Radford, op cit, p31

62 Radford, op cit, p76 (Appendix 1, Derby Works Pullman Erection Table). Wooler quotes them both as sleeping cars, but the Derby table shows 'Ocean' as 'Delivered direct to Great Northern Railway, arranged as day car'.

63 Wooler, op cit, pp31-32. The first quotation is from Oakley's report to the GNR Board (also quoted in Radford, op cit, p38).

64 Kitchenside, op cit, Chapter 2. (Wooler, op cit, p37, however, believes the original fuel was coke.)

65 Bower, op cit, unpublished ts version, p7

66 Radford, op cit, p39

67 ibid, p43

68 ibid, p48

69 Hoole, K. 'The first British railway dining car – a case of mistaken identity', *Railway World*, Sept. 1979, p457

70 *Hotel Guide & Caterer's Journal*, quoted in personal communication from Sue Woodward, Harpenden Railway Museum

71 For details of Villard's career, see McKenzie, op cit, Chapter 4, pp43-55

72 Quoted in ibid, p28

73 McKenzie, op cit, p63

74 Behrend, op cit, p21, gives the arrival date as 1868. Burton, however, p9, gives the date as 1869. His visit lasted a full year.

75 eg Behrend, op cit, facing p32, upper plate

76 Burton, A. *The Orient Express* (London, Amber Books Ltd, David & Charles, 2001), endpaper drawings, top line (originals in Deutsches Museum, Munich)

77 Behrend, G. *History of Trains de Luxe* (Glossop, Transport Publishing Company, 1977), p19

78 Behrend, *Pullman in Europe*, pp32-33

79 Wooler, op cit, p28

Chapter 4

1 Harris, M. *British Main Line Services in the Age of Steam* (Sparkford, Oxford Publishing Company, 1996), p104 (the HR's first restaurant service was 1921)

2 ibid, p54

3 ibid, p27 (buffet for First Class passengers only)

4 ibid, p9 (name in use by 1904)

5 ibid, p31 (name in use by 1898)

6 McKenzie, op cit, p29 (the ban finally collapsed in 1891)

7 Jenkinson, D. *LNWR Carriages* (Easingwold, Pendragon, 1995), p43

8 Reed M. C. *The London & North Western Railway* (Penryn, Cornwall, Atlantic Transport Publishers, 1996), p147

9 Rogers, A. E. *A Century of Meals on Railway Wheels* (1979, unpublished ts in NRM archive, York), Chap 2 p9

10 Wooler, op cit, p38

11 Third Class details from Kitchenside, op cit, Chapter 2

[12] Jenkinson, D. *Historic Carriage Drawings, Vol Two: LMS and Constituents* (Easingwold, Pendragon 1998), pp86-89 & 104-105

[13] Jenkinson, *LNWR Carriages*, pp46 & 47

[14] Wooler, op cit, pp40-41

[15] Harris, op cit, p108

[16] ibid, p43

[17] Rogers, op cit, Chap 2 p10

[18] Wooler, op cit, p39

[19] Smith, W. H. *Norfolk Railways* (Stroud, Sutton Publishing Ltd, 2000), p14

[20] Morel, op cit, p89

[21] Rogers, op cit, Chap 2 pp11-13

[22] Jenkinson, op cit, p10

[23] Jenkinson, *British Railway Carriages*, pp118-121

[24] Harris, op cit, p77

[25] ibid, op cit, p59

[26] ibid, p31

[27] ibid, p77

[28] Jenkinson, *LNWR Carriages*, p51

[29] Wooler, op cit, p47

[30] Harris, op cit, p82

[31] Jenkinson, *Historic Carriage Drawings*, pp114-15

[32] Hoole, K. loc cit above (Chap 3 n 69)

[33] Jenkinson, *British Railway Carriages*, pp205-207

[34] Jenkinson, *LNWR Carriages*, p64

[35] Vincent, M. and Green, C. (eds) *The InterCity Story* (Sparkford, Oxford Publishing Company, 1994), pp58-59

[36] Jenkinson, *British Railway Carriages*, pp203-204

[37] Behrend, *Pullman in Europe*, p34

[38] Smith, op cit, p64

[39] Jenkinson, op cit, p204

[40] ibid, p58; drawing reference is W10

[41] Jenkinson *Historic Carriage Drawings* Vol 2, p105

[42] Wooler, op cit, p44

[43] quoted in Wooler, p45 (The Midland under Towle kept its own wine cellars.)

[44] ibid, pp47-48

[45] ibid, pp50-51

[46] ibid, pp23-25

[47] Harris, *British Main Line Services*, pp7-11

[48] Griffin, J. J. 'Birmingham (Snow Hill) Station Restaurant', *Great Western Railway Magazine*, 1909, p81 (reprinted at p29 of Vol 2 Reprint No 5, March 1985)

[49] Rogers, op cit, Chap 2 p13

[50] Jenkinson, *British Railway Carriages*, p201

[51] Boston, H. L. 'Kitchen Service', *Great Western Railway Journal* 12, Autumn 1994, p505

[52] Russell, J. H. *Great Western Coaches, 1903-1948* (Shepperton, Oxford Publishing Company, 1973 (n.i. 1999)), p47

[53] Jenkinson, op cit, p204

[54] Weddell, G. R. *LSWR Carriages in the 20th Century* (Hersham, Oxford Publishing Company, 2001), p99

[55] Harris, op cit, p16; see also Weddell, loc cit above

[56] Weddell, op cit, pp109-111

[57] ibid, pp153-54

[58] ibid, pp118-19 (The original source is *The Railway Magazine* for May 1910)

[59] Dow, op cit, pp92-94

[60] Simmons and Biddle, op cit, p558 (likewise epithets describing Watkin)

[61] Robotham, R. *The Great Central Railway's London Extension* (Shepperton, Ian Allan Publishing Ltd, 1999), p5

[62] ibid, pp8-9

[63] ibid, p89

[64] Wooler, op cit, pp42-43 (Dow also provides an early photograph, p276)

[65] Kitchenside, op cit, Chapter Three

[66] Fryer, op cit, pp25-27; see also Kitchenside, op cit, Chapter Two

[67] Fryer, op cit, p36

[68] Jenkinson, op cit, pp186-87

[69] Edwards, D. and Pigram, R. *The Golden Years of the Metropolitan Railway* (London, Midas Books, 1983, repr Baton Transport, 1985), p11

[70] Robotham, op cit, p121

[71] Bradshaw for May 1913, pp26 & 40

[72] Behrend, *Pullman in Europe*, p58

[73] Edwards and Pigram, op cit, p89

[74] Kitchenside, op cit, Chapter Three

[75] Bradshaw for May 1913, pp19-47

[76] Jenkinson, op cit, p210

[77] Fryer, op cit, p25

[78] Radford, op cit, p82

[79] Fryer, op cit, p37 (details from an LBSCR Timetable of 1912)

[80] ibid, p38 (quoting a 1910 Pullman brochure)

[81] Jenkinson, op cit, p213

[82] Behrend, op cit, p60

[83] Weddell, op cit, p106

[84] ibid, p108

[85] Behrend, op cit, p52

[86] ibid., p30

[87] Behrend, *History of Trains de Luxe*, p19

[88] Des Cass, J. A. and Caracalla, J. P (trs Behrend, G.) *The Orient Express* (London, Grand Express Books, 1984), p22

[89] ibid, p24

[90] Burton, op cit, p18

[91] Cookridge, E. H. *Orient Express* (London, Allen Lane, 1978), p39

[92] Burton, op cit, pp46-48

[93] Behrend, G *Grand European Expresses* (London, George Allen & Unwin, 1962), pp191-92

[94] Burton, op cit, pp44/5

[95] ibid, p55 Fig 2

[96] Des Cass & Caracalla, op cit, p54 Fig 78

[97] Behrend, op cit, p102

[98] Harris, op cit, p359

[99] McKenzie, op cit, p29

[100] Bryant, op cit, p328 (menus quoted by permission of University of Nebraska Press; Copyright © 1974 by Keith L. Bryant, Jr)

[101] Baker and Kunz, op cit, p56

[102] McKenzie, op cit, p69

[103] Mitchell, op cit, pp14-15 (capitalisation of baked potato menu item taken from Baker & Kunz, loc cit below)

[104] Baker & Kunz, op cit, p139

[105] McKenzie, op cit, pp70-73

[106] E. S. Hanger, by personal communication

[107] McKenzie, op cit, p8 and Chap 1 passim (similarly for commissary stocking information below)

[108] Bryant, op cit, p331 (reproduced by permission of University of Nebraska Press)

Chapter 5

[1] Palmer, op cit, pp145-47

[2] Reed, op cit, pp201-206

[3] Rogers, op cit, Chap 4 p2

[4] Simmons and Biddle, op cit, p557

5   Reed, op cit, pp209-10

6   Harris, *British Main Line Services*, p62

7   ibid, p34

8   ibid, p79

9   ibid, p56

10 ibid, pp12 & 17

11 ibid, pp29-30

12 ibid, p25

13 Fryer, op cit, pp92-93

14 Reed, op cit, p211

15 Burton, op cit, p64

16 Behrend, *Trains de Luxe*, p103

17 ibid, p42

18 Des Cass and Caracalla, op cit, pp147 & 148

19 Ryan, D. and Shine, J. *Southern Pacific Passenger Trains, Vol 2 (Day Trains of the Coast Line)* (La Mirada, CA, Four Ways West Publications, 2000), pp22-24

20 Tayler, op cit, pp109-110

21 Laut, A. C. *The Romance of the Rails* (New York, Tudor Pub Coy, 1936), p529

22 Harris, *British Main Line Services*, p104

23 Booth, G. *The Tilling Group* (Shepperton, Ian Allan, 1998), p14

24 Ryan and Shine, op cit, p26

25 Doughty, G. H *The New Haven Railroad's Streamline Passenger Fleet* (Lynchburg, VA, TLC Publishing Inc, 2000), pp10-11

26 Fletcher, M. and Taylor, J. *Railways: The Pioneer Years* (London, Studio Editions, 1990), p285

27 Burton, op cit, p89

28 Charman, M. *At Your Service* (Great Addington, Silver Link Publishing Ltd, 1999), p22

29 Fryer, op cit, p78

30 Jordan, A. and Jordan, E. *Away For The Day: The Railway Excursion in Britain* (Great Addington, Silver Link Publishing Ltd, 1991), p177.

31 Hughes, G. *LNER*, p61

32 Campling, N. *Historic Carriage Drawings: LNER and Constituents* (Easingwold, The Pendragon Partnership, 1997), pp54-55

33 Austin, S. *Portrait of the Atlantic Coast Express* (Shepperton, Ian Allan Publishing, 1997), pp84-85

34 Kitchenside, op cit, Chap 4

35 Jenkinson, *British Railway Carriages*, p359

36 ibid, p365

37 Harris, *Standard Gresley Carriages*, pp145-46

38 Hughes, op cit, pp137-38

39 Ryan and Shine, op cit, p44

40 Simmons and Biddle, op cit, p43

41 Palmer, op cit, p151

42 Ryan and Shine, op cit, p74

43 Harris, op cit, pp151-52

44 Charman, op cit, p18

45 Doughty, op cit, pp28-37

46 Harris, *British Main Line Services*, p154

47 Wooler, op cit, pp120-22

48 Campling, op cit, pp18-19 & 54-57

49 Kitchenside, op cit, Chapter Five

50 Jenkinson, D. and Essery, R. *LMS Standard Coaching Stock: II – General Service Gangwayed Vehicles* (Sparkford, Oxford Publishing Company, 1994), p74, diagram

51 ibid, p75

52 Jenkinson, op cit, p364

53 Harris, op cit, pp167-68

54 Behrend, *Pullman in Europe*, pp67-68

55 Jenkinson, op cit, p370

56 ibid, pp457-58

57 *GWR Magazine*, August 1934, p347

58 Jenkinson, op cit, pp460-61

59 Ryan and Shine, op cit, pp108-109 & 267 (middle diagram)

60 ibid, plus pp254-255

61 Fletcher and Taylor, op cit, p285

62 Behrend, *Trains de Luxe*, p109

63 Winchester, C. and Allen, Cecil J. (eds) 'The Flying Hamburger', *Railway Wonders of the World*, Vol 1 Part 6 (8 March) (London, Amalgamated Press, 1936), p175

64 ditto, 'The Union Pacific Streamlined Express', *Railway Wonders of the World*, Vol 1 Part 1 (1 February) (London, Amalgamated Press, 1936), pp34-36

65 Tayler, op cit, p131

66 Winchester, C. and Allen, Cecil J. (eds) 'The Rail-Cars of France', *Railway Wonders of the World*, Vol 1 Part 3 (15 February) (London, Amalgamated Press, 1936), pp88-92

67 Burton, op cit, pp76-81

68 Behrend, *Grand European Expresses*, pp106ff

69 Des Cass and Caracalla, op cit, p78

70 Winchester, C. and Allen, Cecil J. (eds) 'International Sleeping Cars', *Railway Wonders of the World* Vol 1 Part 37 (11 October) (London, Amalgamated Press, 1936), p1157

71 Burton, op cit, pp79-80

72 Winchester, C. and Allen, Cecil J. (eds) 'The Taurus Express', *Railway Wonders of the World* Vol 2 Part 48 (27 December) (London, Amalgamated Press, 1936), p 1526

73 Behrend, *Trains de Luxe*, pp103-106, quotation courtesy of Transport Publishing Company

74 Winchester, C. and Allen, Cecil J. (eds) 'Germany and Holland: The Railway Systems of Two Progressive Countries', *Railway Wonders of the World* Vol 1 Part 19 (7 June) (London, Amalgamated Press, 1936), pp582-83

75 Morel, op cit, p62

76 Behrend, *Grand European Expresses*, pp36ff

77 Fryer, op cit, pp72-73

78 ibid., pp68-81

79 Quoted in ibid, p82

80 Hughes, *LNER*, p47

81 Fryer, op cit, pp82-88

82 ibid, pp84-96

83 ibid, pp97-101

84 Winchester, C. and Allen, Cecil J. (eds) 'The Golden Arrow', *Railway Wonders of the World* Vol 1 Part 8 (22 March) (London, Amalgamated Press, 1936), p232

85 Harris, *British Main Line Services*, pp138-39

86 Austin, S. *Portrait of the Pines Express* (Shepperton, Ian Allan, 1997), p20

87 Harris, op cit, pp139-40

88 Harris, *LNER Standard Gresley Carriages*, pp154-57 & 167

89 Jenkinson, *British Railway Carriages*, pp323-30 (the quotation is from p330)

90 Harris, op cit, pp167-70

91 Jenkinson, op cit, p331

92 Jenkinson, op cit, pp373-80

93 Jenkinson and Essery, *LMS Standard Coaching Stock II*, pp44-45 & 236-39

94 Winchester, C. and Allen, Cecil J. (eds) 'The "Royal Scot" Route',

Railway Wonders of the World Vol 1 Part 2 (8 February) (London, Amalgamated Press, 1936), pp40-46, and 'The Flying Scotsman', *Railway Wonders of the World* Vol1 Part 6 (8 March) (London, Amalgamated Press, 1936), pp183-88

95 Russell, op cit, pp128-33

96 Jenkinson, *British Railway Carriages*, pp362-64

97 Russell, op cit, pp155-61 & 202-15

98 Austin, *Portrait of the Atlantic Coast Express*, pp79-81

99 Harris, *British Main Line Services*, p141

100 Boston, op cit, p513

101 Nock, O. S. *British Locomotives of the 20th Century* (Cambridge, Patrick Stephens Ltd, 1984), Vol II p77

102 Winchester, C. and Allen, Cecil J. (eds) 'The Silver Jubilee', *Railway Wonders of the World* Vol 2 Part 45 (6 December) (London, Amalgamated Press, 1936), p1442

103 Jenkinson, op cit, p484

104 Hughes, op cit, p46

105 Harris, op cit, p155 (Hence Jenkinson's claim, op cit p489, that the LNER's 'Coronation' was 'a counterblast to the "Coronation Scot"', cannot stand.)

106 Jenkinson, op cit, pp488-91

107 Harris, op cit, p157

108 Jenkinson, *British Railway Carriages*, p486

109 Petchey, Tim 'Railway Catering' in Kardas, H. (ed) *A Collector's Guide to Railwayana* (Hersham, Ian Allan Publishing, 2001), p78

110 Ryan and Shine, op cit, pp125 & 132

111 Doughty, op cit, pp25-31

112 Tayler, op cit, p131

113 ibid, pp123-24

114 McKenzie, op cit, p66

115 ibid, p74

116 ibid, p89

117 ibid, pp86-90

118 E. S. Hanger (by personal communication)

119 Tayler, op cit, p124

120 Bryant, op cit, pp334-36

121 Winchester, C. and Allen, Cecil J. (eds) 'The Santa Fé "Chief"', *Railway Wonders of the World* Vol 1 Part 9 (29 March) (London,

Amalgamated Press, 1936), pp282-84

122 Bryant, op cit, pp339-41 (reproduced by permission of University of Nebraska Press)

Chapter 6

1 Thorne (ed), *Modern Trains and Splendid Stations*, p14

2 Wooler, op cit, pp124-25

3 Harris, *British Main Line Services*, p162

4 Whitehouse, P. and St John Thomas, D. *The Great Days of the Southern Railway* (London, BCA by arrangement with David St John Thomas, 1992), p97

5 Wooler, op cit, pp134-38

6 Brogan, M. *Home Sweet Home* (Great Addington, Silver Link Publishing Ltd., 1999), p11

7 Whitehouse and St John Thomas, pp96-97

8 Brogan, op cit, p10

9 Rogers, op cit, Chap 6 pp4-5

10 Palmer, op cit, p131 (both quotations)

11 Behrend, *History of Trains de Luxe*, p76

12 For further details, see Wooler, op cit, p173

13 Wooler, op cit, p130

14 Gourvish, T. R. *British Railways 1948-73: A Business History* (Cambridge, CUP, 1986), p579

15 ibid., p578

16 Wooler, op cit, p132

17 Austin, *Portrait of the Atlantic Coast Express*, p84

18 Wooler, op cit, p131

19 Kitchenside, op cit, Chap 7, opening page

20 Wooler, op cit, p141

21 Jenkinson and Essery, *LMS Coaching Stock*, II, pp48-49 & 82-83

22 Parkin, K. *British Railways Mark I Coaches* (Easingwold, Pendragon Books, 1991, 2nd repr 1999), p146

23 ibid, pp149-52 (diagrams)

24 ibid, p138

25 ibid, p142

26 ibid, pp147-48

27 Wooler, op cit, p18

28 Travellers' Fare Press Releases, 1984-85, in NRM boxed archive, York

29 Morel, op cit, p117

30 Fryer, op cit, p115

31 ibid, p117

32 Thus on NRM York Poster 1978-81

33 Morel, op cit, pp163-64

34 ibid, p161

35 Fryer, op cit., pp163-65

36 ibid, p169

37 ibid, pp170-73

38 Morel, op cit, pp93-94

39 Parkin, op cit, pp161-68

40 Fryer, op cit, pp174-78

41 Morel, op cit, p95

42 St John Thomas, D. and Whitehouse, P. *SR 150: A Century and a Half of the Southern Railway* (Newton Abbot, David & Charles, 1988), pp33-39

43 Fryer, op cit, pp126-30

44 Morel, op cit, p45

45 Fryer, op cit, p138

46 Behrend, *Trains de Luxe*, p124

47 Morel, op cit, p63

48 ibid, p67

49 ibid, p68

50 Behrend, *Grand European Expresses*, pp38-39

51 Behrend, G. and Buchanan, G. *Night Ferry* (St Martin, Jersey Artists Ltd., 1985), pp90 & 95

52 ibid, pp95-96

53 Gourvish, op cit, pp615-19

54 Wooler, op cit, pp193 & 200

55 Fryer, op cit, p166

56 ibid, pp170-79

57 Harris, *British Main Line Services*, p180

58 Fryer, op cit, pp179-211 passim

59 ibid, p188

60 Behrend, *Trains de Luxe*, p109

61 Morel, op cit, pp38-39

62 Behrend, op cit, pp138-39

63 Burton, op cit, pp93-99

64 ibid, pp100-101

65 ibid, pp101-102

66 Behrend, op cit, p144

67 Behrend, *Grand European Expresses*, pp107, 144-55 & 230-31

68 Behrend, *Trains de Luxe*, pp139-40

69 Ryan and Shine, op cit, p167

70 ibid, p163

71 Bryant, op cit, p347

72 ibid, p348 (reproduced by permission of University of Nebraska Press)

73 McKenzie, op cit, p92

74 ibid, pp92-96 (cooking time from recipe at p141)

75 Bryant, op cit , pp348-49 (reproduced by permission of University of Nebraska Press)

76 Ryan and Shine, op cit, p158

77 ibid, pp153 & 163 (top)

78 ibid, p148

79 ibid, p165

80 Tayler, op cit, p151

81 Ryan and Shine, op cit, p176

82 Hanger, op cit, Foreword, ppii-iii

83 Ryan and Shine, op cit, p161

84 ibid, pp188-89

85 ibid, p167, chapter epigraph

86 Bradley, R. *Amtrak: The US National Railroad Passenger Corporation* (Poole, Blandford Press, 1985), p25

87 Ryan and Shine, op cit, menu p244. The wine advert showed a wine waiter serving a bottle to the left of the text quoted.

88 ibid, p245

89 ibid, p267

90 ibid, menu p250

91 ibid, menu and comment p258

92 ibid, pp326-33

93 ibid, p327

94 Bryant, op cit, pp352-56 (reproduced by permission of University of Nebraska Press)

95 ibid, pp357-58

96 McKenzie, pp106 & 107 (photograph)

97 E. S. Hanger, by personal communication

Chapter 7

1 quoted in Thorne, *Modern Trains*, p45

2 Vincent and Green, *The InterCity Story*, p13

3 ibid, p10

4 ibid, p33

5 ibid, pp23-24

6 ibid, p102

7 Nicholas, R. 'Dinner is Served', *The Railway Magazine*, November 1979, pp427-28

8 Vincent and Green, op cit, p58

9 ibid, p61

10 ibid, Preface, ppix-x, main text p59

11 Wooler, op cit, p193

12 ibid, p207

13 Vincent and Green, op cit, pp91-92

14 Wooler, op cit, pp203-205

15 Kitchenside, op cit, Chapter Eight

16 David Small, interview, 21 November 2001

17 Vincent and Green, op cit, p95

18 Fryer, op cit, pp212-18

19 Vincent and Green, op cit, pp104-105

20 David Small, On Board Services Menu and Tariff Guide, 1992/3, p2

21 Paul Freeston, InterCity Cuisine 2000 Menus, May-October 1988, p3

22 Vincent and Green, pp99-100

23 ibid, pp98-99

24 Wessner, C. 'Designing for their Needs', in Thorne, M. (ed) *Modern Trains and Splendid Stations* (London, Merrell/The Art Institute of Chicago, 2001), p33

25 ibid, p27

26 Bryant, op cit, pp257-58

27 Bradley, *Amtrak*, pp50-51

28 Johnston, Bob 'Brer Amtrak', *Trains*, June 2001, Vol 61 No 6 p54

29 Wessner, op cit, p25

30 Bradley, op cit, pp74-77

31 Bob Johnston, by personal communication

32 Bradley, op cit, pp84-86

33 ibid, pp138-41

34 ibid, p137

35 Wessner, op cit, pp32-33

36 ibid, p29

37 Johnston, Bob 'Brer Amtrak', op cit, pp56-57

Chapter 8

1 David Small, interview, 21 November 2001

2 Steve Jones, interview, 16 February 2001

3 David Crome, interview, 16 February 2001

4 John Dykes, interview, 23 April 2001

5 Lucy Evans, interview, 19 February 2001

6 Rob Mulder, interview, 22 November 2001

7 Robin Crook, comment during Duncan Fraser interview listed below

8 Rob Mulder, letter to author, 4 January 2002

9 Roger Field, by personal communication

10 Duncan Fraser, interview, 27 April 2001

11 Perren, B. 'Virgin's Catering Revolution', *Modern Railways*, Vol 58 No 639, pp56-58

12 Behrend, *Trains de Luxe*, pp144-45

13 ibid, p145-46

14 *Modern Railways*, April 2003, Vol 60 No 655, pp66-67

15 Thorne, *Modern Trains*, p16

16 Heaps, C., Hunter, D. and Le Jeune, B. 'Dutch Railways in the 21st Century', *Modern Railways*, October 2000, p34

17 Wessner, op cit, pp28 & 32

18 Ferguson-Kosinski, L. *Europe by Eurail* (Guilford, Connecticut, USA, The Globe Pequod Press, 2000), p15

19 Lydia Contreras, Rail Gourmet España, by personal communication

20 Heaps, Hunter and Le Jeune, op cit, pp34-35

21 Locke, T. (ed) *Europe 2002* (Peterborough, Thomas Cook), p35

22 David Small, interview, 21 November 2001

23 Wessner, op cit, p28

24 *Today's Railways*, No 72, Dec 2001, International News Roundup, p37

25 Johnston, Bob 'Amtrak Responds, Reacts ... and Hopes', *Trains*, Vol 61 No 12 p19

26 Johnston, Bob 'Acela Report: Will Amtrak Prove Itself?', *Trains*, Vol 61 No 12, pp56-57

27 Johnston, Bob, draft for article in *Trains* for March 2003

28 Bob Johnston, by personal communication

29 Crome, D. 'Is Anyone Taking Dinner Tonight?', Section 8